Christmas 2007

With love at Christmas —
happy "Journeying into
God" Kathleen

The Journey into God:

A Forty-Day Retreat *with* Bonaventure, Francis and Clare

Josef Raischl, S.F.O,
and
André Cirino, O.F.M.

With a new translation of
The Journey of the Human Person into God
by Zachary Hayes, O.F.M.

ST. ANTHONY MESSENGER PRESS
Cincinnati, Ohio

Scripture citations are taken from *The New Revised Standard Version Bible*, copyright ©1989 by the Division of Christian Education of the National Council of Churches of Christ in the United States of America, and used by permission. All rights reserved.

We are grateful for permission to quote material printed by the following publishers:
Reprinted by permission of Franciscan Institute Publications, excerpts from *Song of Brotherhood and Sisterhood*, by Eric Doyle, copyright ©1997. Reprinted by permission of Our Lady of the Angels Motherhouse, excerpts from *Mystical Expressions: A Book of Poetry*, by Lois Roselle Schafer, O.S.F., copyright ©1997. Reprinted by permission of Crossbush Publications, excerpts from *Fourth Letter to Agnes of Prague*, translation by Sr. Theresa Francis Downing. Reprinted by permission of Paulist Press (www.paulist-press.com), excerpts from *Jacapone da Todi: The Lauds,* translated by Serge and Elizabeth Hughes, copyright ©1982. Reprinted by permission of New City Press, excerpts from *Francis of Assisi: The Early Documents*, Regis J. Armstrong, O.F.M. CAP., J.A. Wayne Hellmann, O.F.M. CONV., William J. Short, O.F.M., editors, copyright ©2000.

Cover and book design by Mark Sullivan
Cover photos by Gene Plaisted, O.S.C.

Library of Congress Cataloging-in-Publication Data
Raischl, Josef.
   The journey into God : a forty-day retreat with Bonaventure, Francis and Clare / Josef Raischl, André Cirino.
        p. cm.
Includes bibliographical references.
   ISBN 0-86716-499-9 (pbk.)
   1. Spiritual retreats—Catholic Church. 2. Francis, of Assisi, Saint, 1182-1226. 3. Bonaventure, Saint, Cardinal, ca. 1217-1274. 4. Clare, of Assisi, Saint, 1194-1253. I. Cirino, André. II. Title.
   BX2375 .R35 2003
   269'.6—dc21
                                        2002011486

ISBN 0-86716-499-9
Copyright ©2002, Josef Raischl, S.F.O., and André Cirino, O.F.M.
Published by St. Anthony Messenger Press
www.AmericanCatholic.org
Printed in the U.S.A.

For Elizabeth Enoch, O.S.C.,
former abbess of Poor Clares in New York,
whose loving interest in the beginning
launched us on this Journey.

For my family, my wife Bernadette,
my first companion on this Journey.
For my children Jona, Elia and Chiara,
our gifts who journey with us.

~Josef Raischl, S.F.O.

For Octavius Checcacci, O.F.M.,
Father Peter Gavigan,
Juvenal Lalor, O.F.M.,
Elaine Bane, O.S.F.,
my trusted and wise guides along the Journey.
For my grandnephews,
River Lee, Knox Christian, Cole Joseph, Jack Michael,
beginners on this Journey.

~André Cirino, O.F.M.

Contents

In February, 1995, I participated in the experiential retreat
on *The Soul's Journey into God* created by Josef Raischl and
André Cirino. My purpose was twofold: to make my annual
retreat and to encounter the work of the great Franciscan
theologian Saint Bonaventure in a new way. At the time
Bonaventure and I had what might be called an adversarial
relationship; my experience with scholastic theology up to
that point had been fraught with struggle and uncertainty.
There was always the question, "What has this to do with my
life?" and not much clarity about the answer. My time with
Bonaventure in the *Journey* retreat forever
changed my perspective with respect to
scholastic theology while also deeply enrich-
ing my personal relationship with God. I
moved into a new sense of how closely God is involved in my
life and how present to reality Bonaventure's theology is.

The wonder and grace of the *Journey* experience is
now available in this new book by Josef and André. Those
seeking to know God more intimately can enter into a
process of spiritual deepening through the texts and exercises provided in this book. Certainly, in this volatile and
troubled world, we all need tools for rooting ourselves in
God, for developing attitudes of peace and compassion
toward ourselves and others, and for making decisions that
emerge from solid Christian values, such as right knowledge,
justice and love.

This is a workbook that will enable individuals and
groups to intensify their desire for inner peace and open
their "spiritual ears." It lays out in clear and practical language the basic theological concepts found in *The Journey of
the Human Person into God* and presents daily readings and
exercises for our prayerful consideration. The structure of

each week is thematic; readers are supported by a three-part structure for each day's reflection: texts for prayerful reading, shared reflections from Josef and André, and exercises of body, mind and spirit for integration. Days flow from one to the next in an efficient arrangement that allows a reader to move through the daily readings into an integrative piece at the end of each week. Some texts are used more than once, thus allowing time for renewed reflection and calling forth new insights over the course of the forty days. The materials of successive weeks progress into ever more challenging and complex readings while never losing sight of the need for practical application and internalization.

For hearts and souls hungering for God, this book opens up new vistas. We meet Francis and Clare through their own writings and through the lens of Bonaventure's reflections upon the values they embraced. We learn, as they did, that being loved by God is our ultimate strength; we learn to surrender to a belief in our personal capacity for contemplation. Not only that, Raischl and Cirino also show us how to get inside the heart of Bonaventure and how to embrace his understanding that all the universe is a ladder by which we can ascend to God. Very creative and powerful excerpts from *The Journey* and from other spiritual and theological resources offer solid examples of how to feed our desire for God. We are invited to use our senses, to seek the revelation of the divine in the ordinary events of day-by-day living. Tension and peace, giving and receiving, intimacy and mission are indispensable elements in the journey of every human person into God. The illustrations and exercises developed here gently but firmly lead us into an exploration of this truth. Those who partake of the banquet of texts will be fed internally and secretly transformed.

This project is not a scholarly treatise in the academic sense. It is, rather, a work that facilitates personal theological reflection and spiritual growth. The authors invite us to develop our spiritual senses and to release memories of past pain and sorrow so that God can fill us with new awareness, deeper delight and clearer judgments about who God is and who we are as God's beloved sons and daughters. They invite each of us to embrace the truth that sets us free— Franciscan spirituality's most precious gift may be its dimensions of adoration, gratitude and praise, as well as a positive, joyful acceptance of goodness. We are set free to embrace the gift.

There should be no fear about attempting to use this work for one's individual benefit. And one of the beauties of the book is that it is also geared for use in group reflection. It can be used for parish groups, Secular Franciscan Order groups, ongoing formation in local houses of religious congregations. It can be used for a private retreat, a directed retreat, a Lenten focus group. One of its great virtues is its adaptability and versatility. The authors encourage creative responses to the movement of the Spirit of God and do not intend any measure of rigid adherence to the suggestions made. However, it should be said that anyone who enters into the texts and exercises in good faith can expect surprises of great grace and surpassing beauty. That is because this *Journey* is a work of God.

~ROBERTA MCKELVIE, O.S.F.

Francis (1181/82–1226) and Clare (1193/94–1253) of Assisi, with their companions, initiated a new direction for religious life in the church during the thirteenth century and their movement attracted many followers. Their experience inspired, spread and changed both the religious and social life of their time. In our own day the Franciscan movement continues to touch and involve thousands of people all over the world. Having entered into the third millennium, the search for our spiritual roots continues to be a crucial question—a question of survival—for our world and society.

This original Franciscan experience of God and the world has had various forms of expression throughout the centuries. The  Order of the Friars Minor experienced its "second founder"[1] only thirty years after Francis' death. A physician's son and professor at the University of Paris, Giovanni di Fidanza (1217–1274), called in the Order Bonaventura, composed *The Journey of the Human Person into God (Itinerarium mentis in deum)*[2] after a profound experience he had on Mount LaVerna[3] in Tuscany in 1259. The Franciscan Order was in crisis, wondering how it could sustain its original ideal and yet adapt to new challenges and situations, when Bonaventure became general minister in 1257.

At the beginning of the twenty-first century—nearly 750 years later—we desire to share Bonaventure's beautiful and profound text with the people of the new millennium.

In 1987 to 1988, we—Josef Raischl, a Secular Franciscan from Dachau, Germany, and André Cirino, a Friar Minor of the Immaculate Conception Province, New York—met in Rome. At that time André dreamed that this spiritual treasure could be broken open and made more available for larger segments of the Franciscan family using the structure of an experiential retreat. At first it seemed to be risky, if not absurd, to use this seemingly dry, philosophical-theological treatise as the basis for an experiential retreat. But the dream gradually became reality. We worked for many months, studying the text in several languages. More and more we became enraptured by the genius of Bonaventure's thought.

The Poor Clares of New York, through their abbess at the time, Sister Elizabeth Enoch, o.s.c., invited us to conduct such a retreat for the sisters in their monastery. We owe inestimable gratitude to these Poor Clares who encouraged us to make *The Journey* with them, and because of their active participation we were gifted with many new ideas. These spiritual exercises developed into an eight-day Franciscan retreat experience.

Since 1988 we have worked intensely with this masterpiece of Christian spirituality in several countries. The fruit of our work is the book you have in your hands. We divided it as follows:

- Bonaventure relates his own life story, giving us some flavor of his historical background.
- A collection of ideas for use of this book lays the groundwork for personal application.
- Daily readings, reflections and exercises help reinforce the main themes of the text.

For each day you will find a selected reading of Bonaventure's original text. For the context of the passage chosen, the complete original text is found at the end of the book.

Our suggestions are designed as a companion for making *The Journey* through Lent or any other forty-day time of solitude. So we begin with a Sunday and conclude on a Thursday, or from the first Sunday of Lent concluding on Holy Thursday.

We concentrate on the main ideas of the text rather than interpreting the text in its scientific depth and detail. In this way, many questions still remain open and unresolved.

- The daily exercises suggested should help to root the reflections in your own personal life, the crucial point being the present, not the past.
- Should you prefer to make *The Journey* in companionship with others, the guide for group meetings suggests an outline for a weekly session. Our suggestions can be adapted to your own circumstances.

Since this book was first published in German,[4] Nancy Celaschi, O.S.F.., our good friend and an excellent linguist, provided us with the first translation of the manuscript, for which we express our deep gratitude.

We also needed a new English translation of Bonaventure's *Itinerarium mentis in deum*. We thank Zachary Hayes, O.F.M., prominent Franciscan and Bonaventurian scholar, who offered to do so. The result is found in the citations of every chapter and the complete text at the end of the book.

We express our appreciation to Roberta McKelvie, O.S.F., who made *The Journey* with us and offered priceless suggestions in preparation of this text for publication.

We are grateful to Paul Perkins, S.F.O., for his generous assistance that helped move this project through its initial stages.

And we thank Jeremy Harrington, O.F.M., and Lisa

Biedenbach of St. Anthony Messenger Press for their confidence and interest in our work with Bonaventure's *Journey*.

Finally, a word of thanks to the more than seven hundred retreatants who have journeyed with us. We were frequently asked by them to publish our material. Their enthusiastic response and helpful suggestions were crucial in the growth and development of this book.

~JOSEF RAISCHL AND ANDRÉ CIRINO
DACHAU / NEW YORK

NOTES

[1] John Moorman, *A History of the Franciscan Order From Its Origins to the Year 1517* (Oxford: Clarendon Press, 1968), p. 154.

[2] Hereinafter referred to simply as *The Journey*.

[3] Known also as La Verna or Mount Alverna.

[4] Josef Raischl, s.f.o., and André Cirino, o.f.m., *Auf Gott Zugehen*, (Munich: Claudius Verlag, 1999).

Part One

PREPARING FOR THE JOURNEY

I was born in Bagnoregio, a small town in central Italy, located between Viterbo and Orvieto in the year 1217.[1] My father, Giovanni di Fidanza, was a physician. My mother's name was Maria di Ritello. When they baptized me they gave me the name of my father, Giovanni.

I was a post-conciliar person, born right after the Fourth Lateran Council. I was born when the Franciscan Order was peaking in its early development. Francis and Clare had many followers. The friars had opened a *convento*, that is, a friary, in my hometown, where I received my preliminary education.

"When I was a boy (about eleven years old), as I still vividly remember, I was snatched from the jaws of death (and restored to perfect health) by Saint Francis' invocation and merits. So if I remained silent and did not sing his praises, I fear that I would be rightly accused of the crime of ingratitude. I recognize that God saved my life through him, and I realize that I experienced God's power in my very person."[2]

I enjoyed my life in Bagnoregio. I had many friends and was as content as I thought anyone could be. But God had plans for me. And when I turned seventeen in the year 1234, I found myself enrolled in the University of Paris in the faculty of arts, a long way from my beloved Bagnoregio.

But life in Paris began to take hold of me. The university filled me with new ideas, theories and questions. And I had some very fine instructors, too. My favorite instructor was Alexander of Hales, an archdeacon of Coventry. In my second year at the university, in 1236, this illustrious Englishman and professor decided to join the Order of

Friars Minor, sending shock waves not only through me but also through the entire academic community. And this step brought his doctoral chair—and me with it—to the Franciscan house, thus establishing the school of the Friars Minor as an official part of the University of Paris. Little did I know what that move would mean to me.

Alexander continued his lectures. More and more I felt myself come under the spell of the Poor Man of Assisi. And by the year 1243 I found myself a novice in this same Order. By 1245 my tutor and mentor Alexander was dead. I continued with my studies. By 1248 I was licensed as a bachelor of Scripture. I lectured on the Bible for the next two years. From 1250 to 1252 I lectured on the *Sentences*[3] of Peter Lombard and wrote a *Commentary on the Sentences*. It was in 1253 or 1254, I cannot remember exactly, that I became a master in theology and was designated to occupy the same chair which my brother, Alexander of Hales, had held as master of the Franciscan school of theology.

I continued my writing, research and lectures with enthusiasm. I also became embroiled in the controversy that broke out in Paris in 1256. The new mendicant orders, our own included, were all under attack. So I set to writing my own *Defense of the Mendicants*. And victory was ours when Thomas Aquinas and I were accepted as regent masters of the university, the title being less important than the full accreditation now granted to the mendicants.

Those were exciting times. And I had some fascinating students, too. There was Peter John Olivi (d. 1298), who wrote in behalf of the Spirituals,[4] John Pecham (d. 1292), an archbishop of Canterbury and Raymond Lull (d. 1315), mystic, missionary and martyr.

And news traveled quickly, even in my day. We heard in Paris of tensions in the Order between those who wanted to follow the ideals of Francis in stark simplicity and those who favored adaptation as the Order expanded. The news got worse, because some friars espoused the teachings of Joachim of Fiore.[5] Rumors reached us, too, that our general minister, John of Parma, was influenced by Joachimism. It was right after these rumors reached Paris that the bottom fell out of my life, my academic life.

Pope Alexander IV had secretly ordered John of Parma to resign his office as general minister.[6] I was rather sad, for John was a good man, well loved by the brothers. Another bit of news, no longer a rumor but a fact, reached us in Paris. When John resigned, he suggested my name as his successor.[7] So on February 2, in the year 1257, I was elected the seventh general minister of the Order of Friars Minor, thirty-one years after Francis had died.

I was forty years old. I guess you could say I was in midlife and I was not completely ready for what lay ahead of me. However, I jumped right in and did the one thing I knew best: I wrote. I composed a letter to all the provincial ministers. Let me tell you a bit about this letter, for I believe it was a lack of response from the friars to this letter that led me to LaVerna panting for peace. I began the journey of my own soul into God.

First, the letter: I wrote and said "that the splendor of our Order has been clouded; the (brothers) were not living up to (our) ideals."[8] I then wrote of ten points where I felt reform was needed:

1. the multiplicity of ways in which money is being obtained;

2. the laziness of the friars;

3. their wandering about;

4. their importunate begging, whereby people are as fearful of meeting a friar as of meeting a robber;

5. the grandeur of their buildings;

6. their over-friendliness with certain people (presumably the rich and the influential);

7. the unwise bestowal of office in the Order;

8. a greedy desire for burials and legacies;

9. frequent changes from simple dwellings to more sumptuous ones;

10. and a general luxuriousness of living.[9]

I decided to visit Italy, France, Germany and England. But before going, I had to deal with the man who had been my predecessor in the Order as general minister, John of Parma. John was accused of the heresy of Joachimism. I liked John very much, and the brothers liked him. He was older than I, "learned, humble and devout."[10] Why could he not steer clear of the Joachimites? "Heresy (is) an evil . . . which must be rooted out. Nothing would do more harm to the Order than to receive charges of shielding heretics. Nothing would give greater delight to its critics than to be able to accuse the Order of slipping into heresy."[11] So I was bound to act. How could I deal fairly with such an obviously good man? Even Cardinal Ottobono was pleading with me for leniency. Finally, I knew what to do. I sent him to Greccio where he lived out his years in peace. To some, it looked like imprisonment, but at least he was alive and taken care of by the brothers.

Little did I know what a response this move would evoke from some of the friars. Angelo of Clareno described the resignation of John and my election as general minister with my being the one "under whom the fourth persecution began."[12] It was not fair. He did not understand my motives. But I was getting hit with criticism from others, too. My work often took me away from Paris. Yet I managed to be there for a considerable part of each year to continue with my studies. I wanted to show the brothers it was possible to be a theologian and a scholar and yet remain faithful to the ideals of Saint Francis. In spite of my efforts, the brothers did not understand. I was very hurt by this remark of Brother Giles: "Paris, Paris, why do you destroy the Order of Saint Francis?"—a cry later echoed by Brother Jacopone da Todi in his lament: *Mal vedemmo Parisci, c'hane destrutto Ascisi* ("Evil be of Paris said! By it is Assisi dead!"). But was this true? Was Paris really destroying Assisi?[13] I could barely take any more.

I had been content with my work at the university. I never asked to be thrust into the position of general minister. I was in my middle years, still full of energy and ideas. But this ministry to the friars as their minister drained me of all my zeal. So in October of 1259, I found myself unsettled, disturbed and "seeking this peace with panting spirit (so) I withdrew to Mount LaVerna, seeking a place of quiet and desiring to find there peace of spirit."[14] I wrote my reflections, *The Journey of the Human Person into God.*

Coming down from this glorious mountain, I was rested and fortified in my being for what was ahead of me in the new year 1260, namely a general chapter[15] which we held at Narbonne. We were in desperate need of a thorough revision of the Order's legislation, which task we assumed by writing a new set of Constitutions. And if this writing was not enough, the same chapter commissioned me to compose another biography of Saint Francis to supersede and replace all that had been written thus far. Later, at the general chapter of Paris, in the year 1266, the brothers ordered all former biographies of Saint Francis to be destroyed, establishing my work as the Order's official biography.

In the preceding year, in 1265, I had just turned forty-eight; the pope nominated me to become archbishop of York, but I refused on the grounds that I must work for the friars. I gathered with the friars in general chapters at Pisa in 1263, at Paris in 1266, Assisi in 1269, Lyon in 1272. These chapters alone were enough to keep me busy and consume all my energy. I remember the chapter of Pisa in 1263 Francis had always desired that the friars provide and care for the Poor Ladies. Clare respected this desire of Francis and wrote it into her Rule of 1253. Now the friars were "asking to be released from all responsibility towards the Poor Clares."[16] Pope Urban IV opposed this separation. I "wrote to Brother Lothario at the end of September pointing out how suitable it was that the friars should look after the (sisters)."[17] But the new Rule issued by Urban IV on October 18, 1263, and imposed on the Poor Ladies accepted the fact that the friars were unwilling to care for them. I regretted the separation that finally emerged.

One day in the year 1273, I was in the kitchen of one of our friaries washing dishes[18] when the news arrived that I had been made a cardinal and was summoned to join the papal curia in autumn of that same year. I was consecrated Bishop of Albano in November, 1273, at Lyon. That winter I participated in the Council of Lyon and then in the general chapter of the Order in May, 1274. I resigned at the chapter, for illness was upon me, and Sister Death came to meet me here at Lyon on July 15 in the year 1274. I was fifty-seven years old.

Before my death one of my friars approached me with the question: Can only the learned become saints? I replied: "'If God gives (one) only the grace to love, that is enough.' Giles asked: 'So a dunce can love God as much as a doctor?' The graduate of Paris answered: 'A poor little old woman can love (God) even more than a doctor of theology.' Then Giles, all enthusiasm, leaped to his feet, ran to the garden's edge . . . and raising his arms began shouting: 'Poor little old woman! Plain and ignorant as you are, love the Lord God and you can become greater than Brother Bonaventure.'"[19]

To my surprise, the church saw fit to enroll me in the catalogue of the holy ones by canonizing me on April 14, 1482. With this recognition through canonization came the acceptance of all that I had written. By this the church said "yes" to a Franciscan theology and confirmed this "yes" on March 14, 1588, by proclaiming me Seraphic Doctor.

NOTES

[1] This text originally was composed for an audiovisual presentation on Bonaventure's life. In order to give a more immediate impression of his person we chose to use the first-person I rather than the third-person he. While imaginatively written, the text is based on historical data. See also Zachary Hayes, O.F.M., *Bonaventure: Mystical Writings* (New York: The Crossroad Publishing Co., 1999), pp. 16–18; *Bonaventure: The Soul's Journey Into God, The Tree of Life, The Life of Saint Francis,* Ewert Cousins, trans. (New York: Paulist Press, 1978), pp. 2–8; *Bonaventure: Mystic of God's Word,* Timothy Johnson, ed. (Hyde Park, N.Y.: New City Press, 1999), pp. 10–26.

[2] *The Life of Saint Francis* P:3, in Cousins, *op. cit.,* p. 182.

[3] The "*Sentences,* compiled in the twelfth century . . . was an anthology of the thoughts or judgments (*sententiae*) of the Fathers on the dogmas of the Christian Faith" (From C. H. Lawrence, *The Friars* (London: Longman,

1994), p. 141).

[4] For further information concerning the Spirituals, see Duncan Nimmo, *Reform and Division in the Medieval Franciscan Order* (Rome: Capuchin Historical Institute, 1987) and William Short, O.F.M., *The Franciscans* (Wilmington, Del.: Michael Glazier, 1989), p. 40 ff.

[5] For further information concerning Joachim of Fiore, see Marjorie Reeves, *Joachim of Fiore and the Prophetic Future* (Gloucestershire, England: Sutton Publishing, Ltd., 1999).

[6] Lazario Iriarte, O.F.M. CAP., *Franciscan History* (Chicago: Franciscan Herald Press, 1982), p. 39.

[7] *Ibid.*, p. 40.

[8] Moorman, *op. cit.*, p. 145.

[9] *Ibid.*

[10] *Ibid.*, p. 146.

[11] *Ibid.*

[12] *Ibid.*

[13] *Ibid.*, p. 246.

[14] *The Soul's Journey Into God* P:2, in Cousins, *op. cit.*, p. 54.

[15] A chapter is a meeting or assembly of religious on a regular basis for prayer, discussion and election of leadership.

[16] Moorman, *op. cit.*, p. 214.

[17] *Ibid.*

[18] Efrem Bettoni, *St. Bonaventure* (Notre Dame, Ind.: University of Notre Dame Press, 1964), p. 11.

[19] Nello Vian, *Golden Words: The Sayings of Brother Giles of Assisi* (Chicago: Franciscan Herald Press, 1966), p. 36.

Bonaventure concludes his Prologue with this sound advice: "It is important that you not run through these reflections in a hurry, but that you take your time and ruminate over them slowly" [P:5]. It is our hope that you will have both the desire and the time to enter deeply into these reflections, avoiding a superficial run through them. Bonaventure invites us to ruminate, to chew, to mull the text over and over again. So we encourage you to take just one passage daily, for this is certainly no spiritual fast-food menu.

We recommend two thirty-minute sessions daily, if possible; plan your schedule and content the night before. It is certainly helpful to choose a place for the entire experience of the forty days, a place of quiet where you can rest with this book and with a Bible[1] without disturbance. It might be a good idea to talk this through with your family or community, especially concerning your responding (or not) to telephone and doorbell.

We suggest following this schedule for the first part (thirty minutes):

1. Time of preparation (five minutes)
   Quiet yourself.
   Focus on inner rest.
   Choose some physical exercise to relax and settle down.
2. Reading of *The Journey*
   You will find a selection from *The Journey* for each of the forty days. Please start with the Prologue. In the beginning of every week it is helpful to read the entire chapter as found in the last section of the book.
3. Observe silence for at least two or three minutes.

4. Read the reflection of the day.

5. Meditate silently for at least ten minutes.

6. Reserve two or three minutes for slowly concluding the exercise! Physical exercise or movements could be very helpful, perhaps some deep breathing or vigorously shaking one's arms and legs.

The second thirty minutes should be spent exclusively with one of the suggested daily exercises. These exercises are crucial for a holistic understanding of *The Journey*. The place for performing the exercises can alternate.

Before going to sleep we recommend a short reflection on the past day, especially the exercise of the day. You may want to keep a diary of your personal journey.

If you should have a free day anywhere along *The Journey* of these forty days, we suggest the following schedule:

7:30 A.M.	Morning Prayer
8:00 A.M.	Breakfast and reading of
	The Journey text
	A quiet walk
	Reading and reflection on the
	commentary
	Lunch
	Rest
	Exercise
	Quiet time
5:00 P.M.	Eucharist
	Supper
8:00 P.M.	Evening Prayer
	Quiet time

For groups making *The Journey* together over these forty days, we suggest a similar schedule. It is not necessary that all the participants follow the same route. A weekly meeting offers the opportunity to share *The Journey*, discussing problems or questions. If there is one person coordinating or leading the group, this person should be available for questions throughout the whole time.

It might also be a good idea to form smaller groups of three or four participants who could meet more often for common exercises for certain parts of *The Journey*. You can experiment with many alternatives. Please make sure that the schedule or rhythm you choose does not become a torture or burden for you. Then *The Journey* will lose its direction as you lose a sense of leisure and freedom.

NOTES

[1] The translation of the Scriptures outside the text of *The Journey* cited here is the *New Revised Standard Version*. Scriptures cited within *The Journey* are the translation of Zachary Hayes, O.F.M., from Saint Bonaventure's original.

Part Two

DAILY READINGS, REFLECTIONS AND EXERCISES

DESIRE FOR PEACE

Sunday

Breathless

Bonaventure writes in the Prologue 1 and 2:

1. To begin my reflections,

I call upon that First Beginning

from whom all illumination flows as from *the God of lights*

and from whom comes *every good and perfect gift* [James 1:17].

I call upon God through the divine Son, our lord Jesus Christ,

that through the intercession of the most holy virgin Mary,

the mother of the same Lord, Jesus Christ,

and through that of blessed Francis, our leader and father,

God might grant *enlightenment to the eyes* of our mind

and *guidance to our feet on the path of peace—*

that peace *which surpasses all understanding.*

It is that peace which our Lord Jesus Christ

proclaimed and granted to us

[Ephesians 1:17; Luke 1:79; Phillippians 4:7].

It was this message of peace which our father Francis

announced over and over, proclaiming it at the beginning and

the end of his sermons.

Every greeting of his became a wish for peace;

and in every experience of contemplation he sighed for an

ecstatic peace.

2. Moved by the example of our most blessed father, Francis,

I eagerly desired this peace—I a sinner who, unworthy as I am,

had become the seventh general minister of the brothers

after the death of the most blessed father.

It happened around the time of the thirty-third anniversary of

the death of the saint

that I was moved by a divine inspiration
and withdrew to Mount LaVerna since it was a place of quiet.
There I wished to satisfy the desire of my spirit for peace.
And while I was there reflecting on certain ways
in which the human person might ascend to God,
I recalled, among other things,
that miracle which the blessed Francis himself had experienced
in this very place,
namely the vision of the winged Seraph in the form of the
Crucified.
As I reflected on this,
I saw immediately that this vision pointed
not only to the uplifting of our father himself in contemplation
but also to the road by which one might arrive at this
experience.

JOSEF

In my work for hospice, I regularly encounter people who
are suffering from incurable diseases, some of whom constantly face death because of a difficulty with breathing. They
are prone to terrible attacks of anxiety because of the short-
ness of breath they endure for weeks or months. One day a
seventy-five-year-old man suffering from lung cancer confronted me with a long list of restless nights, saying, "Every
night when I went to bed, I would lie there for about ten
minutes, but soon I would have to get up again because of
severe coughing attacks and try to catch my breath. After fifteen minutes I was able to lie down again. This routine went
on for the whole night. I have kept an exact list of all the
times this has happened. I'm a nervous wreck! I'm done for."
This list of terror, minute for minute, touched me deeply.

Losing our breath triggers anxiety about death—and anxiety in turn causes breathlessness. It's a vicious circle. This disastrous spiral is not simply a difficulty faced by terminally ill people. Our economic and social lives run more and more at a breathless pace. Time, it seems, is experienced only as delay, waiting and even threat. We run after it and never seem to close in on it. We try to kill time or push it away. We might even be tempted to abolish time completely—or hoard it. A twenty-seven-year-old man was dying. A brain tumor had robbed him of a great degree of his consciousness. His life's companion, who had remained loyal to him to the end, pointed to his collection of watches and said, "He wanted to hoard time. And now there's no time left for us!" The person who cannot find time, cannot find breath, cannot find peace. Anxiety and racing propel us into despair, if not into the hands of insurance companies offering no guarantees of anything.

Another phenomenon of our age is the burnout syndrome that leaves us feeling empty, depleted, completely drained and barely functioning. This problem frequently afflicts people who serve others without limits or boundaries. Their ideals and motives cause destruction, usually self-destruction. An authentic, responsible, peaceful, joyful life is threatened by death.

ANDRÉ

Bonaventure uses the word *pax* ("peace") ten times in the first paragraph of his Prologue alone. His biographical background gives us an explanation: during his first two years as general minister of the Franciscan Order, he writes a letter to all the friars listing ten abuses for correction in their lives. His letter was all but ignored. He is forty-two years old with only fifteen years left to live—Bonaventure sees his energy begin to wane. The huge throng of friars has lost focus and is living in tension and the danger of splitting into factions. This young professor who leads them is wondering: how can this go on? What can unite us once again as followers of Francis? Everything seems to be shifting course. Bonaventure is breathless; like a dog he is panting for peace. His wisdom is depleted.

So, like many people seeking peace before him, he sets out for his mountain of revelation. Moses climbs a mountain to receive the Law and his face is transformed. Jesus climbs Mount Tabor and his face is transfigured. Jesus climbs another mountain and proclaims the Beatitudes, his road map to happiness. Francis climbs Mount LaVerna, faces the Seraph and is stigmatized with the wounds of Jesus. Bonaventure climbs Mount LaVerna searching for peace beyond the tensions of his life. He is looking for direction for himself and his brothers. He wants to confront himself with the gospel in a new way; he uses the Latin word *evangelizavit*. Bonaventure wants to be evangelized, "gospel-ized." He wants to be touched anew by the Good News of Jesus Christ. He wants to re-root himself in the Scriptures, to dig into the nourishing soil of the Word of God.

During this very difficult time, Bonaventure does not content himself with mere political or administrative strategies. He becomes a mystic! As a mystic he tries to put his feet on solid ground once again. More than thirty years after Francis' death, Bonaventure tries to recapture his original charism. The spiritual basis of Franciscanism has to be translated into a new and unique formula!

The fruit of these forty days on Mount LaVerna will be

a gift of God, not the result of scientific findings. Bonaventure does not present a study with logical conclusions. No, here is a mystic trying to open himself to the mystery.

Peace here is not an eschatological vision, nor a truce between warring parties; nor is it a slogan for calling people to self-restraint. Rather, peace here is a new certainty in the core of the human person, like a pregnant woman feeling new life in her body. Perhaps peace begins in us simply as an intuitive glimpse. This new life is entirely gift. However, the road to birth demands courage and an openness to risk, with much patience and trust every step of the way.

In our world of fast food and instant communication, waiting is sometimes beyond our human powers, beyond our patience. The Latin word for "patience" is *patientia*, which has its root meaning in the verb *pati*, "to suffer" or "to endure." We Northern and Western people are accustomed to an economic and social system where everything money can buy has to be fast, cheap, enjoyable.

The Prologue of *The Journey of the Human Person into God* places this work in an entirely different world. It speaks of a gift that is meant to be received. Francis received it like a woman receives and conceives life. This reminds us of the basic Christian and spiritual attitude of radical openness, an inclination to greater receptivity and a readiness to take risks. "Will the baby be all right?" "What will this child be like?" The risk-taking of the mystic is comparable to the courage of an expectant mother. This is probably what some spiritual writers mean by the term *virginitas*—virginity for the sake of the kingdom. Those who embark on *The Journey* dispose themselves to an encounter with Peace itself.

EXERCISES

- Find a place where you can remain quiet, away from the telephone, doorbell, family. Simply concentrate on your breath as you inhale and exhale. Try to do or think of nothing special for thirty minutes!

    In the beginning it might be helpful to use some music or a song to draw you into quiet and rest, in order to recollect yourself. Or perhaps a silent walk is better for you.

- Try some creative activity such as painting. Just take a piece of paper and start to draw or paint. You can choose a theme like "peace" or "What is bothering me right now?" Or just begin without any special idea! The result will not be judged. In the end let the picture touch you, speak to you or just be for you.

MIRROR, MIRROR

Bonaventure writes in the Prologue 4:

Therefore, I first of all invite the reader

to groans of prayer through Christ crucified,

through whose blood we are purged from the stain of our sins

[Hebrews 1:3].

Do not think that

reading is sufficient without unction,

reflection without devotion,

investigation without admiration,

observation without exultation,

industry without piety,

knowledge without charity,

intelligence without humility,

study without divine grace,

or the reflecting power of a mirror without the inspiration of

divine wisdom.

To those who are already disposed by divine grace—to the

humble and pious;

to those who are devout and sorrowful for their sins;

to those anointed with the *oil of gladness* [Psalms 44:8];

to those who are lovers of divine wisdom and are inflamed

with desire for it;

and to those who wish to give themselves

to glorifying, admiring, and even savoring God,

I propose the following reflections.

At the same time I ask them to keep in mind

that the mirror of the external world is of little significance

unless our interior mirror is cleansed and polished.

Therefore, O child of God,

awaken yourself first to the remorseful sting of conscience

before you raise your eyes to those rays of wisdom
that are reflected in its mirrors.
Otherwise it might happen that the very act of looking on
these rays
might cause you to fall into an even more treacherous pit of
darkness.

ANDRÉ

Have you have ever driven a car in bad weather? The windows are foggy, the outside mirror so blurred that you can barely see it at all. As you try to get oriented, you want to see, but you cannot. Without a mirror, driving a car is quite a dangerous undertaking. With the help of inner and outer mirrors, you can look all around you in seconds and see what's happening without moving yourself at all.

How often during a given day do you look at yourself in the mirror? What do you see in your reflection? Do you see more than just what is wrong, crooked or in disarray? Do you see only that which you don't like about yourself or what you think others don't like about you? Sometimes when I get up in the morning, I can hardly get out of bed, and looking into the mirror, I think: Oh no, it's you again! What do your eyes see in the mirror? Do you start your day by concentrating on your defects? You probably have some kind of an ideal in your head, or an idea of how you wish you looked!

Caravaggio's *Narcissus* has always touched me in a special way. The artist depicts the young Narcissus sitting at the water's edge, completely absorbed in his own reflection. He fell in love with his image. Of course, looking at ourselves in the mirror probably isn't as attractive for most of us as it was for the young and handsome Narcissus.

In the spiritual literature of the Middle Ages, the word *speculum* (Latin for "mirror") was a frequently used term. In the Franciscan sources, for example, we find *The Mirror of Perfection* (*Speculum perfectionis*). This type of literature strove to offer direction by presenting some saintly persons as examples—mirrors—of how Christians should live.

Quiet surfaces of water or ice offered the earliest mirror-effects. Later, people would hammer and polish metal for a long period of time until they could see their faces in it. Even today the quality of a mirror depends on the material used, its cleanliness and the right amount of light. The best mirror is of no help at all in darkness. A large part of the art of photography and cinematography is the knack of observing and using light, the balance of shadow and light. The most important partners of photographers and cinematographers are the lighting crew, the people behind the lens.

In chapter 1:7, Bonaventure speaks of the original state in which the human person was still upright and could see with his or her eyes. That was paradise! Now people are bent over and they miss the opportunity of gazing "in the mirror."

JOSEF

For Saint Clare of Assisi, it was Christ himself who is the mirror. In her *Fourth Letter to Agnes of Prague*, written in 1253—the year of her own death—Saint Clare writes:

> Certainly, she is happy who has been given to drink deeply
> at this sacred banquet
> so that she might cleave with all her heart to him
> whose beauty all the blessed hosts of heaven wonder

unceasingly at,

whose love stirs to love;

whose contemplation remakes;

whose kindliness floods;

whose sweetness fills;

whose memory glows gently;

whose fragrance brings the dead to life again;

of whom the glorious vision will make all the citizens

of the Jerusalem above most blessed,

since she is the splendour of eternal glory,

the brightness of everlasting light and an unspotted mirror.

Gaze into this mirror daily, O queen, bride of Jesus Christ,

and continuously study your face in it,

so that you may adorn your whole being, within and without,

in robes set about with variety,

adorned, as is only fitting, with virtues like flowers

and with garments every bit as ornate

as those of the daughter and dearly beloved bride of the Most

High King.

In that mirror, then, shine

blessed poverty, holy humility, and love beyond words,

as, by the grace of God, you can contemplate in the whole mirror.[1]

Being a Christian is quite aesthetically challenging. Your very first moves each morning, your waking moments each day, can symbolize and be part of your entire attitude and goal in Christian living, namely, to become like—to mirror—Jesus, to conform yourself to his life and to his gospel. What should you look like if you want to have *his* charisma? What would it cost you to afford *his* clothing and resemble *his* appearance?

EXERCISES

• Sit in front of a mirror and observe your face in it. After five minutes, slowly read Psalm 139. Move your view again and again in the mirror and look at your face and figure from different angles. Repeat individual verses of your choice as often as you like. Say them out loud or just in your mind. Then meditate again for five minutes on your own image in the mirror.

• Today, try in a special way to be conscious of the gaze of people you meet. Notice the difference between superficial and intense gazes. Notice the difference between the gazes of those you know very well and those you know only superficially.

• Practice looking into the eyes of someone near to you. What reaction does this gazing awaken in you and in the other? Do you become uncomfortable, or are you able to let yourself be seen as you are? Are you able to see your own image in the other's eyes?

NOTES

[1] Translation of Saint Clare's *Fourth Letter to Agnes of Prague*, verses 9-18, is that of Sister Frances Teresa Downing, O.S.C. (Arundel, England: Crossbush Publications, Convent of Poor Clares). In this passage, Saint Clare quotes a text from the Legend of Saint Agnes, the Roman martyr, used on her feast in the Liturgy of the Hours, the Office of Readings (part of the Office which includes longer readings from spiritual writers). The senses are involved here in an impressive way. Saint Clare seems to use this passage as a central exercise for herself. See also her *Third Letter to Agnes of Prague*, verses 3–28, and her *Testament*, verses 18–23.

Tuesday

THIS IS WHAT I DESIRE WITH MY WHOLE HEART!

Bonaventure writes in the Prologue 3:

For those six wings can well be understood
as symbols of six levels of uplifting illuminations
through which the soul is prepared, as it were by certain stages
or steps,
to pass over to peace
through the ecstatic rapture of Christian wisdom.
There is no other way but through the most burning love of
the Crucified.
It was that sort of love
which lifted Paul into the *third heaven*
and transformed him into Christ
to such a degree that he could say:
With Christ I am nailed to the cross.
It is now no longer I that live, but Christ lives in me
[2 Corinthians 12:2; Galatians 2:20].
This sort of love so absorbed the mind of Francis also
that his spirit became apparent in his flesh;
and for two years prior to his death,
he carried the holy marks of the passion in his body.

The image of the six wings of the Seraph, therefore,
is a symbol of six stages of illumination
which begin with creatures and lead to God
to whom no one has access properly
except through the Crucified. . . .
This means that no one can enter into the heavenly Jerusalem
by means of contemplation
without entering through the blood of the Lamb as through a
door.

For no one is disposed in any way for those divine
contemplations
which lead to spiritual ecstasies
without being, like Daniel, *a person of desires* [Daniel 9:23].
But desires of this type are enkindled in us in two ways,
namely through the *cry of prayer*
which makes us cry aloud with *groaning of the heart*
[Psalms 37:9],
and through the *brightness of speculation*
by which we turn our attention most directly and intently to
the rays of light.

JOSEF

"Desire" is another keyword of the Prologue. I remember
quite well a small hermitage near Spello—opposite Assisi on
the other end of Mount Subasio—where I spent some time
one winter. It was cold, wet and not very comfortable in the
room attached to an empty cattle stall, with a hole in the
floor leading to a dark cave. The environment mirrored my
inner being. I so greatly desired light and warmth in my life
I was looking for direction. I, too, had come to a mountain
of revelation in my life.

In daytime, I would gather some branches so I could
light a fire at least once a day. The wood was wet and when I
finally succeeded in lighting it, I was rewarded with a most
beautiful concert. It crackled, sighed, ached. These burning,
self-consuming branches touched me at a very deep level,
the level of my desire and thirst for peace and reconciliation.
It is interesting that fire in most religions and cultures is a
sacred symbol, speaking of yearning rather than fulfillment.

Even in my childhood, religious practices involving

the mystery of light and fire fascinated me. I can recall the processions of light leading us through the evening darkness, the whispered prayers of hundreds of people winding their way around the dark plaza of our town's shrine to Mary, carrying candles and torches. More than anything else, this sign still speaks to me. In today's civil society torch-lit marches and chains of candles speak for themselves. Surely, this is a holy sign!

In the phenomenology of religion, the symbol of fire is linked to blood, to sexuality and the relationship to the entire cosmos, to salvation, fortune and the intimate union with the divine. Especially in the Judeo-Christian tradition, the central manifestations of God are connected with the symbol of light and fire. We need only recall the burning bush in Exodus 3, Yahweh's revelation in the old covenant and Jesus, who says, *I am the light of the world* [John 8:12]. Is God not a God of desire? God wants to be in communion with all of creation. How else could we offer a decent explanation for the Incarnation? And at Pentecost, when the church was born, the symbol is once again *fire*, which hints at the core of this new religious life, the heart of a powerful new beginning.

Christians do not profess a belief in a God who is remote from this world and a stranger to it, a distant philosopher-God enthroned high above the valleys of this world and untouched by it. During the flow of Christian history, it is precisely Franciscan spirituality that rediscovered the I-Thou relationship with God. Our whole person, in all our human powers and desires, our height and depth, is challenged in this relationship, which is all about falling in love and being in love!

The Franciscan sources are full of this idea and symbolism. Bonaventure writes in his biography of Francis:

> From that time on he (Francis) was removing himself from the pressure of public business, he would eagerly beg the divine kindness to show him what he should do. When the flame of heavenly desire intensified in him by the practice of frequent prayer, and already, out of his love for a heavenly home, he *despised* all earthly things *as nothing*, he realized that he had found a *hidden treasure*, and like a wise merchant, planned to buy *the pearl he had found by selling everything*. Nevertheless, how he should do this, he did not yet know. . . .[1]

Later in this same biography of Saint Francis, we read:

> Who would be competent to describe the burning charity with which Francis, *the friend of the Bridegroom*, was aflame? Like a thoroughly burning glowing coal, he seemed totally absorbed in the flame of divine love. For as soon as he heard "the love of the Lord," he was excited, moved and on fire as if these words from the outside were a pick strumming the strings of his heart on the inside. . . .
>
> Jesus Christ crucified always *rested like a bundle of myrrh in the bosom* of his soul, into Whom he longed to be totally transformed through an enkindling of ecstatic love.[2]

In one of the most delightful traditional Franciscan stories, Clare had an ardent desire to share a meal with Francis and, after some reluctance on his part, Francis acceded to her wish. Francis had some of his friars accompany her from San Damiano to Saint Mary of the Angels:

> Nearby they found a clean surfaced stone, and there they sat down on the grass while Clare's companion and one of the brothers served them both with crusts of bread and cups of fresh water. The sun flickered through the trees as the branches swayed in the breeze. Overhead the birds were celebrating their spring songs. However, before placing any food to his mouth, Francis began to speak of the Lord and his charity and love. This love of which Francis spoke became like a flame of fire, which from the first utterance entered the souls of those present and sent them into ecstasy. This light spread to the woods with such brilliance that the sun was overshadowed. The Portiuncula became one great mass of light. From Assisi it seemed as though the woods were on fire. From far away people came running to put out the flames. As they neared the place they could see that there was nothing burning in the woods, which nevertheless was full of light.[3]

André

Surely this historically late source is relating the flames of divine love and ecstasy with desire. After many dark periods in the history of Christian theology, I find it very consoling that the Second Vatican Council again picks up this symbolic language in its most important document, *Lumen gentium* (*A Light to the Nations*), thus moving away from a rather juridical understanding of the relationship between God and the world. This burning desire within us is capable of changing the whole world. The Danish philosopher-theologian, Søren Kierkegaard (1813–1855) once noted that only transformed people can effect transformation.

Anthony de Mello (1931–1987), the Indian Jesuit teacher, told this story:

> Each day the disciple would ask the same question: "How shall I find God?" And each day he would get the same mysterious answer: "Through desire." "But I desire God with all my heart, don't I? Then why have I not found God?" One day the Master happened to be bathing in the river with the disciple. He pushed the man's head under water and held it there while the poor fellow struggled desperately to break loose. Next day it was the Master who began the conversation. "Why did you struggle so when I held your head under water?" "Because I was gasping for air." "When you are given the grace to gasp for God the way you gasped for air, you will have found God."[4]

Those who are on fire belong to God, to Christ and to his body, the church. They hunger and thirst for justice and peace and for an encounter with the *living* One. The human path toward union with God is the way of desire, of an inner burning. We need to have some kind of spiritual discipline to keep this inner flame lit. In the beginning of our "ascent," therefore, it may be very helpful to carry enough wood to burn. Desire is the heart of prayer, and prayer is the motor that transports us further along the journey.

The French poet and pilot Antoine de Saint-Exupéry (1900–1944) is reported to have said that if you are going to build a ship, don't go out and gather people together, collect wood, prepare tools and assign jobs. First, instill in the people a desire for the wide and endless sea.

EXERCISES

Try to be present to all your senses by becoming aware of each one!

- Go for a walk focusing on inner concentration. Experience in quiet and meditation a sunrise or sunset or a walk through the night with the bright stars or other images of desire.
- Ask yourself the following questions:

  Where do I sense a desire for peace in my life now?

  What areas of my life lack inner or outer peace?
- Write some answers to those questions on paper.

  For each answer use a separate small sheet of paper.
- Then burn the pieces of paper, lighting a candle from this new flame while praying for peace, using, for example, the Taizé chant, *Da pacem domine.*

Like the fire that consumes these papers, may your desire for reconciliation, renewal and peace never die.

NOTES

[1] *The Major Legend of Saint Francis* 1:4, in *Francis of Assisi: Early Documents—The Founder, Volume II,* Regis J. Armstrong, O.F.M. CAP., J. A. Wayne Hellmann, O.F.M. CONV., William J. Short, O.F.M., eds. (New York: New City Press, 2000), p. 533.

[2] *Ibid.,* IX:1–2, pp. 596–597.

[3] Piero Bargellini, *The Little Flowers of St. Clare,* Edmund O'Gorman, O.F.M. CONV., trans. (Assisi: Edizioni Porziuncola, 1988), pp. 53–54; see also *The*

Little Flowers of St. Francis 15, Raphael Brown, ed. and trans., in *Omnibus of Sources*, Marion A. Habig, ed. (Chicago: Franciscan Herald Press, 1983), pp. 1332–1334.

4 Anthony de Mello, *One Minute Wisdom* (Garden City, N.Y.: Doubleday, 1986), p. 43.

Wednesday

Look into My Eyes!

Bonaventure writes in the Prologue 1 and chapter 7:6:

P:1. He was like a citizen of that Jerusalem about which the
man of peace—
who was peaceable even with those who despised peace—says:
Pray for those things that are for the peace of Jerusalem.
For he knew that it is only in peace
that the throne of Solomon exists, since it is written:
His place is in peace, and his dwelling is in Sion
[Psalms 119:7; 121:6; 75:3].

7:6. Now if you ask how all these things are to come about,
ask grace, not doctrine;
desire, not intellect;
the groaning of prayer and not studious reading;
the Spouse not the teacher;
God, not a human being;
darkness not clarity;
not light, but the fire that inflames totally and carries one into
God
through spiritual fervor and with the most burning affections.
It is God alone who is this fire,
and God's *furnace is in Jerusalem* [Isaiah 31:9].
And it is Christ who starts the fire
with the white flame of his most intense passion.

Josef

In paragraph one of the Prologue, Bonaventure not only
speaks about mirrors, but also about eyes. He prays: "God . . .
grant enlightenment to the eyes of our mind." *Oculus*, the
Latin word for "eye," is etymologically linked to the word

speculum, the Latin word for "mirror." Let's consider for a moment our eyes.

What have you experienced with your eyes? Certainly there were important impressions picked up at the beginning of your life. How did your parents look at you? Were you "re-spected" by them? For eyes are linked to trust and acceptance.

I remember a pilgrimage we made on foot from Greccio to Assisi. It was February, very dry and cold. Since I am very nearsighted, I can see better by wearing contact lenses, which are subject to problems, especially in windy weather. One day we had to walk along a dusty road with many cars passing by, and suddenly some dust nested in my eyes. I could neither open my eyes nor did I have anything with me to remove the lenses. So I had to trust my companions in my blindness. Eyes closed, I was led along the road. But the eyes of my heart were wide open.

Often our first eye contact determines whether we are attracted to or repulsed by someone. Is there sympathy or antipathy? Or, imagine that you are standing in the midst of a crowd and suddenly realize that a complete stranger is staring at you with a critical eye. You may feel threatened: am I known by someone without being loved? Or, a slightly different feeling may emerge from the passing glance of a stranger as you walk by. Your eyes meet fleetingly, but you do not gaze upon one another.

If two persons are arguing and become estranged from one another, unable to speak to one another, they may often glance at one another, but they avoid looking each other in the eye. They refuse to see and to be seen, to be loved. Conversion then, would mean being able to look into the mirror and gaze lovingly upon my own face, or that of the other, as well. But are we not afraid to do so? Many times we cannot take the full light of conversion and, so, we retreat into the twilight. Desire, however, draws us to the full light.

The age of Francis and Clare was an age of itinerant singers and musicians, the so-called troubadours. Francis loved them and their world; he himself preferred to sing in French, or more exactly, in the dialect of Provence. He knew the troubadours' rituals. If a singer would offer a song to his lady to court her, she would signal her acceptance or rejection with her eyes. The lady who was the object of his affection would, if she accepted his homage, look him straight in the eye. If she were rejecting his song, she would keep her eyes cast down. She would not look at him, signaling that his love and attention were rejected.

Francis alludes to this ritual in his *Letter to a Minister*. The minister is frustrated trying to serve the friars:

> I wish to know in this way if you love the Lord and me, His servant and yours: that there is not any brother in the world who has sinned—however much he could have sinned—who, after he has looked into your eyes, would ever depart without your mercy, if he is looking for mercy. And if he were not looking for mercy, you would ask him if he wants mercy. And if he would sin a thousand times before your eyes, love him more than me so that you may draw him to the Lord.[1]

In my marriage, I constantly experience this tension. Our two eldest children are boys, and their brotherly love is at times nerve-racking. Quite frequently our sleep is interrupted; household affairs demand much attention and time. Situations like these remind us how necessary it is for us parents to pause for a while and gaze quietly into each other's eyes. We need to recognize and know one another anew. And this may require that we step back a bit from the daily demands made upon us.

There is a further experience of the eyes. When I meet a good friend whom I love, I know he enjoys seeing me. Gazing into the eyes of such a person is not simply a fleeting glance, but a loving and desiring one. This communication develops beyond words, even beyond mirrors. It means being present to the other person in the silence.

In literature, this experience has been expressed so wonderfully in *The Little Prince* in the story of how he became the fox's friend. The author, Antoine de Saint-Exupéry, calls the process that develops between the two of them "taming":

> "Just that," said the fox. "To me, you are still nothing more than a little boy who is just like a hundred thousand other little boys. And I have no need of you. And you, on your part, have no need of me. To you, I am nothing more than a fox like a hundred thousand other foxes. But if you tame me, then we shall need each other. To me, you will be unique in all the world. To you, I shall be unique in all the world. . . ."
>
> "What must I do, to tame you ?" asked the little prince.
>
> "You must be very patient," replied the fox. "First you will sit down at a little distance from me—like that—in the grass. I shall look at you out of the corner of my eye, and you will say

nothing. Words are the source of misunder-
standings. But you will sit a little closer to me,
every day."[2]

One could say that the experience of faith is related to a new
way of being looked at or "re-spected," a new image. And this
image is a gift!

A text that fascinates me in this context is the
prophet Ezekiel 16. Yahweh does not pass by the newborn
child lying in the desert wilderness wallowing in its blood
and crying. God looks at the child, and that is life! And that
is the way human beings come to life. They are looked at in
joy and excitement, contemplated and cherished. From the
very beginning God is someone who looks upon us in love.
How great it would be if more people could have this life-giving experience. This is healing medicine for all forms of self-
doubt, as well as for the bitter statement: "Nobody loves me."
Is not this image of how we are loved by God our ultimate
stronghold?

ANDRÉ
And this, I think, is the core of Christian contemplation. We
are not the initiators of contemplation. God looks at us in
love. That is a gift. We reach the fullness of life by accepting
and responding to this loving gaze.

And this is the experience of peace for Clare and
Francis of Assisi and the deepest reason for their joy. In
Francis' life there are two central experiences that directly
exemplify this:

- his encounter with the leper in his youth, when his
  life was turned upside-down;
- and on Mount LaVerna, when he was eye-to-eye

with the Seraph who gifted him with painful consolation and divine confirmation.

There on Mount LaVerna, I think Francis felt God's loving gaze. He felt so well-accepted that from that point on he had nothing to lose, so he could walk the path of poverty. He no longer depended on the superficial and fleeting perception of his society. This enabled him to live in relaxed freedom, a free and joyful attitude of letting go. This is the background of the scene where he strips himself naked in front of the bishop, his father and the people of Assisi. Having let go of what is security for most people, he discovers his new way of life.

In one of his sermons, Anthony of Padua, whose role as teacher of the brothers was acknowledged in a personal letter from Francis,[3] said:

> Do you want to carry God in your heart every day? Look constantly at yourself. Where your eye is, there is your heart. Keep your eyes fixed constantly on yourself. I mention three items: your heart, your eye, yourself. God is in your heart, your heart is in your eye, your eye is in you. So, if you are looking at yourself, you are looking at God in you. Do you want to have God in your heart every day? Then, be what God has created you to be. Do not look for another I in yourself. Do not try to be anything other than what God created you to be, and you will constantly have God in your heart.[4]

EXERCISES

- Watch a child at play. The child is deeply involved and absorbed in what is happening in the game. Maybe you would like to join the child in playing, just for the sake of playing.

- Sit down in a quiet place and try just "to be" there. Let yourself be contemplated by God. An empty chapel or church might serve this purpose.
- Read and meditate on Ezekiel 16. God's relationship with the human person is described as a love relationship:

> I passed by you, and saw you flailing about in your blood. As you lay in your blood, I said to you, "Live! And grow up like a plant of the field.". . .
>
> I pledged myself to you and entered into a covenant with you . . . and you became mine. (Ezekiel 16:6–8)

NOTES

[1] *A Letter to the Minister 9-10*, in *Francis of Assisi: The Saint—Early Documents, Volume I*, Regis J. Armstrong, O.F.M. CAP., J. A. Wayne Hellmann, O.F.M. CONV., William J. Short, O.F.M., eds. (New York: New City Press, 1999), p. 97.

[2] Antoine de Saint Exupéry, *The Little Prince*, Katherine Woods, trans. (New York: Harcourt, Brace & World, Inc., 1971), pp. 80–84.

[3] *A Letter to Brother Anthony of Padua*, in *Francis of Assisi: The Saint, op. cit.*, p. 107.

[4] *Leben des Evangeliums. Ausgewählte Texte aus den Predigten des Heiligen Antonius von Padua (Gospel Life. Text excerpts from the Sermons of St. Anthony of Padua)*, introduction and commentary by Sophronius Clasen, O.F.M., in *Franziskanische Quellenschriften* IV (Werl: Dietrich Coelde Verlag, 1954), pp. 248-249. Authors' translation. Anthony (1195-1231), born Ferdinand in Lisbon, Portugal, joined the Franciscan movement around 1220. He became a professor of theology at Bologna and attracted huge crowds by his preaching in southern France, northern Italy and, finally, in Padua where he died and was buried.

Thursday

FRANCIS BERNARDONE

Bonaventure writes in the Prologue 2 and chapter 7:3:

P:2. Moved by the example of our most blessed father, Francis,
I eagerly desired this peace—I a sinner who, unworthy as I am,
had become the seventh general minister of the brothers
after the death of the most blessed father.
It happened around the time of the thirty-third anniversary of
the death of the saint
that I was moved by a divine inspiration
and withdrew to Mount LaVerna since it was a place of quiet.
There I wished to satisfy the desire of my spirit for peace.
And while I was there reflecting on certain ways
in which the human person might ascend to God,
I recalled, among other things,
that miracle which the blessed Francis himself had
experienced in this very place,
namely the vision of the winged Seraph in the form of the
Crucified.
As I reflected on this,
I saw immediately that this vision pointed
not only to the uplifting of our father himself in
contemplation
but also to the road by which one might arrive at this
experience.

7:3. All this was shown also to blessed Francis when,
in a rapture of contemplation on the top of the mountain
where I reflected on the things I have written here,
a six-winged Seraph fastened to a cross appeared to him.
This I myself and several others have heard about from his
companion

who was with him at that very place.
Here he was carried out of himself in contemplation and
passed over into God.
And he has been set forth as the example of perfect
contemplation
just as he had earlier been known as the example of action,
like another Jacob transformed into Israel [Genesis 35:10].
So it is that, through Francis,
God invites all truly spiritual persons to this sort of passing over,
more by example than by words.

JOSEF

This is not the place to go into detail about the life and work of Francis of Assisi (1181/82–1226), for in recent years much good material about him has been published.[1] In this first week you might spend some time with a biography, getting acquainted or reacquainted with Francis. His life provided source material for Bonaventure and all those men and women who have followed him throughout these last eight centuries.

Dynamic leader of a band of young men, Francis was always ready for action: a party, a feast or some prank. He lacked nothing. He was supposed to inherit his merchant-father's cloth business. The socio-economic situation of his day was undergoing radical change. Money was taking over the world of business and finance. Francis Bernardone could certainly expect the best, for his father was one of the most successful entrepreneurs of his day. Certainly he was not just another face in the crowd; his personality served him well. His motto might have been, "the more, the better."

During and after his imprisonment in Perugia for a year, he began to think about the path he had begun to pursue. Years later he would write in his *Testament*:

> The Lord gave me, Brother Francis, thus to
> begin doing penance in this way: for when I
> was in sin, it seemed too bitter for me to see
> lepers. And the Lord Himself led me among
> them and I showed *mercy* (cf. Sirach 35:4) to
> them. And when I left them, what had seemed
> bitter to me was turned into sweetness of soul
> and body. And afterwards I delayed a little and
> left the world.[2]

The *Legend of the Three Companions* states:

> After a few days, he moved to a hospice of lep-
> ers, taking with him a large sum of money. . . .
> With the help of God's grace, he became such
> a servant and friend of the lepers, that, as he
> testified in his *Testament*, he stayed among
> them and served them with humility.[3]

Raoul Manselli writes in his biography of Saint Francis:

> Francis began to appear even more in the grip
> of a profound inner crisis. We will never know
> its deep wellsprings, because there exist no
> confidences from him to anyone on the mat-
> ter. The sources remain, then, closed off in
> the silence of a conscience, about which we
> know only that it became even more restless,
> full of uncertainties, of vacillation, of perplex-
> ity, until the decisive event arrived, that fact
> that determined the break from his former
> way of life: his conversion.[4]

Then, through embracing minority or powerlessness in soli-

darity with the poor and a new lifestyle of poverty by "living
. . . without anything of (his) own,"[5] his whole being was filled
with overflowing joy and gratitude. We are convinced that
this remarkable joy and this playful, creative unpredictabili-
ty have been part of the core of the Franciscan movement
throughout the centuries. Francis puts his trust in the ever-
flowing, abundant fountain of life. And that makes him—in
the depths of his being—a brother of all creatures.

One of his most moving texts is to be found in chapter 23 of the *Earlier Rule:*

With our whole heart,
our whole soul,
our whole mind,
with our whole strength and fortitude,
with our whole understanding
with all our powers
with every effort,
every affection,
every feeling,
every desire and wish
let us all love *the Lord God*
Who has given and gives to each one of us
our whole body, our whole soul and our whole life,
Who has created, redeemed and will save us by His mercy
alone,
Who did and does everything good for us . . .
the only true God,
Who is the fullness of good,
all good, every good, the true and supreme good
Who alone is good,
merciful, gentle delectable and sweet . . . .[6]

ANDRÉ

Francis' radical poverty, rigorous asceticism and rejection of all possessions open a path leading to exuberant joy and gratitude in opposition to all of life's bitterness and despair. In choosing LaVerna, Bonaventure makes a direct reference to the sign that had quite often become a sign of contradiction: the stigmata. In September 1224, on that mountain Francis had the wounds of the crucified Jesus miraculously imprinted on his own body. Every fiber of Francis' being became transparent with the love of God. The bleeding wounds of his hands and feet and side show his identification with Jesus' radical option for the life of the world:

> In his theology of history Saint Bonaventure understands Saint Francis as the angel of the rising sun mentioned in Revelation 7:2: "Then I saw another angel ascend from the rising of the sun, with the seal of the living God." The seal of the living God had been impressed on him when he received the stigmata on Mount LaVerna two years before he died. As such he heralded the new order of contemplatives in the age of the Holy Spirit predicted by Joachim of Flora.
>
> We noted earlier that Dante wanted Assisi to be called Orient because from that city a new sun arose on the world in the person of St. Francis. But perhaps the most attractive words about the connection between St. Francis and the sun are those which conclude the second chapter of G. K. Chesterton's *St. Francis of Assisi*. There Francis is described so beautifully as herald of the sun: "While it was yet twilight a figure appeared silently and sud-

denly on a little hill above the city, dark
against the fading darkness. For it was the end
of a long and stern night, a night of vigil, not
unvisited by stars. He stood with his hands lifted, as in so many statues and pictures, and
about him was a burst of birds singing; and
behind him was the break of day."[7]

EXERCISES

• In Francis' "sermon on the mount," his Admonitions, he
  summarizes his attitude toward life, his philosophy of life:

> Where there is charity and wisdom,
> there is neither fear nor ignorance.
>
> Where there is patience and humility,
> there is neither anger nor disturbance.
>
> Where there is poverty with joy,
> there is neither greed nor avarice.
>
> Where there is rest and meditation,
> there is neither anxiety nor restlessness.
>
> Where there is fear of the Lord to guard an entrance,
> there the enemy cannot have a place to enter.
>
> Where there is a heart full of mercy and discernment,
> there is neither excess nor hardness of heart.[8]

• Try to "play" with the contrasting pairs. Perhaps you can
  find a symbol for each of the terms, or some image, or perhaps even some bodily movement. For contrast, place the
  two sides of the text in two separate columns.

• Take some meditation time and reflect on the selection
  from chapter 23 of *Francis' Earlier Rule* (above).

NOTES

[1] Biographies of Saint Francis of Assisi are bountiful. Authors such as Sabatier, Englebert, Jörgensen, Fortini, Manselli, Boff, Kazantzakis, Frugoni, Robson, Mueller, House and countless others have penned biographies of Francis. The basic Franciscan sources in three comprehensive volumes have been published recently, edited by Regis J. Armstrong, O.F.M. CAP., J. A. Wayne Hellmann, O.F.M. CONV., and William J. Short, O.F.M., *Francis of Assisi: Early Documents—The Saint, The Founder, The Prophet* (3 vols.) (New York: New City Press, 1999, 2000, 2001).

[2] *Testament* 1–3, in *Francis of Assisi: The Saint, op. cit.*, p. 124.

[3] *The Legend of the Three Companions* 4:11, in *Francis of Assisi: The Founder, op. cit.*, p. 74.

[4] Raoul Manselli, *St. Francis of Assisi* (Chicago: Franciscan Herald Press, 1988), p. 50.

[5] *The Later Rule* I:1, in *Francis of Assisi: The Saint, op. cit.*, p. 100.

[6] *The Earlier Rule* XXIII:8–9, *ibid.*, pp. 84–85.

[7] Eric Doyle, O.F.M., *St. Francis and the Song of Brotherhood and Sisterhood* (New York: Franciscan Institute Publications, 1997), p. 87. See also, Joseph Ratzinger, *The Theology of History in St. Bonaventure*, Zachary Hayes, O.F.M., trans. (Chicago: Franciscan Herald Press, 1971), pp. 1–55, 166–190; G. K. Chesterton, *St. Francis of Assisi* (London: Hodder and Stoughton, 1923), p. 39.

[8] *The Admonitions* XXVII, in *Francis of Assisi: The Saint, op. cit.*, pp. 136–137.

Friday

CLARE FAVARONE

Bonaventure writes in chapter 7:4:

If this passing over is to be perfect,
all intellectual activities must be given up,
and our deepest and total affection must be directed to God
and transformed into God.
But this is mystical and very secret,
which *no one knows except one who receives it*
[Revelation 2:17].
And no one receives it except one who desires it.
And no one desires it
but one who is penetrated to the very marrow
with the fire of the Holy Spirit
whom Christ has sent into the world [Luke 12:49].
Therefore the Apostle says [1 Corinthians 2:10 ff.]
that the revelation of this mystical wisdom comes through the
Holy Spirit.

JOSEF

It often happens that those who write Franciscan history lose sight of the woman at Francis' side—Clare of Assisi. Just who was Clare Favarone?

Clare, about twelve years younger than Francis, came from a noble family.[1] In her book, *The First Franciscan Woman*, Margaret Carney gives us an early portrait of Clare as:

a young woman who from childhood was seen
to be especially gifted in the things of the
Spirit . . . she was charitable . . . respected for
her purity of life and desire to avoid worldly
gossip . . . devoted to prayer, almsgiving, peni-

tential practices, fasting . . . held in high
regard. . . . (A)quaintances and relations
affirm . . . that her intentions toward a dedicated life had been visible even before the dramatic events of her Palm Sunday flight to join
Francis and his brothers. What is most striking
in this mosaic is the pattern of practices
ascribed to Clare . . . a "form of life" even at
this early stage. It was, in fact, a form of life
consonant with the elements of lay penitential
spirituality then in flower. How else can such
details as the desire to remain hidden, the
choice of sober dress, the use of a penitential
garment, the prayer, fasting, almsgiving and
the consistent ministry to the poor be
explained. . . . Such was the young woman to
whom Francis would turn to fulfill the prophecy made in the Spirit some years earlier, for
whom he had undertaken the radical renova-
tion of the church of San Damiano, trans-
forming the repaired edifice into a structure
of "living stones. [2]

Clare received a good education—her Latin is far better
than that of Francis. Although Clare "had been educated
with a view to a good marriage,"[3] Clare was able to evade her
family's plans for her life.

The penitential movement, including that of Francis
himself, was blossoming and women were seeking to join it.[4]
People were roaming the roads, living penitential lives and
preaching the gospel. Some of them even started to celebrate sacraments without permission. The institutional
church was very concerned because of the chaos that

ensued. A cardinal was put in charge of solving this problem.[5] His task was to enclose all the women as quickly as
possible!

Regarding the early encounters between Francis
and Clare, her sister Beatrice witnessed: "After Saint Francis
heard of the fame of her holiness, he went to preach to
her."[6] Before Francis and Clare begin to interact with each
other, the reputation of Clare's holiness seems to have been
already established in Assisi. Hearing of her reputation,
Francis "whispered in her ears of a sweet espousal with
Christ, persuading her to preserve the pearl of her virginal
purity for (her) blessed Spouse. . . . Immediately an insight
into the eternal joys was opened to her."[7] This espousal invitation gave her the "insight" that Murray Bodo, Franciscan
poet, describes: "The words were simple and unadorned, but
they touched her like a deep and purifying shaft of light. Her
whole being seemed bathed in a light that came from some-
where inside her own heart."[8]

What did Francis and Clare really mean to one
another? There is a story that gives us some indication:

> Clare would have liked to have seen Francis
> frequently. There were so many things that
> she wanted to ask him! She could manage
> with very little material food, but she required
> much more of that spiritual nourishment
> which came from the words of the master. On
> the other hand, Francis kept himself well away
> from San Damiano . . . to set an example for
> the rest. . . . Clare was saddened by this, and
> her sorrow came to the ears of Francis. . . .
> Certainly he loved them all, these "Poor
> Ladies" who followed his teaching. . . . From

time to time Francis did visit her, but his appearances at San Damiano were momentary. He knocked at the door and greeted them: "Peace and good will." He glanced inside and noted that the convent was "a strong tower of sovereign poverty."

One cold winter's day Francis stood, ready to leave, as he had come, without having any other comfort than the knowledge that true poverty was being observed. . . . So he walked toward the door. Outside the wind whistled and blew through the branches of the olive trees, and snow was settling in little droves and sleet was forming upon the front pathway. Francis' bare feet stepped out onto the snow and Clare followed after him a few paces away. She hoped to detain him a little. At least she hoped to get a promise from him of another visit very soon.

Francis pulled his hood up over his head: "Sister Clare, it is better that we go our own ways because of what the world might think. I will leave you to manage on your own." Clare, standing in the brightness of the ground, felt lost: "What will I do without you? You are my guide and support." Francis raised his eyes to the somber sky: "Our blessed Lord will guide you." "And we will not see you again?" Francis looked about. Considering the weather conditions and seeing a thorny rosebush covered with snow, he said to Clare: "We will meet again when the roses re-flower." It was the beginning of winter and the roses would not flower again until well into the spring. He wanted to place a complete season between himself and Clare.

"Let it be as you wish," answered Clare, "but also as Our Lord wishes." And she bowed her head. Francis made to move away, but almost immediately he involuntarily stopped. On the bush that was near him suddenly and miraculously groups of roses had flowered! Clare, under her double veil, smiled to herself; and when Francis had gone off towards Spello in the snowstorm, she went back into San Damiano with a bunch of roses in her hands which she placed at the feet of the Crucifix.[9]

In *The Form of Life* given to Clare and her sisters, Francis proclaims: "I resolve and promise for myself and for my brothers to have that same loving care and special solicitude for you as (I have) for them."[10] Another story from *The Little Flowers of Saint Clare* illustrates this "loving care and special solicitude":

> Though far away from San Damiano, he thought of Clare and her Poor Ladies. He was afraid lest their shining example should be hidden and their splendor obscured. . . . Far from her, Francis prayed that her light might shine ever clearer before people. Standing in prayer during the night, he raised his eyes to the stars and asked the Lord to let the Poor Ladies shine with splendor even as those heavenly bodies. . . . One night when there was a full moon, he was out on a long journey with Brother Leo . . . and they arrived, tired and

dusty, at an open well. Francis went up to it and for a long time stood there gazing down into the darkened shaft of the well as though attracted by something in the water below. When he went away from the parapet, he seemed in a state of ecstasy; he had not even asked for a drink, but continued walking, singing and praising the Lord.

After a while, as though sensing the perplexity of Brother Leo who was walking behind him, he stopped and asked his companion: "Brother Leo, what do you think I saw reflected on the water down in that well?" "My Father," said Brother Leo, "you would have seen the moon that was shining in the sky." "No, Brother Leo, I saw there the face of our Sister Clare who I thought was suffering under temptation. Instead, she was all peace and brightness. Because of this my heart is now set at peace in her regard, and full of joy and gratitude to my Savior."[11]

André

The friendship and closeness of these two people was also marked by much suffering. Francis died the evening of October 3, 1226, and was canonized in 1228. Clare became more aware of the "responsibility she bore for the growth of the Franciscan vocation in the church during that span of twenty-seven years after the death of Francis in which she continued to govern, to write, and to legislate."[12]

At San Damiano, she struggled resolutely with church leaders to maintain the form of life given her by Saint Francis. "Pope Gregory IX . . . pleaded with Clare to accept some possessions, but Clare was unwilling to yield."[13] Pope Innocent IV "brought new problems, this time serious ones, for Clare. . . . [H]e issued a new rule . . . allowing the sisters to possess property in common."[14] Remembering the privilege of poverty granted her grudgingly by Gregory IX, Clare began to write her own *Rule*, the first woman to write a rule approved by the church.[15]

The richness of her spiritual strength speaks to us through her writings, especially her letters to her friend Agnes of Prague. They are a beautiful treasure of Franciscan spirit, a source for meditation and for a deeper insight into the soul of a great woman. Poor Clare Sister Frances Teresa Downing writes:

> Her letters are densely packed with thoughts, and constructed in a way quite different from ours today. They are more like a piece of architecture than a casual communication to a friend, and this must always be borne in mind. The bonus is that we can scrutinise her words, constructions and parallels with a reasonable confidence that she did indeed mean the things we are reading into them.[16]

We would like to quote here some passages from her *Third Letter to Agnes of Prague*, which was composed around 1238 when Clare was forty-four years old and already quite ill:

> Truly I can rejoice, nor can anyone make me a stranger to such joy, since that which under heaven I had desired, I already hold. For I see that you, sustained by the wonderful privilege of wisdom from the mouth of God himself, have overthrown in a terrible and unexpected

way the shrewdness of the astute enemy and the pride that destroys human nature and the vanity which infatuates the human heart.

A treasure beyond compare is hidden in the field of the world and in human hearts. With it, that by which everything was made from nothing has been bought. You have embraced it by humility, by the power of faith and the arms of poverty. And, to use the very words of the Apostle himself, I judge you a co-worker of God himself and one who holds up the members of his ineffable Body who are giving way.

Who could tell me not to rejoice at such wonderful joys? Therefore, you too, my dearest, rejoice in the Lord always, and, O Lady most beloved in Christ, joy of the angels and crown of the sisters, may neither bitterness nor clouds overwhelm you.

Place your mind in the mirror of eternity;
place your soul in the splendor of glory
Place your heart in the icon of the divine substance
and transform your whole self through contemplation
into an image of the Godhead.

Do this in order that you yourself may feel what his friends feel on tasting the hidden sweetness, which God himself has kept from the beginning for those who love Him. And completely passing over all those things with which an untrustworthy and perturbed world entangles its blinded lovers,
love totally
the One who gave his whole self for your love,
the One at whose beauty the sun and the moon wonder,

the One whose rewards, with their value and greatness,
have no end;
I am speaking of
the One who is Son of the Most High,
Whom the Virgin brought to birth
and after whose birth remained a virgin.
Cleave to his most sweet Mother
who begot such a Son as the heavens could not contain,
And yet received him within the small confines of her holy
womb
and held him on her young girl's lap.
See how obvious it already is,
that through the grace of God the faithful human soul,
that most worthy creation,
is far greater than the heavens,
while the heavens, with other creatures, cannot contain the
Creator,
and only the faithful soul itself is his mansion and throne,
and this only through love
—which the ungodly lack.

Truth itself having said: anyone who loves me will be loved by
My Father,
and I shall love him, and we shall come to him and make our
home with him.
As the glorious Virgin of virgins materially,
so will you, spiritually,
certainly be able to carry him in your chaste and virginal body,
by following in her footprints,
particularly the prints of humility and poverty,
containing him by whom you and everything are contained,
possessing that which,
in comparison with the other transitory possessions of this
world,
you will possess more completely.[17]

EXERCISES

- Reread the passage from Saint Clare's *Third Letter to Agnes of Prague* in quiet. Try to imagine the author, her joy, her strong will, her strength of faith and life.

    And "place your mind into the mirror of eternity!"

- Against the background of the same letter, think about the mystery of "spiritual motherhood."[18] Is this not the primary dignity of Christians? According to Marian theology, is not her central mission to be mother and model of the church?

- Asian cultures have a deep sense of reverence, which they express in rituals of greeting or leave-taking. Try to become aware today of reverence when meeting others. Some people of India have a saying: "I reverence the divinity within you."

NOTES

[1] See Gemma Fortini, *The Noble Family of St. Clare of Assisi*, in *Franciscan Studies* (New York: Franciscan Institute Publication, 1982), pp. 48–65.

[2] Margaret Carney, O.S.F., *The First Franciscan Woman* (Quincy, Ill.: Franciscan Press, 1993), pp. 31–32.

[3] Marco Bartoli, *Clare of Assisi*, Frances Teresa Downing, O.S.C., trans. (London: Darton, Longman & Todd, 1989), p. 35.

[4] See Carney, *op. cit.*, p. 33.

[5] See *Clare of Assisi: Early Documents*, Regis J. Armstrong, O.F.M. CAP., ed. and trans. (New York: Franciscan Institute Publications, 1993), pp. 87–88.

[6] *Ibid.*, p. 173.

[7] *Ibid.*, p. 257.

[8] Murray Bodo, O.F.M., *Clare: A Light in the Garden* (Cincinnati: St. Anthony Messenger Press, 1992), p. 6.

[9] Bargellini, *op. cit.*, pp. 65–68.

[10] *The Form of Life Given by Francis to Clare and Her Sisters*, in *Clare: Early Documents, op. cit.*, p. 12.

[11] Bargellini, *op. cit.*, pp. 83–85.

[12] Carney, *op. cit.*, p. 22.

[13] Ingrid Peterson, O.S.F., *Clare of Assisi* (Quincy, Ill.: Franciscan Press, 1993), p. 327.

[14] *Ibid.*, pp. 329–330.

[15] See Jean François Godet-Calogeras, *Clare of Assisi: A Woman's Life* (Chicago: Haversack, 1991).

[16] Frances Teresa Downing, O.S.C., *This Living Mirror* (London: Darton, Longman and Todd, 1995), p. 45. See also Downing's *Living the Incarnation.*

[17] Translation of Saint Clare's *Third Letter to Agnes of Prague,* 5–26, is that of Sister Frances Teresa Downing, O.S.C., *op. cit.*

[18] See introduction to *Bringing Forth Christ: Five Feasts of the Child Jesus of St. Bonaventure,* Eric Doyle, O.F.M., ed. and trans. (Oxford: SLG Press, Convent of the Incarnation, Fairacres, 1984).

Saturday

MAPPING OUT THE JOURNEY

Bonaventure writes in the Prologue 5 and chapter 1:3–5:

P:5. It seemed good to me to divide this tract into seven
chapters. . . .

I ask, therefore, that you give more attention to the . . . truth
than to attractiveness,
more to the stimulation of affect than to intellectual
enrichment.
So that this might happen,
it is important that you not run through these reflections in a
hurry,
but that you take your time and ruminate over them slowly.

1:3. This, therefore, is the three-day journey in the solitude of
the desert [Exodus 3:18];
this is the triple illumination of a single day;
the first is like evening, the second like morning, and the third
like noon. . . .
This also relates to the triple substance in Christ who is our
ladder;
namely the corporal, the spiritual, and the divine.

1:4. . . . In the ascent to God,
all three of these ought to be used so that God will be loved
with the whole mind, the whole heart, and the whole soul
[Mark 12:30; Matthew 22:37; Luke 10:27].
In this we see perfect fidelity to the Law together with
Christian wisdom.

1:5. Each of these foregoing ways may be doubled
depending on whether we consider God as the *alpha and the
omega* [Revelation 1:8],

or whether in each of the above-mentioned ways
we consider God as *through* a mirror or as *in* a mirror.
Or we may consider each of these ways
as related to another with which it is connected,
or simply in itself in its purity.
Thus, it is necessary that these three principal levels of ascent
be increased to six.
Just as God completed the entire world in six days and rested
on the seventh,
so the microcosm (i.e. humanity) ought to be led in a most
orderly way
through six levels of illumination to the quiet of
contemplation.
This was symbolized by the *six steps*
with which one ascended to the throne of Solomon
[2 Chronicles 10:18].
Similarly, the Seraphim which Isaiah saw had *six wings*
[Isaiah 6:2];
the Lord called Moses from the midst of the cloud
after six days [Exodus 24:16];
and, as Matthew writes,
after six days Christ led the disciples to the mountain
and was transfigured before them [Matthew 17:1 ff.].

ANDRÉ

Bonaventure begins by offering us various symbols to
describe this journey: a ladder, a spiral staircase, a step-by-step
ascent. He structures this journey in seven chapters, or steps.
The illustration below on page 70 attempts to show the pattern he used. Bonaventure begins *The Journey* where Francis
of Assisi concluded his life with his *Canticle of the Creatures*.
Francis announces his great thanksgiving through all of creation: "Be praised, my Lord, with all your creatures. . . ."[1]

Through (*per*, the Latin preposition) all of creation surrounding him, Francis praises God. So the *Canticle of the Creatures* seems to be the springboard for *The Journey*.

In chapters 1 through 6 of *The Journey*, Bonaventure alternates between the prepositions *per* and *in* ("through" and "in"). This is comparable to the basic composition of steps on a staircase: *Through* is the equivalent of the vertical rise of a step and *in* the horizontal plane of the same step. Bonaventure uses this combination of "through" and "in" three times—so there are three steps in the illustration on page 70.

In the first step, chapters 1 and 2, Bonaventure searches outside himself for the footprints, or vestiges (*vestigia*), of God in creation; this is nature mysticism. Here, he is dealing with all created things, including their natural perception by way of the senses. The illuminations of this step are like the light of evening or dusk. Bonaventure compares this step to entering the court of the temple of Jesus' day or to the two lower wings of the Seraph.

In the second step, chapters 3 and 4, Bonaventure looks inside himself for the images (*imagines*) of God in the soul, a type of soul mysticism. The middle step describes our inner human life in its psychic functions. This is where all concrete inner spiritual and religious experience takes place. In chapter 4 the human reality comes to an end when human and divine meet with divine power taking the lead. The illuminations now are stronger and compared to the light of morning or dawn. Bonaventure likens this step to entering the sanctuary of the temple or to the two middle wings of the Seraph.

In the third step, chapters 5 and 6, Bonaventure looks beyond himself for the likenesses (*similitudines*) of God in the divine names of being and goodness, a type of "God" mysticism. We reach the mysticism of the divine. We are capable of reflecting on something that is beyond our limited experience. The illuminations are strongest now, like the light of noon. Bonaventure likens this step to entering the holy of holies of the temple or to the two upper wings of the Seraph.

7. surrender

6. in	beyond/names of God	
	noon	*LIKENESSES*
5. through	Holy of Holies	
	God mysticism	

4. in	within/soul	
	morning, dawn	*IMAGES*
3. through	temple sanctuary	
	soul mysticism	

2. in	without/creation	
	evening, dusk	*VESTIGES*
1. through	temple court	
	nature mysticism	

↑   *The Canticle of the Creatures* (Francis of Assisi)   ↑

Illustration 1:
Outline of *The Journey*

JOSEF

Bonaventure alludes here to some well-known categories found in mystical writings. The distinction between "through" and "in" and the use of numbers like three were quite common. For example, Hugh of Saint Victor (1100–1141), an influential scholastic theologian, uses a threefold structure when writing of the eye of the flesh, the eye of the mind and the eye of contemplation. Pseudo-Dionysius, an unknown Syrian author of the fifth century after Christ, uses a ladder symbol with three rungs, in Greek *katharsis—ellampsis—teleiosis*, purification—illumination—perfective union, traditionally repeated in spiritual and ascetical literature as *purificatio—illuminatio—perfectio*.

Because these three steps constitute six chapters of *The Journey*, Bonaventure writes:

It is necessary that these three principal levels of ascent be increased to six.

Just as God completed the entire world in six days and rested on the seventh,

so the microcosm (i.e. humanity) ought to be led in a most orderly way

through six levels of illumination to the quiet of contemplation.

This was symbolized by the *six steps*

by which one ascended to the throne of Solomon.

Similarly, the Seraph which Isaiah saw had *six wings*;

the Lord called Moses from the midst of the cloud

after six days;

and, as Matthew writes,

after six days Christ led the disciples to the mountain and was transfigured before them. (1:5)

When making such a *Journey*, it makes sense to follow the actual sequence, going from the bottom step upwards. Skipping a step might disrupt *The Journey*, for each step builds upon the previous one. You cannot just arrive at union or pick it up from some spiritual supermarket, taking as much as you could afford. Bonaventure does not see spirituality as a self-service market pledged to keeping prices low. His *Journey* contains a mystagogy, in the traditional sense of this word. We are led step by step into the mystery, we are drawn into it, we are challenged by it. And prayer is the moving power of *The Journey*, the motor of its movement and progress. He calls "prayer . . . the mother and the origin of the upward movement of the soul" (1:1).

This movement reaches the summit of mystical communication in chapter 7, a mysticism involving at the same time both a deep surrender and fulfillment. It is a mysticism of the cross, of suffering and waiting for the Resurrection, the summit of mystical communication. Looking at Illustration 1 above, one can imagine chapter 7 symbolized by a swimming pool diving board. The great Jesuit Hugo M. E. Lassalle (d. 1990) likens the highest point of illumination to "a death-leap from a mental diving board."[2] It is fascinating that even this highest step of *The Journey* opens up to more. The end is not yet reached, only the end of the ability to describe this experience.

Bonaventure uses symbols to suggest a straight climb. Nevertheless this does not mean that this *Journey* continually advances step by step, one after the other. It is rather a matter of stages that sometimes are entwined together, much like a spiral staircase. The reader is asked not to leave any step behind, but rather to weigh the importance of each step. In our daily living it seems to be of great importance to start this *Journey* wherever we can hit the road and to dig into the depths of its mysteries as far as we can.

EXERCISES

• Think of a journey and/or a road. What comes to mind? Perhaps the road to school, to work, for shopping, a detour, getting lost, a one-way street or a dead end. Choose one of the roads of your life, perhaps an important road that led to a cross and salvation. Try to describe this experience in words or drawing.

First select a journey/road and then take some time to do this exercise.

• Jesus' last journey of his life was to Calvary and, as tradition holds, with many stops along the way. Together with Jesus, walk the Stations of the Cross in a church or outdoors, and pause for some reflection and prayer at each one.

• If you have more time, perhaps a half day, or even a whole day, go on a pilgrimage alone to some holy place. Walk slowly in silent prayer or song. Be aware of the different stages of the journey. Try to be aware of everything around you and everyone you meet. Listen to the silence in yourself!

NOTES

[1] Doyle, *Song of Brotherhood and Sisterhood, op. cit.*, p. 42. This verse is Doyle's translation.

[2] Hugo M. E. Lassalle, S.J., *Zen—Weg zur Erleuchtung. Einführung und Anleitung (Zen—Way to Illumination. Introduction and Instruction)* (Freiburg, Germany: Herder, 1982), p. 33. Author's translation. See Illustration 1, "7. surrender," for diving board symbol.

FOOTPRINTS OF GOD

Sunday

ME, A CONTEMPLATIVE?

Bonaventure writes in the Prologue 5 and chapter 1:7–8:

P:5. I ask, therefore, that you give
more attention to the intent of the writer than to the work itself,
more to the things said than to the uncultivated language,
more to the truth than to attractiveness,
more to the stimulation of affect than to intellectual enrichment.
So that this might happen,
it is important that you not run through these reflections in a hurry,
but that you take your time and ruminate over them slowly.

1:7. According to the way nature was originally instituted,
the human being was created
with the capability of experiencing the quiet of contemplation.
Therefore, *God placed the first human being in a paradise of pleasures* [Genesis 2:15].
But turning from the true light to a changeable good,
the first human was bent over. . . .
The result is that humans, blind and bent over,
sit in darkness and do not see the light of heaven
without the aid of grace together with justice to fight concupiscence,
and knowledge together with wisdom to fight ignorance.
All this comes about through Jesus Christ,
who by *God has been made wisdom and justice and sanctification and redemption.*

1:8. Therefore, a person who wishes to ascend to God
must avoid sin which deforms nature.

The natural powers of the soul described above
must be brought under the power of reforming grace;
and this is done through prayer.
These powers must also be influenced by justice which
purifies;
and this is carried out in everyday actions.
They must also be brought to that knowledge which illumines,
and this happens in meditation.
And they must be brought to the wisdom that perfects,
and this takes place in contemplation.
For just as no one arrives at wisdom
except through grace, justice, and knowledge,
so no one arrives at contemplation
except by means of penetrating meditation, a holy lifestyle,
and devout prayer. Therefore, as grace is the foundation
of the righteousness of the will and the clear enlightenment of
reason,
so it is necessary first of all to pray.
Then we must live in a holy way.
And third, we must concentrate on the reflections of truth;
and gazing on these, we must rise gradually,
until we arrive at the peak of the mountain,
where the God of gods is seen in Sion [Psalms 84:8].

ANDRÉ

In commenting about contemplation, Joseph Chinnici
wrote:

> *Seven Storey Mountain* concluded with a short
> reflection piece entitled *Meditatio pauperis in*
> *solitudine* (the meditation of a poor one in soli-
> tude), a title surely reflective of the first chap-
> ter of Bonaventure of Bagnoregio's *Itinerarium*
> *mentis in Deum,* entitled *Speculatio pauperis in*

deserto (speculation of the poor one in the
desert). In his reflection, Merton . . . pointed
to St. Francis: . . . "Christ implanted His own
image upon St. Francis . . . in order to draw
out some men (and women), not for a few
privileged monks, but all truly spiritual men
(and women) to the perfection of contemplation which is nothing else but the perfection
of love. . . ." It is about being imprinted with,
contemplating, and exemplifying . . . the "perfection of love."[1]

Bonaventure makes a very poignant statement about contemplation in chapter 1.7. "According to the way nature was
originally instituted, the human being was created with the
capability of experiencing the quiet of contemplation."
Bonaventure seems to be pointing out that in original inno-
cence, humanity was made fit for contemplation. Before the
fall, this was the normal, natural state of humanity.

One of the more popular spiritual authors of recent
years, Henri Nouwen, wrote eloquently of contemplation in
this Bonaventurian mode in his essay "The Contemplative
Life," likewise picking up on Merton's thoughts about contemplation. Merton said that "the contemplative life is a life
in which we constantly move from opaqueness to transparency, from the place where things are dark, thick, impenetrable, and closed—to the place where these same things
are translucent, open, and offer vision far beyond themselves,"[2] ultimately pointing to God. Nouwen then takes
Merton's definition and proceeds "to show the need to move
continuously from opaqueness to transparency in three central relationships: our relationship with nature, with time
and with people."[3]

When we view nature simply as a force to be used, our relationship with nature remains opaque. When we view nature as gift, then nature becomes transparent and points beyond itself to God. When we live time simply as "a chronology, a randomly collected series of incidents and accidents over which we have no control,"[4] then time remains opaque—*chronos*. When these same incidents in our lives become opportunities for change, moreso, for conversion, then these daily time experiences become transparent—*kairos*, pointing to the God who lives beyond time. When we respond to people simply as "interesting characters," they basically remain opaque. However, when we let them sound through to us "a greater reality than we ourselves fully know,"[5] then they become transparent.

All of this is to say that contemplation is an integral dimension of our daily experiences. Nature, time and people are daily encounters and experiences for us. This seems to bring about a democratization of contemplation, showing how clearly it is available to all who are willing "to see."

JOSEF

Thomas of Celano, Francis' first official biographer, said of Francis:

> He would often *ruminate* inwardly with unmoving *lips,*
> and, drawing outward things inward,
> he raised his spirit to the heights.
> Thus he would direct all his attention and affection
> toward the *one thing* he *asked of the Lord,*
> not so much praying as becoming totally prayer.[6]

The basic aspects of the contemplative experience in a Franciscan understanding would seem to be:

- God first looks upon me in love.
- I respond to this loving gaze.
- I see the face of God everywhere, at all times and in everyone and everything.

Prayer then is not necessarily something for eloquent people, but rather for those who are good listeners. Listening consists in treasuring words within oneself, pondering them, and repeating them. This means taking a word to heart and, at the same time, lingering or abiding with it.

This exercise is nothing new. Eastern Christian traditions especially use the continuous rumination on the name "Jesus," the so-called "Jesus prayer."[7] Repetitive prayers of diverse religions and denominations—such as the Rosary in the Catholic tradition—are similar.

At the end of the Prologue, Bonaventure admonishes the reader to mull over carefully each part of *The Journey*. Like ruminating animals, we are called to internalize this text slowly. The person who tries to swallow it whole will not experience its fullness. Here, too, it is not so much a matter of intellectual exercise and effort or of theoretical knowledge, but rather involves the whole person—one's emotions, senses, psychic and physical capacities or powers. It is a question of the human person being ready and able to give itself to the Other.

In his Prologue, Bonaventure maps out the spiritual path for the human person from a Franciscan perspective, which is indicated in the illustration following on page 82:

- the motor or power which thrusts you forward—desire

- the important signposts along the way—eyes, mirror, contemplation
- the goal of the journey—peace

This *Journey* is not always undertaken with ready-made answers, as some fundamentalists from various religions or Christian denominations tend to believe. That would seem to be so practical, so easy to handle. But it is just not so. It starts from a desire for peace that must always be kept alive in one's heart, a desire that must sometimes reach into a mysterious and mystifying darkness.

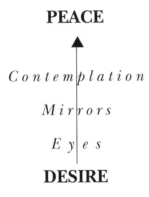

PEACE

Contemplation

Mirrors

Eyes

DESIRE

Illustration 2: Prologue.
The whole Journey *starts with desire and leads to peace.*

EXERCISES

- Ruminate on or "chew" a prayer over and over again: First, repeat it slowly, word by word, as often as you want, and however you wish. It may be simply a word or a sentence or phrase. Francis prayed like this before the crucifix in the dilapidated church of San Damiano:

Most High,

glorious God,

enlighten the darkness of my heart.

and give me

true faith,

certain hope,

and perfect charity,

sense and knowledge,

Lord,

that I may carry out

Your holy and true command.[8]

At the end of the prayer, remain in silence.

• During the day, repeatedly hum, sing or speak a little refrain or saying, for example, one of the many chants from Taizé, or a single word or passage from the Scriptures.

• Write down how you see God in nature, in your time or in persons you meet.

NOTES

[1] Joseph P. Chinnici, O.F.M., "This Is What We Proclaim to You: Facing the Christ Incarnate," in *The Cord*, Vol. 50, No. 1, January/February 2000, pp. 2–3.

[2] Henri J. M. Nouwen, *Clowning in Rome* (Garden City, N.Y.: Doubleday & Co. Inc., 1979), p. 89.

[3] *Ibid.*, p. 91. See Nouwen's essay for further detail.

[4] *Ibid.*, p. 95.

[5] *Ibid.*, p. 99.

[6] Thomas of Celano, *The Remembrance of the Desire of a Soul (The Second Life of Saint Francis)*, in *Francis of Assisi: The Founder, op. cit.*, p. 310.

[7] See R. M. French, *The Way of a Pilgrim and the Pilgrim Continues His Way* (San Francisco: Harper, 1991).

[8] *The Prayer before the Crucifix*, in *Francis of Assisi: The Saint, op. cit.*, p. 40.

Monday

LET FLOWERS SPEAK!

Bonaventure writes in chapter 1:2, 9, 10, 15:

> 2. When we pray in this way we are given the light
> to recognize the steps of the ascent to God.
> For it is in harmony with our created condition
> that the universe itself may serve as a ladder
> by which we can ascend to God. . . .

> 9. Now since we must ascend before we can descend on Jacob's
> ladder [Genesis 28:12],
> let us place the first step of our ascent at the bottom,
> putting the whole of the sensible world before us as a mirror
> through which we may pass to God, the highest creative Artist. . . .
> *For in the greatness and beauty of created things*
> *their Creator can be seen and known* [Wisdom 11:21].

> 10. The supreme power, wisdom, and goodness of the Creator
> shines forth in created things. . . .

> 15. Therefore, any person who is not illumined
> by such great splendors in created things is blind.
> Anyone who is not awakened by such great outcries is deaf.
> Anyone who is not led from such effects to give praise to God is
> mute.
> Anyone who does not turn to the First Principle as a result of
> such signs is a fool.
> Therefore open your eyes,
> alert your spiritual ears,
> unlock your lips,
> and apply your heart [Proverbs 22:17]
> so that in all creation
> you may see, hear, praise, love and adore, magnify and honor

your God
lest the entire world rise up against you.
For because of this *the entire world will fight against the fools*
[Wisdom 5:21].
On the other hand, it will be a cause of glory for the wise
who can say in the words of the prophet:
You have given me delight, O Lord, in your deeds,
and I shall rejoice in the work of your hands.
How wonderful are your works, O Lord.
You have made all things in wisdom,
the earth is filled with your richness [Psalms 92:5; 103:24].

JOSEF

In 1988, when I visited Niagara Falls for the first time, André
and I were pressed for time. However, he could not leave
because I refused to go. I was just fascinated, caught up by
the immense power of the cascading waters. What a spectacular view! The patient and constant resistance of the rocks!
And the wonderful tenderness of the rainbows hanging over
the water here and there. How light and joyful the water
seemed as it was tossed up in the air and fell down in soft
raindrops covering wide parts of the walkway above. When
the wind came up, people walking nearby were soaked
instantly. And there, alongside the incredible force of the
river streaming down into the abyss, were a few flowers, some
grass and trees almost untouched by this spectacular display.
And on the Canadian side there were beautiful flowers in a
park along the promenade. Beauty filled my senses with
enchantment. I strolled along, stopping to gaze in admiration upon these miracles of nature.

All this beauty is no accident. Must not God, the origin and source of all living things, far surpass the beauty, the

power, the tenderness, the freshness, the greatness? On the first step of *The Journey* as demonstrated in Illustration 3 below, Bonaventure does exactly what I have just described. His senses take in all of creation surrounding him and, through its individual parts, he discovers the greatness, beauty and power of God. The following illustration exemplifies this:

Senses ➔ ➔ ➔ Creation ➔ ➔ ➔ Greatness, Beauty, Power of God

Illustration 3: Chapter 1.
How we perceive God through creation

ANDRÉ

What a positive view of nature Bonaventure has! He does not warn us to be wary of creation, categorizing it in terms of good and evil. He does know about the power of an encounter with God, which could even happen in the kitchen while you are washing dishes. God is so close to us; how then can it happen that sometimes we feel so lost and abandoned, left alone by God? Why do we experience God as so alien and remote? Anthony de Mello once said: "You cease to be an exile when you discover creation is your home."[1]

In an era when there are endless streams of refugees, when millions of people are searching for a home, we cannot ignore the fact that many people have a hard time trusting their mother earth or their grandmother, the universe.

Through the flower we can discover how beautiful, how great and how powerful God really is. Everything I can perceive outside of my own person—

- the delightful, soft mattress on which I am lying right now;
- the play of the waves upon the beach;
- the shouts of children;
- my wife's voice as she talks on the phone;
- the speed of a motorbike;
- the tender hands of a nurse changing the bed-clothes of an elderly person;
- pausing for a warm drink at a stand in the Christmas market;
- the fresh air on a winter morning;
- a clear, star-speckled night sky;
- the menacing sound of an approaching storm

—everything bears a trace of God, everything leads us to God. Through all these things the immensity of God, the Creator, is opened up, revealed to us.

In some philosophical-theological treatises, the material world was described as evil, as the negative principle. Therefore, the logical conclusion on the moral level was to flee and despise the world, to turn away from it and live a life of asceticism. Throughout the centuries, Christian spirituality has been tainted by those tendencies toward a negative view of everything surrounding us.

In Francis' day, the Cathars, for example, who lived a life quite similar to the early Franciscans

believed that the universe emanated from two conflicting principles, one good and one evil. God was a spirit, and the world God created was a world of spiritual beings. The visible and material world . . . was the

work of the evil power . . . and it was irre-
deemably evil. The flesh was an evil integu-
ment in which the human soul was imprisoned. It followed that most of the apparatus
of Catholic Christianity, notably the sacraments, which used material things—water,
bread and wine—as vehicles of supernatural
grace, was to be rejected. . . . (I)t touched a
responsive chord in orthodox Christianity,
which contained a strong ascetical tradition
that was all too easily tilted into dualism by
preachers and writers of ascetical theology... At the end of 1207 Innocent (III)
appealed (for) a crusade (against) the
heretics.[2]

The Franciscan movement was contemporaneous with
groups such as the Cathars.[3] However, it was Francis' clear
recognition of creation as the gift of an all-good God that
kept the movement from going the way of the heretical
Cathars. Bonaventure is in complete harmony with his spiritual master. Everything was created in goodness. God is to be
praised for everything! And footprints of God are powerful-
ly present in all creation.

In conclusion, I would like to cite an excerpt from
Eric Doyle's book based upon *The Canticle of the Creatures*:

Being in a district where the local priest was
living with a woman, he was asked by a strict
"Manichaean" Christian: "If a priest keeps a
concubine and so stains his hands, do we have
to believe in his teaching and respect the
sacraments he administers?" Instead of reply-

ing, St. Francis went straight to the priest's house in the sight of everyone. Kneeling down in front of the priest he said:

"I do not really know whether these hands are stained as the other man claims they are. In any case, I do know that even if they are, this in no way lessens the power and efficacy of the sacraments of God . . . that is why I kiss them out of respect for what they administer and out of respect for Him who delegated his authority to them."

This must be one of the most wonderful stories ever related about a holy man in the history of any religion. It speaks volumes about the spirit of St. Francis. He was a passionate man. And any knowledge of his own strong passions is perhaps what produced in him the delicate compassion which comes through this story. We would admire him if he had refused to make any comment; we would be impressed if he had gently reminded the questioner not to judge, so that he would not be judged himself. But there is much more here than this, far more, in fact, than tolerance or forbearance. Francis' reaction was entirely positive. He looked for what was obviously good in the man, found it and emphasized that.[4]

EXERCISES

• Look around you in your home, workplace or your favorite leisure spot. Look at the things around you and try to express their value in a kind of litany:

Praise be yours, my God, because through all things, we are able to
perceive and experience your power, wisdom and goodness.
Through Niagara Falls, *I praise your majesty and power!*
Through my child, *I praise your simplicity!*
Through _____ *I praise your* _____ !

- Take a leisurely stroll in the place where you ordinarily
  walk, or another place. Try to pay close attention to the
  things that speak to you in a special way today. At the end
  of this walk, reflect on an encounter with a specific part of
  creation, for example, on a cold winter day as the icy wind
  touched your face. Pause for a moment to express your
  gratitude for the gift of this encounter and feel the message of the wind. Is God in the wind?

NOTES

[1] de Mello, *op. cit.*, p. 85.

[2] C. H. Lawrence, *The Friars* (London: Longman, 1994), pp. 4–8.

[3] See William J. Short, O.F.M., *Poverty and Joy* (Maryknoll, N.Y.: Orbis Books, 1999), p. 24.

[4] Doyle, *Song of Brotherhood and Sisterhood, op. cit.*, p. 18.

Tuesday

Drink It All In!

Bonaventure writes in chapter 2:3–5:

3. The human being, therefore,

who is said to be a *microcosm,*

has five senses which are like five doorways

through which the knowledge of all things in the sensible world

enter into the interior world. . . .

Therefore, it is through these doorways

that simple and composite or mixed bodies enter into the soul.

In a true sense we perceive not only particular sense objects

such as light, sound, smell, taste,

and the four primary qualities which the sense of touch notices,

but also the common sense objects

such as number, size, shape, rest, and motion. . . .

4. Therefore, the whole sensible world in its three categories of beings

enters into our interior through our basic sense experience.

These external, sensible beings are the first to enter into us

through the doors of the five senses.

It is not the substance of such an object that enters in,

but rather a likeness of the object.

And that likeness is generated in a medium.

And from the medium this likeness passes into the organ,

and from the external organ it moves to the internal organ,

and from here it moves to the faculty of awareness.

So the generation of the likeness in the medium

and its movement from the medium to the organ,

and the turning of the faculty of awareness to it
leads to the knowledge of all those things
which we come to know as external to ourselves.

5. Now pleasure follows from the awareness of a suitable
object.
For the senses delight in an object
that is perceived by means of the likeness that has been
abstracted.
This delight comes either from its beauty, as in the case of
vision,
or sweetness, as in the case of smell and hearing,
or from its healthful quality as in the case of taste and touch,
to speak in terms of appropriation.
For all pleasure flows from proportion. . . .
for the senses are pained by extremes but take delight in
moderation.
Finally, proportion can be viewed in as far as it is active and
impressive.
In this case proportionality is found
when the impression of the agent fulfills a need in the
recipient
and thus preserves and nourishes it. . . .

JOSEF

What is the best way for you to relax? Where do you go to let
go, to rest and enter into your deepest self? Are there times
when you are able to enjoy the world or some part of it more
fully? Are you thinking of a cool drink, a warm bed, a stroll
through a colorful autumn countryside, a hot cup of tea on
a cold winter's day, a tender kiss, a soft touch, an exciting
dance, a funny game with a group of good friends, a deli-
cious dish, a fascinating piece of music or a seductive aroma,

or peacefully reading in a comfortable rocking chair?

The second chapter of *The Journey* deals with the process of sense perception, of taking information from the outside into our being. It describes the way our senses function. How does the world out there manage to register itself inside us? What is the biochemical or psychological procedure involved in the use of our senses?

Living in the thirteenth century, Bonaventure had to rely on the knowledge of the natural sciences available in his day. If we look at a flower, thirteenth-century scientists believed that a copy of this flower is transported into us by the medium of light. The result of this sensual perception is that we have a more or less good copy of the original within us by use of the sense of sight. This process immediately evokes feelings and some type of judgment: Do I like the flower, its shape, its color? For us human beings, every process of our senses will be limited in some way or other. At times the process moves too fast, too superficially. At others, it may be too dark or too far in the distance, or we may have a cold and be unable to smell or taste something. For Bonaventure, even this limited process of the senses is a footprint of a divine process.

The better we perceive something, the better we listen, the more carefully we look at something, the more sensitively we touch something or someone, the more consciously we taste food, and the more deeply we assimilate the aromas around us, the more our action resembles the divine encounter between the Father and Son. The Father and the Son are constantly beholding one another, taking the Other in, so to speak. But when our senses present an object to our mind, we have a copy of it, not the original, and certainly not a perfect copy. As the Father and Son perceive one another, what they take in is not a mere copy, but theology teaches us that their exchange is a perfect one—fully complete, exactly as it is in the Other. One divine person is completely open to taking in the other, without reservation.

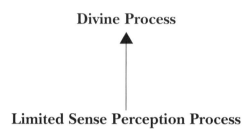

Divine Process

Limited Sense Perception Process

Illustration 4: Chapter 2.
Our sense perception process is a vestige of a divine process.

Bonaventure sees our process of sense perception replicating, in a less than perfect manner, that which constantly goes on within the Trinity. Within this constant functioning of our senses, he detects a vestige of God, for our senses are constantly doing what the Father and Son constantly and eternally have been doing.

ANDRÉ

Having addressed the mere observation of nature, of creation, we now come to the point where we can deal with the encounter between the outer world and the inner world. Just how difficult this experience can be for people today we can learn from the following:

> My dear contemporary! You talk about everything. Through the mass media you have access to the most diverse problems which ear-

lier generations could never imagine. You are enlightened like no one before you has ever been. Yet your inner self is obscured like never before!

Your inner self is encapsulated. Every once in a while you look into the depth of your being, but you flee as quickly as you can, escaping into more work, amusement, into drugs and alcohol, sex and gossip. You find no rest nor quiet. You are faced with the bankruptcy of your inner world, and you have known it for some time already. You have exploited the outer world. Now you stand before yourself, before the court of your conscience that's telling to you: "You have worshiped false gods. You have harmed yourself. You ignored the words I wanted to speak to you in stillness."[1]

In order to enjoy as gift the things and persons we encounter externally through our senses we must exercise a good deal of discipline. It requires practice.

JOSEF

Does God really want us to be happy? Does God want us to enjoy life? Even to the highest degree possible? Some people have a hard time believing that God wants us to be happy and enjoy life in a "sensual" way without feeling somewhat guilty.

Bonaventure is calling us to celebrate using our senses because in their very use is a vestige, a trace, a footprint of God. Jacopone da Todi—a thirteenth-century Franciscan poet—knew well Bonaventure's *Journey*, as seen in his "Laud 82":

> How the Soul through the Senses Finds God
>   in All Creatures:
>
> O Love, divine Love, why do You lay siege to me?
> In a frenzy of love for me, You find no rest.
>
> From five sides You move against me,
> Hearing, sight, taste, touch, and scent.
> To come out is to be caught; I cannot hide
>   from You.
>
> If I come out through sight I see Love
> Painted in every form and color,
> Inviting me to come to You, to dwell in You.
>
> If I leave through the door of hearing,
> What I hear points only to You, Lord;
> I cannot escape Love through this gate.
>
> If I come out through taste, every flavor
>   proclaims:
> "Love, divine Love, hungering Love!
> You have caught me on Your hook for You
>   want to reign in me."
>
> If I leave through the door of scent
> I sense You in all creation; You have caught me
> And wounded me through that fragrance.
>
> If I come out through the sense of touch
> I find Your lineaments in every creature;
> To try to flee from You is madness.
>
> Love, I flee from You, afraid to give You my
>   heart:
> I see that You make me one with You,

I cease to be me and can no longer find
    myself.

If I see evil in someone or defect or
    temptation,
You fuse me with that one, and make me
    suffer;
O Love without limits, who is it You love?

It is You, O Crucified Christ
Who take possession of me,
Drawing me out of the sea to the shore;

There I suffer to see Your wounded heart.
Why did You endure the pain?
So that I might be healed.[2]

How important and fundamental chapter 2 of *The Journey* could be for religious education and human development. It could teach us how to be more fully aware of our surroundings by cultivating the use of our senses.

This cultivation of the senses can begin at any time in our lives, and it is linked especially to the factors of time and silence. We are able to drink in something fully only when we can let go of everything else and focus on that thing alone. What do you really feel when you breathe deeply a certain fragrance, when you gently touch a person you love, or when your favorite dish is just melting on your tongue? What do you feel when you behold a meadow filled with colorful wildflowers in the springtime or sit in a concert hall listening to one of your favorite musical pieces? Part of this experience is concentration, undivided attention, which is also an act of communication. Perhaps when we learn to go this deep within ourselves, the fullness of the emptiness will begin to open up to us!

EXERCISES

- Treat yourself to a "sensual" day!

  Feast your eyes upon nature or a person.

  Open your ears to a melody of instruments or voice.

  Take note of some special fragrance—perfume or the aroma of cooking.

  Treat yourself to your favorite food; savor its taste.

  Hold someone/thing precious in your hands—a loved one or keepsake.

  Reflect and alert yourself to whatever your senses present to you.

- Choose a common routine task, such as washing dishes or brushing your teeth, and try to be aware of what is happening. Spend a little more time at it than usual. A pause before and afterward may help you in this exercise of meditation. Conclude with prayers of gratitude and praise!

NOTES

[1] Josef Dirnbeck and Martin Gutl, *Ich began zu beten (I Began to Pray)*, 6th ed. (Graz, Austria: Styria Verlag, 1982), pp. 126–127. Authors' translation.

[2] *Jacopone da Todi: The Lauds*, Serge and Elizabeth Hughes, trans. (New York: Paulist Press, 1982), pp. 239–240.

Wednesday

Life's Contradictions

Bonaventure writes in chapter 5:8:

8. Looking over the way we have come,

let us say that the most pure and absolute being,

because it is being in an unqualified sense,

is first and last;

and therefore it is the origin and consummating end of all things.

Because it is eternal and most present,

it embraces and enters into all things that endure in time,

simultaneously existing as their center and circumference.

Because it is most simple and greatest,

it is within all things and outside all things,

and hence "it is an intelligible sphere

whose center is everywhere and whose circumference is nowhere."

Because it is most actual and immutable,

therefore "remaining unmoved, it imparts movement to all things."

Because it is most perfect and immense,

therefore it is within all things but is not contained by them;

and it is outside all things but is not excluded;

it is above all things but not distant;

and it is below all things, but not prostrate.

Because it is supremely one and all-embracing,

it is *all in all* [1 Corinthians 15:28],

even though all things are multiple and this is simply one.

And because this is most simple unity,

most peaceful truth,

and most sincere goodness,

it is all power, all exemplarity, and all communicability.

Therefore, *from him and through him and in him are all things*
[Romans 11:36],
for he is all-powerful, all-knowing, and all-good.
And to see him perfectly is to be blessed, as it was said to
Moses:
I will show you all good [Exodus 33:19].

ANDRÉ

The Journey in its opening chapters 1 and 2 seems to take up where Francis leaves off in his poem *The Canticle of the Creatures.* In chapters 42 through 45, *The Legend of Perugia*[1] describes in very precise details the circumstances under which Francis composed this song. Francis was very ill and, in the spring of 1225, he stayed for about fifty days in a simple hut near San Damiano. Due to the pain in his eyes he could not bear the light of the day or even a fire at night. The marks of Christ's passion, the stigmata, had weakened him considerably. He could only lie there in the dark, and if the pain did not keep him from sleeping, the mice did. Night and day they scurried over and around him. Francis' companions, and he himself, claimed they were some kind of diabolical manifestation. While Francis was enduring all these troubles, it was in this very situation while at prayer, that he heard a voice that gave him new hope and meaning. All of a sudden he understood why he had to bear all of this pain and discomfort. He was overcome with a wave of peace.

> Therefore, for (God's) praise, for our consolation, and for the edification of our neighbor, I want to write a new *Praises of the Lord* for (God's) creatures, which we use every day, and without which we cannot live. Through them the human race greatly offends the Creator,

and every day we are ungrateful for such great graces, because we do not praise, as we should, our Creator and the Giver of all good.[2]

Then Francis sat down, meditated and soon cried out his song to the whole world:

Most High, all-powerful, good Lord,
Yours are *the praises, the glory,* and *the honor,* and all *blessing,*
To You alone, Most High, do they belong, and no human is worthy to mention Your name.
Praised be You, my *Lord,* with all *your creatures,*
especially Sir Brother Sun,
Who is the day and through whom You give us light.
And he is beautiful and radiant with great splendor;
and bears a likeness of You, Most High One.
Praised be You, my Lord, through Sister *Moon* and *the stars,* in
heaven You formed them clear and precious and beautiful.

Praised be You, my Lord, through Brother Wind,
and through the air, cloudy and serene, and every kind of weather,
through whom You give sustenance to Your creatures.
Praised be You, my Lord, through Sister *Water,*
who is very useful and humble and precious and chaste.
Praised be You, my Lord, through Brother *Fire,*
through whom *You light the night,*
and he is beautiful and playful and robust and strong.
Praised be You, my Lord, through our Sister Mother *Earth,*
who sustains and governs us,
and who produces various *fruit* with colored flowers and herbs.

. . . .

> Praised be You, my Lord, through our Sister Bodily Death,
> from whom no one living can escape.
> Woe to those who die in mortal sin.
> Blessed are those whom death will find in Your most holy will,
> for *the second death* shall do them no harm.
> *Praise* and *bless* my *Lord* and give Him thanks
> and serve Him with great humility.[3]

Francis taught the melody to his companions so that they could sing the song to the people. Some time later, however, a serious scandal arose in Assisi. The bishop had excommunicated the mayor and the mayor forbade the people from having any kind of transaction with the bishop. Francis was quite concerned because the peace of the city had been severely disturbed. So he added a verse to his new song:

> Praised be You, my Lord,
> through those who give pardon for Your love,
> and bear infirmity and tribulation.
> Blessed are they who endure in peace,
> for by You, Most High, shall they be crowned.4

Next, he set up a meeting between the belligerent parties and arranged for one of his brothers to sing the entire *Canticle* to them. Both the mayor and the bishop were moved to tears, asked each other's forgiveness and embraced.

JOSEF

The Canticle of the Creatures is filled with opposites, and these opposites or extreme poles—pain and joy, despair and consolation, losing meaning and finding it anew, hatred and reconciliation—blend into one another within this little person, Francis. The blind man who cannot leave his hut because light pains his eyes, sings in praise of the brilliant light of the sun. The one who cannot abide the putrid odor of the lepers[5] finds in the embrace and kiss of a leper the path that leads to healing and a pleasing fragrance—"sweetness of soul and body"[6] as he notes in his *Testament*. Might we not say that only the person who confidently risks stepping into the abyss of one pole will experience the depth of the opposite pole?

In my ministry as a counselor, I know that the first step in a healing process is empathy, a kind of feeling for or with another's life situation and being. There is a price to pay for this empathy in time, patience and energy. I have to be able to bear a sense of powerlessness and despair and only the person who bears this long enough will eventually find light in the darkness. If I try to move a person into the light too quickly, the person might end up in an even deeper darkness.

Thomas of Celano tells us of a weighty conflict Francis experienced when he was about twenty years old. His father and brother used to curse him when they saw him begging in the streets of Assisi, so Francis asked a companion to walk with him and bless him whenever his relatives would curse him.[7] And the companion did so. The Latin words for "cursing" and "blessing" are *maledicere* and *benedicere,* which literally mean "to speak badly" and "to speak well." Francis proved time and again that he could find something joyful and wholesome even in an unchanged, critical situation.

And he could make something whole from what was broken, turning the *diabolon* (Greek for "thrown apart") into a *symbolon* (Greek for "parts brought together again," or "the whole"). A symbol is always something that stands for the whole! It integrates all the opposites within itself. It does not deny the opposites but maintains a healthy, unified tension as life continues to unfold.

The Christian symbol par excellence for the coincidence of opposites is Jesus Christ himself, the Alpha and Omega, the crucified and the risen one, divine and human, creator and creature. Faith in him is filled with opposites and contradictions. In him all of life's opposites converge.

Therefore, we can describe Francis as a second Christ, because there is a convergence of opposites in him as well. However, the same holds true for all of us. As Christians we are called to become a symbol, and we are shown how by Christ. As Christians, each of us, too, is called to become a second Christ.

Many ritual dances perform symbolic movements, such as drawing us on a deeper level into the center. Here, different parts and aspects of ourselves and our lives that have become separated and alienated are symbolically reunited. In light of this, it may be helpful to reconsider the therapeutic effect of dance, including its use in liturgy.

EXERCISES

• Meditate on each verse of *The Canticle of the Creatures.* Repeat words or sentences as you like. Take some paper and paint or draw each of the verses and let the pictures speak to you. Try to put the verses to music or a familiar melody!

• Recall a dry time in your life, perhaps a time of crisis. Did you experience that "bitterness" turned into "sweetness"? Note these experiences on paper in opposite columns and try to remember what brought about the change. You might use colored arrows between the columns to mark the powers or factors of change on your chart.

NOTES

[1] See *The Assisi Compilation* 83–85, in *Francis of Assisi: The Founder, op. cit.*, pp. 184–186. In this edition, *The Legend of Perugia* is called *The Assisi Compilation* and the paragraph numbers have been changed as well.

[2] *Ibid.*, p. 186.

[3] *The Canticle of the Creatures*, in *Francis of Assisi: The Saint, op. cit.*, pp. 113–114.

[4] *Ibid.*, p. 114.

[5] See Thomas of Celano, *The Life of Saint Francis* VII:17, *ibid.*, p. 195.

[6] *The Testament* 3, *ibid.*, p. 124.

[7] See Thomas of Celano, *The Remembrance of the Desire of a Soul* VII:12 (*The Second Life of Saint Francis*), in *Francis of Assisi: The Founder, op. cit.*, p. 251.

Thursday

Let's Talk about Sex!

Bonaventure writes in chapter 2:5, 6, 8:

5. . . . Thus it is through pleasure
that external delights enter into us
by means of a likeness and in terms of three kinds of pleasure.

6. Awareness and delight are followed by judgment
through which one judges not only whether a thing
is white or black—
for this pertains to a particular sense;
and not only whether it is healthful or harmful—
for this pertains to the interior sense;
but one judges and explains why this object gives pleasure.
And in this act, one asks about the cause of the enjoyment
which the senses derive from the object.
When we ask why an object is beautiful, sweet, or wholesome,
the cause for this is found in a proportion of equality.
Now the nature of equality is the same in large things or in
small things;
it is not extended in dimensions
nor is it changed by movements through successive stages,
nor does it pass away with transitory things. . . .
And in this way the entire world enters into us
through the doorways of the senses
in accord with the three operations cited above.

8. In like manner, the likeness that gives delight
in its beauty, sweetness, and wholesomeness
suggests that in that first likeness
there is a first beauty, sweetness, and wholesomeness
in which is found the highest proportionality and equality
in relation to the one that generates it.

And there is power suggested not by means of the phantasm,
but by means of the truth that floods our awareness.
It suggests also an impression
that nourishes and is sufficient to fulfill all the needs of the
knower.
Therefore, if "delight is the union of two beings
that are proportionate to each other,"
and if it is only in the likeness of God that one finds
that which is by nature supremely beautiful, sweet and
wholesome;
and if that likeness is united in truth,
and intimacy,
and in a fullness that transcends our every need,
it can be seen clearly that it is in God alone
that the true fountain of delight is to be found.
So it is that from all other delights we are led to seek this one
delight.

JOSEF

Christianity has had its problems dealing with human sexuality. Through the centuries of church history, sex and the enjoyment of bodily intimacy became the important sin. All too frequently confessors dealt primarily with the sixth commandment. Some who were trained to live an asexual life pressured the people of God, at times condemning any kind of sexual desire. Terms such as "purity," "holiness" or "asceticism" almost automatically evoked anti-sexual associations. Accordingly, marriage and sexuality have had a rough history in the church.

How might we see marriage and sexuality in a positive way in the Catholic tradition in light of what we read in *The Journey*?

With chapter 2 as our starting point, we can speak only of an entirely positive approach to all human realities. In a sexual encounter a person can have such a deep, total experience of the other, as well as of the person's own self, casting a spell, as it were, upon the person's whole being. With Bonaventure, you could say that the more your senses are involved, the more present and aware you are in this sexual exchange, the more you are able to enjoy this psychosexual capacity and lose yourself deeply in the other, the closer you can approach the mystery of divine truth. That does not mean that closeness to God is necessarily related to sexual experience or a full sexual life, but it would suggest that the church's attitude toward sexuality may need to be renewed.

It could mean that sexuality might be discussed more freely and openly within communities and parish groups. It could mean appreciating the daily routine of family life, not only peripherally or for its utility, but accepting sexual intimacy between married couples as an essential realization of the Incarnation and God's gifting us with meaning and love. It could mean freeing religious education from the burdens of a pessimistic view of the world and of humankind, and leading people toward a freer, more responsible and respectful attitude toward themselves, toward members of their own sex and of the opposite sex. Bonaventure says, "In this way the species which delights as beautiful, pleasant and wholesome suggests that there is primordial beauty, pleasure and wholesomeness in that first Species" (2:8).

Bonaventure talks about created things in an incredibly positive way. The sensuality of a sexual encounter is one of the most concrete and clear expressions of God's close-ness and presence. One might say it is a type of sacrament with a small "s," bringing God's gift—grace—into our life, a sign of the union of God with creation. When a woman and man join in a bodily union, a new asceticism is required. It involves the practice of a new attentiveness, of being present, open to the other, with a deep perception and enjoyment.

Sexual life, however, must be understood much more broadly than just sexual intercourse. Tenderness, touch and closeness require constant care and attention from everyone. No one lives without sexuality. The question is: how do we perceive it and how do we live it?

I think that we are all being called to help create a new culture of sexual behavior in both the public and private sectors. The starting point for all of us is the cultivation and sharpening of our senses and a deep respect for all that God has given us as an image of God's own being. It is in our sex-ual giving to the other that we reflect the highest form of divine self-giving and communication.

EXERCISES

• On a piece of paper write the label "Sexual Life." Alone or with your spouse, write under this term on the paper every-thing that comes to your mind on this theme, especially everything connected to it in your daily life. An alternative might be to jot down free associations in the form of metaphors or images: *Sex is like* . . . At the end of the exer-cise you might want to continue by sharing this with your spouse. In line with Bonaventure's thought, express your gratitude for this gift in your life.

• Relax and enjoy a massage from your spouse or a profes-sional massage therapist. Feel how your skin tingles; feel the power of life and warmth, of energy and acceptance that flow into you from this touch. Simply try to *be* in this touch!

Friday

CREATION—SACRAMENT OF GOD

Bonaventure writes in chapter 2:10–12:

10. . . . Therefore, since all things are beautiful and in some
way delightful;

and since there is no beauty or delight without proportion;

and since proportion resides first of all in numbers;

it is necessary that all things involve number.

From this we conclude that

"number is the principal exemplar in the mind of the
Creator,"

and in creatures it is the principal vestige leading to wisdom.

Since number is most evident to all and is closest to God,

it leads us very close to God by its seven-fold distinction;

and it makes God known in all bodily and sensible things

when we become aware of numerical realities,

when we take delight in numerical proportions,

and when we come to make irrefutable judgments

by means of the laws of numerical proportions.

11. . . . For creatures are shadows, echoes, and pictures

of that first, most powerful, most wise, and most perfect
Principle,

of that eternal source, light, and fullness;

of that efficient, exemplary, and ordering Art.

They are vestiges, images, and spectacles proposed to us

for the contemplation of God.

They are divinely given signs.

These creatures are copies or rather illustrations

proposed to those who are still untrained and immersed in

things of the senses,

so that through sensible objects which they do see

they may be lifted to the intelligible realities which they do not
see,
moving from signs to that which is signified.

12. For the created beings of this sensible world
signify the invisible things of God [Romans 1:20]
partly because God is the origin, exemplar, and goal of all
creation,
and every effect is a sign of its cause;
every copy is a sign of its exemplar;
and the road is a sign of the goal to which it leads. . . .
For every creature is by nature a kind of copy and likeness of
that eternal Wisdom.

ANDRÉ

For Francis of Assisi, each part of creation has its own value,
its unique dignity and special message. Nature as a fraternity of sisters and brothers reflects God in all its facets. The
entire universe becomes a sacrament, a holy sign of the One
Who is "Wholly Other."

The Franciscan mystic, Blessed Angela of Foligno
(1248–1309), experienced this deep union with nature surrounding us in a very impressive way.

> Everywhere she looked—"This creature is
> mine," God said—she saw the created uni-
> verse resplendent with God's presence and
> herself one with it. . . . In (a) vision, one so
> thoroughly Franciscan, Angela reports: I
> could perceive nothing except the divine
> power . . . so that . . . marveling my soul
> cried with a loud voice, saying: "this whole
> world is pregnant of God.". . . (T)he world
> (is) so charged with the grandeur of God.[1]

Within the Catholic tradition the number of sacraments was limited to seven, which number symbolizes fullness. However, instead of allowing the seven to embrace all things mystical, practice at times has reduced these divine processes to magical rituals demanding little or no human participation, causing these holy signs to lose much of their deeper meaning.

JOSEF

I would like to share with you a memory that haunts me from time to time. I was seventeen years old and was sitting at the bedside of my dying father. In our helplessness, my mother had started to pray. We prayed the rosary together, holding his hands, since my father was unconscious. His breathing began to falter. We continued our prayer, taking comfort in the familiar words. After he had breathed his last, a priest walked in. Without greeting us or even acknowledging our presence, he began to administer the "last rites." The Latin words of his prayer distanced us even more. I was so angry I wanted to throw him out of the room. His performance of this almost meaningless ritual complemented the clinical, sterile way dying happens in hospitals. This sacrament of anointing could have been a sign of the holy appearing at a crucial moment in one's life and received with great reverence and respect. This mechanical manner of celebrating sacraments diminishes both the sacrament and the human experience it attempts to mark by the presence of the holy.

And yet, the whole world is full of signs and wonders of the holy! Francis in his love for all of creation—rocks, trees, plants, animals, insects—established a remarkable relationship with every aspect of God's world. A look at two of our stories shows us how Francis lived with creation:

> A nobleman from the area of Siena sent a pheasant to blessed Francis while he was sick. He received it gladly, not with the desire to eat it, but because it was his custom to rejoice in such creatures out of love for their Creator. He said to the pheasant: "Praised be our Creator, Brother Pheasant!" And to the brothers he said: "Let's make a test now to see if Brother Pheasant wants to remain with us, or if he'd rather return to his usual places, which are more fit for him." At the saint's command a brother carried the pheasant away and put him down in a vineyard far away. Immediately the pheasant returned at a brisk pace to the father's cell.
>
> The saint ordered it to be carried out again, and even further away, but with great stubbornness it returned to the door of the cell, and as if forcing its way, it entered under the tunics of the brothers who were in the doorway. And so the saint commanded that it should be lovingly cared for, caressing and stroking it with gentle words. A doctor who was very devoted to the *holy one of God* saw this, and asked the brothers to give it to him, not because he wanted to eat it, but wanting rather to care for it out of reverence for the saint. What else? The doctor took it home with him, but when separated from the saint it seemed hurt, and while away from his presence it absolutely refused to eat. The doctor was amazed, and at once carried the pheasant

back to the saint, telling him in order all that happened. As soon as it was placed on the ground and saw its father, it threw off its sadness and began to eat with joy.

A cricket lived in a fig tree by the cell of the *holy one of God* at the Portiuncula, and it would sing frequently with its usual sweetness. Once the blessed father stretched out his hand to it and gently called it to him: "My Sister Cricket, come to me!" And the cricket, as if it had reason, immediately climbed onto his hand. He said to it: "Sing, my Sister Cricket, and with joyful song praise the Lord your Creator!" The cricket, obeying without delay, began to chirp, and did not stop singing until the *man of God*, mixing his own songs with its praise, told it to return to its usual place. There it remained constantly for eight days, as if tied to the spot. Whenever the saint would come down from the cell he would always touch it with his hands and command it to sing, and it was always eager to obey his command. And the saint said to his companions: "Let us give permission to our Sister Cricket to leave, who has up to now made us so happy with her praises, so that our *flesh may not boast vainly in any way*."[2]

A contemporary brother of Francis in the Order, Saint Anthony, is associated with an event in his life that has become known as "the sermon to the fish":

Once when St. Anthony was in Rimini, where there was a great number of heretics, wishing to lead them back to the light of the true faith and on to the path of truth, he preached to them. . . . But they were stubborn and hard-hearted, and . . . they refused to listen to him. So one day, by an inspiration from God, St. Anthony went to the . . . river. . . . And standing on the bank . . . he began to call the fishes in God's name, saying: "You fishes, listen to the word of God since the faithless heretics refuse to hear it!" As soon as he said that . . . a great throng of large and small fishes gathered before him . . . and . . . held their heads a bit out of the water, gazing intently at St. Anthony's face. . . . At this miracle the people of the city, including the heretics, came running. And when they saw the marvelous miracle of the fishes listening to St. Anthony, all of them felt remorse and sat down at his feet so that he should preach a sermon to them.[3]

These two holy friars—Francis and Anthony—had a marvelous respect and rapport with creation. They saw it all as a sacrament of God. A deep and interior union, a knowledge of the desires and natural calling of all living things and a respectful approach to them are certainly part and parcel of a truly Christian and Franciscan spirituality.

The Catholic writer Ida Friederike Görres (1901–1971) once said, "Creation is a collection of 'holy pictures' made by God."[4] This certainly would be a worthwhile evening meditation! Which "holy pictures" will I take to bed with me today?

EXERCISES

- Experience water! It can be a shower, a bath, swimming or diving, washing hands or dishes or a car. Does the water "speak" to you of the presence of God? The sole purpose of this exercise is to "encounter" the water.

- In our highly developed Western industrial countries, we are plagued by fast-food establishments. We eat and drink too much too fast! Take some leisurely time to enjoy a meal and try to identify its various "holy pictures."

To conclude the exercise—which we hope you enjoyed—sing or listen to a song of praise or offer some spontaneous prayer.

NOTES

[1] Paul Lachance, O.F.M., *The Spiritual Journey of the Blessed Angela of Foligno According to the Memorial of Frater A.* (Rome: Pontificium Athenaeum Antonianum, 1984), pp. 174, 212–213. Angela's journal was compiled by her confessor, Brother Arnoldo. Lachance published his work on Blessed Angela in *Angela of Foligno: The Complete Works* (New York: Paulist Press, 1993).

[2] Thomas of Celano, *The Remembrance of the Desire of a Soul*, CXXIX:170 and CXXX:171, in *Francis of Assisi: The Founder, op. cit.*, pp. 356–357.

[3] *The Little Flowers of St. Francis* 40, in *Omnibus of Sources, op. cit.*, pp. 1391–1393.

[4] Ida F. Görres, *Die Leibhaftige Kirche* (Freiburg, Germany: Johannes Verlag, 1994), pp. 27–28. Authors' translation.

Saturday

WHAT'S IN A NAME?

Bonaventure writes in chapter 2:1; 7:1; 2:13:

2:1. With respect to the mirror of things perceptible to the
senses,
it is possible that God might be contemplated not only
through them,
but also in them in as far as God is present in them
by essence, power, and presence.
This way of reflecting is higher than the previous one.
Therefore it follows as the second level of contemplation
by which we ought to be led to contemplate God in all those
creatures
that enter into our consciousness through our bodily senses.

7:1. We have covered these six meditations,
comparing them to the six steps by which one ascends to the
throne of the true Solomon where we arrive at peace.
It is here that the true person of peace rests in the quiet of the
mind
as in an interior Jerusalem.
They are also compared to the six wings of the Seraphim
by which the mind of the truly contemplative person is filled
with the light of heavenly wisdom and can come to soar on
high.
They are also like the first six days during which the mind
needed to be trained
so as to finally arrive at the Sabbath of rest. . . .

2:13. From all that has been said above
we may conclude that *from the creation of the world*
the invisible things of God are seen,
being understood through those things

that are made so that *they are without excuse* [Romans 1:20]
who do not wish to pay attention to these things,
or to know, bless, and love God in all things,
since such people do not wish to be lifted
from darkness to the marvelous light of God.
But *thanks be to God through Jesus Christ our Lord
who has lifted us out of the darkness
into his marvelous light* [1 Corinthians 15:57; 1 Peter 2:9],
since because of the lights that come to us from outside
we might be disposed to re-enter the mirror of our mind
in which divine realities shine forth.

JOSEF

Now it is time to meditate more closely on the title of
Bonaventure's work—*Itinerarium mentis in deum—The Journey
of the Human Person into God.* The Latin word *itinerarium* can
be translated by the words "journey," "itinerary" or "trave-
logue." In a religious context, the word could also designate
a prayer for protection and safety as one sets out on a journey. It can also mean "pilgrimage"—usually, the pilgrimage
to the Holy Land. The Second Vatican Council (1962–1965)
rediscovered the people of God on pilgrimage[1] as a central
ecclesiological theme. Christians are people on the road.
They have not yet arrived at their goal, not even as a church
with all its teaching, its witness and its theology. Christians
must always seek constant direction and change. Nevertheless, God is present and God's power can be felt everywhere,
not just at the finish line. God is with people on the road,
and God is also the goal.

Journeying is an archetype for human existence.
Every culture and religion has some type of procession or
pilgrimage as a symbolic representation of this basic struc-

ture of life. At the start of the third Christian millennium our desire for mobility has increased to such a degree that it seems to be threatening our very survival. Each year thousands of people are killed in traffic accidents. Our air is being poisoned by the burning of fossil fuels, putting all life forms on earth at risk. Humankind—and the church as the People of God within it—is caught between the danger of standing still and aimlessly running around helter-skelter, searching everywhere in vain! The word *itinerarium* implies a balance between these two extremes: knowing where I come from and where I am going, with awareness and direction along the way.

Mentis, from the Latin *mens*, the second word of the title, is especially difficult to translate. Our word "mental" implies primarily the mind's ability to reason. If we take into consideration Bonaventure's entire work, the best translation may be "the entire human person with all one's capacities, powers and possibilities," or "the human person in one's physical, psychological and spiritual dimensions."

Bonaventure, therefore, does not infer only the mental processes but all possible expressions of human existence. Reducing this word to the mental meaning alone would lead us to misunderstand the whole book. And this is not just some trivial matter; it involves Bonaventure's main purpose and touches upon the key element of it. All aspects of human life are indispensable elements and parts of this *Journey*.

The shortest word of the title seems to be the simplest as well: *in*. Nevertheless, it hints at another central theme: mystical union, the flowing into one another, the unifying process between God and the human person. This implies something more than and qualitatively different from a mutual rapprochement or the person's crawling humbly towards God. The Latin alternative to *in* would have been *ad*: "toward" someone. *In* implies a personal encounter of depth, an encounter of hearts. It means a loving unification as the aim of *The Journey*. And yet the journey remains full of tension; there is no fast or superficial melting of opposites into one another. *The Journey* ends in the seventh step in a wordless, powerless waiting.

Deum (from the Latin *deus* for "God") comes as no surprise in a treatise such as this. Nevertheless, it seems noteworthy that Bonaventure does not speak exclusively of the Christian God. As we continue along the way this will become quite clear. This *Journey* is not just some familiar tour for insiders. The very title highlights the Parisian professor's thesis that embraces all serious religions. Encountering God, even union with God, is not exclusive to the Christian journey. Rather, the exact opposite is true, for Bonaventure believes that this path is open to everyone as a path of salvation and healing.

At a time in history when crusades and persecution and execution of heretics were the usual ways of dealing with non-believers (or believers whose faith was different), Bonaventure's thoughts have to be noted as extraordinary signs of resistance. He gives us a signal that far transcends his era. The "second founder" of the Lesser Brothers stands in a direct line with Francis, who counted the Egyptian sultan among his friends. How might things have been different for the church and the world if the fifty-seven-year-old minister general of the friars had become pope?

ANDRÉ

Bonaventure wrote primarily for himself, for his own needs and his own situation.[2] Only afterward, perhaps, when he had returned to the realities of his Order and church, did he feel the need to pass his work on to the others. And he undertook to do so himself. He composed a longer and a shorter biography of Saint Francis of Assisi, called by their Latin titles respectively the *Legenda Maior* and the *Legenda Minor*.[3] If we listen and look carefully at the stories of Francis' life, which are not recounted in chronological order, we discover parallels to his more theoretical steps in *The Journey of the Human Person into God*. Bonaventure wanted to offer a summary or an overview of Franciscan spirituality that could give the Franciscan Order some direction, even during this difficult stage of its growth and development. This aim, however, could be achieved only if it were made accessible to more than just intellectuals and scholars.

For the intellectual person, rational knowledge is not everything; rather, it is a part of the whole. Although Bonaventure is an intellectual, rational knowledge is not everything for him, for his focus is much more a heart filled with desire, a surrendering that includes all the dimensions of human life.

Today, many people speak of the holistic approach to the human person. Bonaventure took this route long before it became fashionable. Nothing human is left out of *The Journey*. There is nothing that is senseless, meaningless or to be disregarded. The holy is everywhere and in everything, in all processes and development happening in us and around us.

In his work *De reductione artium ad theologiam (On the*

Reduction of the Arts to Theology), Bonaventure amplifies this theme. Zachary Hayes writes, "The title of this small work of Bonaventure . . . implies the long-standing conviction of the Seraphic Doctor that the ideal for the spiritual-intellectual life is to draw all the varied forms of human knowledge into a unity to serve the human person in the spiritual journey. . . . As a metaphysical term, the word (*reduction*) has to do with the circle of creation as it emanates from God eventually to return to its point of origin."[4] The arts, that is, all knowledge, serve theology, which teaches that we have come from God and return to God.

Perhaps you have read the book or seen the film *Awakenings.* The story takes place in the first half of the twentieth century. A mysterious illness causes a man to fall into a coma and be sent to an institution where an alert and creative psychiatrist experiments with some drugs to reawaken him briefly to life.

For Bonaventure, theology is something like this. In the midst of everyday life, it helps raise us out of a kind of listlessness or lifelessness, a life devoid of meaning. It helps us to understand with our heart and mind that God's presence is much greater than many preachers of various religious denominations would have us believe. God and the knowledge of God are to be sought—and found—right in the midst of life.

This *Journey,* therefore, encompasses everyone and everything. But you will be able to get a taste of it only if you proceed by shifting down a gear, taking time to slow down with the desire to relearn the art of living.

EXERCISES

• Write your own resumé or *curriculum vitae,* as if you were preparing a job application. Indicate the various stages of your life. Try to give different titles to the various stages; you might want to borrow them from film or book titles. What title would fit your life now?

• Moses' people called their experience of God and life *Exodus.* The *Pesach* (Passover) celebration recalls their central experience of being liberated from Egypt. Meditate on Exodus 15:1–21 and let the images used speak to you. As you do this exercise, repeat individual words or verses you come across. Allow those images to connect with your own life and your experience of God in your life.

NOTES

[1] See *Dogmatic Constitution on the Church (Lumen Gentium)* 48, in *The Documents of Vatican II*, ed. Walter M. Abbott, S.J. (New York: Guild Press, 1966), p. 79, which speaks of "the pilgrim Church."

[2] See *Life of Saint Bonaventure*, pp. 3-10.

[3] See *Francis of Assisi: The Founder, op. cit.*, pp. 525–717.

[4] *On the Reduction of the Arts to Theology*, Zachary Hayes, O.F.M., trans. (New York: Franciscan Institute Publications, 1996), p. 1. See the introduction to this text for further explanation.

IMAGES WITHIN

Sunday

ETERNAL ART

Bonaventure writes in chapters 2:7, 9; 3:3:

2:7. Now these actions are vestiges in which we can see our
God.

For the species of which we become aware is a likeness
generated in the medium
and then impressed on the organ itself;
and through that impression it leads to its source as to the
object to be known. This clearly suggests that the eternal light
generates a likeness of itself,
or a splendor that is coequal, consubstantial, and coeternal.
It suggests that the one who is *the invisible image of God*
and the splendor of God's glory
and the figure of God's substance
[Colossians 1:15; Hebrews 1:3],
exists everywhere by virtue of an original generation
just as an object generates its likeness in the entire medium.
It suggests also that this one is united to an individual rational
nature
by the grace of union as the species is united to the bodily
organ
so that through this union
He might lead us back to the Father as to the fontal principle
and object.
If, therefore, it is in the nature of all knowable things
to generate a likeness of themselves,
they clearly proclaim that in them as in mirrors
we can see the eternal generation
of the Word, the Image, and the Son eternally emanating from
God the Father.

2:9. . . . (I)f all our more certain judgments are made by virtue
of such a reality,
then it is clear that this reality itself is the reason for all things
and the infallible rule and light of truth in which all things
shine forth
in a way that is infallible, indelible,
beyond doubt and beyond questioning or argumentation,
unchangeable, having no limits in space and no ending in
time,
in a way that is indivisible and intellectual.
Therefore those laws by which we judge with certitude
concerning all sense objects that come to our consideration,
since they are infallible
and beyond doubt to the intellect of the one who is aware of
them;
and since they cannot be removed from the memory of one
who recalls,
for they are always present;
and since they are beyond question and beyond the judgment
of the intellect
of the one who judges. . . .
it follows that these laws must be changeless and incorruptible
They are not made but are uncreated,
existing eternally in the eternal Art
from which, and through which, and in accordance with which
all beautiful things are formed.
Therefore they cannot be judged with certainty
except through that eternal Art
which is the form that not only produces all things,
but also conserves and distinguishes them;
for this is the Being that sustains the form in all things
and the rule that directs all things.
And it is through this that our mind comes to judge
about all those things which enter into it through the senses.

3:3. It comes, therefore, from the exemplarity of the eternal
Art,
according to which things have an aptitude and a relation to
each other
which is grounded in their representation in the eternal Art.

ANDRÉ

Do you like museums? Do you like to look at paintings and
sculptures? Once Josef and I were walking through the Uffizi
Gallery in Florence in Italy. We went our separate ways in
each of the galleries. At one point I looked to see where Josef
was and saw him across the room almost laughing aloud.
This continued for some time as he moved from painting to
painting. Becoming a bit concerned about his behavior, I
went over to inquire about the reason for his laughter. He
said he was concentrating on the child Jesus in each painting, thinking it was really quite funny to see all those different infants, in various positions, stark naked or dressed in
royal robes, with the stern, adult look of a judge or the smile
of a playful child.

Each artist has inside herself or himself an inner
meaning, an idea, a whole complex of concepts even before
picking up a brush or hammer and chisel. At some point in
time, a work of art is created, given external form and
engages the senses of people viewing it. And then you find
yourself standing in front of a painting, looking at its form
and color, searching for meaning in it. What is the painting
saying to you? Realize that the meaning you give to it today
is your meaning. Over and over again a new, interpretative,
unique creation emerges between each observer and this
same work of art. The encounter between an objective
observer and the art-object is complete. And something new

comes into existence, a new and unique meaning that exists only in this moment. Of course, you might succeed in understanding the original intention and meaning of the artist, but nonetheless, yours is a slightly different understanding.

The same holds true for our understanding of God. God is an artist and God's inner ideas, God's profound and complex meanings, are expressed in the created world around us. Therefore, as we come into contact with creation and encounter the external world in so many different forms, we also encounter the artist who created all of this. We can also discover the artist's meaning if we but look for it. We experience God, the Eternal Artist. Bonaventure writes, "(All) these . . . are vestiges in which we can see our God" [2:7].

Moreover, in the process of taking in the external object through our senses, we create a copy of the object in us, a copy that resembles the original external object. Because of our limited capacity for attention and awareness, it is only a relatively good copy. Christians, however, believe that between God the Father and God the Son there is a total and perfect exchange that has existed from all eternity. The Eternal Artist has created an Eternal Art, God's masterpiece, an identical copy, a copy that is equal to the original. In chapter 2, Bonaventure says that our senses constantly produce new copies of some original, external objects. And this process of the senses reflects what is happening in God all the time, "the eternal generation of the Word, the Image, and the Son eternally emanating from God the Father" [2:7]. This most perfect emanation is God's Eternal Art.

There is a story told about the young Michelangelo Buonarotti.[1] As a boy walking through the streets of his village to school each day, he had to pass by the studio of a sculptor. One day as he walked by he stopped and wondered why the man was diligently pounding away at a huge piece of stone. What was that man doing? School vacation came around, and it wasn't until two weeks later that the boy again passed by the sculptor's studio. As he walked by the large window, he halted in his tracks and stood there with his eyes and mouth wide open. Running into the studio, he blurted out, "Where did this huge lion come from?" The sculptor told the boy that before he saw the lion in the stone, he saw the lion in his heart.

A sculptured lion now sat there in place of the block of stone. An artwork is born when an idea is actually painted or sculpted. The artist then gives external form or shape to the idea first conceived in his or her head. Of course, how closely the artwork resembles the original idea depends upon the artist's skill.

This world existed first as an eternal idea before being birthed in all its wonderful variety. Filled with awe like the boy in our story, we can run up to God and ask, "Where did creation come from?" And God may respond, "From within my heart!" And our eyes, too, will be opened wide.

EXERCISES

- Walk through your home, not in the usual way or at your normal speed or concentrating on the disorder or anything that bothers you. Rather, look at paintings or art objects you might have there. Then, choose one item and study it. What does this piece of art evoke in you? Do you have an idea of what the artist wanted to express with it? Where does this piece of art lead you today? What inspiration does it give you?

• Look at the Crucifix of San Damiano, which spoke to Saint
Francis and which today hangs in the Basilica of Saint Clare
in Assisi.[2] What is Jesus saying to you? What do the individual figures around the cross say to Jesus? What are they saying to you? What would you like to say to the various figures or images (the empty tomb, the rooster, the lance)? If
you prefer, choose a different crucifix, one that has more
personal meaning for you.

NOTES

[1] Henri Nouwen repeats this story in *Clowning in Rome, op. cit.*, p. 87.

[2] This Syro-Byzantine style crucifix was named for the Church of San
Damiano, where it spoke to Francis early in his conversion (c. 1205–1206).
Many books have been written about it, but its meaning has yet to be
exhausted. A good example is by Marc Picard, O.F.M. CAP., *The Icon of the
Christ of San Damiano* (Assisi: Casa Editrice Francescana, 2000).

Monday

FORGET ME NOT!

Bonaventure writes in chapter 3:1–2:

1. . . . (I)n this third stage,
as we leave the outer court and enter into ourselves,
we should try to see God through a mirror, as it were, in the
holy place—
namely in the area in front of the tabernacle. . . .
Therefore, enter into yourself and recognize
that your mind loves itself most fervently.
But it cannot love itself if it does not know itself,
And it would not know itself unless it remembered itself,
for we do not grasp anything with our understanding
if it is not present to us in our memory. . . .

2. The function of the memory is to retain and to represent
not only things that are present, corporal, and temporal,
but also things that are successive, simple, and everlasting.
Memory holds past things by recall,
present things by reception,
and future things by means of anticipation. . . .
In its first function,
the actual retention of all temporal things past, present, and
future,
the memory is similar to eternity
whose undivided presentness extends to all times.
In its second function,
it is clear that memory is formed not only by phantasms from
external objects,
but also from above by receiving and holding within itself
simple forms
which cannot enter through the doorways of the senses

or by means of sensible phantasms.
In its third function,
we hold that memory has present within itself
a changeless light by which it remembers changeless truths.
So through the operations of memory,
it becomes clear that the soul itself is an image of God
and a similitude so present to itself
and having God so present to it
that it actually grasps God
and potentially "has the capacity for God and the ability to
participate in God."

JOSEF

Some years ago I was working in a secured ward in a nursing home. The elderly residents had no idea where they were nor who was caring for them. Most of them were suffering from some form of senile dementia. Some seemed to have lost their memory completely, while others retained long-term memory.

One day I began to sing a Bavarian song to an elderly lady—eighty-eight years old, to be exact—an innkeeper's daughter. I was completely amazed when she continued to sing another ten verses of the song, while I remembered only three of them. Of course, she sang the song for the rest of the day with great joy. There I was, fifty years younger, living with the illusion that I knew and remembered so much. And what a joy that lady felt! Because of a simple melody, the sound of familiar words—in the midst of a situation that seemed to be without consolation and hope—a past world opened up to her with all of its wonder and attraction and she felt alive again and full of energy. This elderly, disoriented woman was able to experience such joy that I, the so-called normal person, envied her.

Is it not true that any joy I feel today, at this very moment, is to some degree the memory of some happiness I once experienced? What would humanity be without the power of memory? Would we be able to feel our own human individuality? Usually, it is tragic when someone loses memory. But at times it could be a grace, the masterly performance of our psyche protecting us from something that is too difficult or terrible to recall. If we remembered everything, it is possible that our life would no longer be a happy one. Speaking of memory, Bonaventure also mentions its reaching into the future: "Memory holds past things by recall, present things by reception, and future things by means of foresight" [3:2]. The ability to remember is tied up with both past and future because it deals with thoughts which come together in the here and now.

What would humanity be without special days and times for remembrance? What would we be without fixed rhythms, recurring festivals and celebrations? What would we be without our ancestors and our own personal history?

Memory seems to be the source of everything else in us. At every moment it is being fed, always at work through our senses and their impressions. This sense perception and its transformation, which we call memory, will accompany me and this process will mark me to a certain degree as an individual person.

What Bonaventure does at the beginning of chapter 3 is very simple. Sitting alone or in a group, we could follow our thoughts and ideas from one to the next without stopping. Each word or thought may call to mind another memory. The apparent endlessness of memory is an image of the eternity of God. We are made in God's image, and God is eternal, like the endless chain of our memories leading us into the future.

Eternity

remembers changeless truths

receives and holds simple forms

retains past, present and future

Memory

Illustration 5: Chapter 3.

Through memory and its three functions one glimpses an image of the eternity of God.

For the German people, the Nazi past is a heavy burden and challenge as well. There will be neo-Nazis for as long as people are not increasingly prepared to remember what happened. Memory is the necessary starting point for any healing process. Elie Wiesel, a Jew who suffered in body and soul at the hands of this regime, once wrote:

> My key word is memory. . . . (There is a) necessity to remember and thus live in truth. The people are not responsible for their forebears, but they are responsible for the memories created by their forebears. . . Memory is already a protest. . . . [1]

Sigmund Freud's brilliant discovery of the psychoanalytical technique originates with the importance of this basic human capacity, memory. Memories of early childhood, dreams and fantasies, free associations and ideas offer the key to successful therapy. It is no wonder that Freud, like Wiesel, was Jewish. The Jews as a religious community have a most intense appreciation for this human capacity, and they used it. Tradition and remembering can sum it up for them. Both theologically and socially, it is at the core of Jewish culture, as the book of Deuteronomy, the fifth and last book of the Pentateuch, tells us:

> Now this is the commandment—the statutes and the ordinances—that the Lord your God charged me to teach you to observe . . . so that you . . . may fear the Lord your God all the days of your life, and keep all his decrees and his commandments that I am commanding you, so that your days may be long. Hear therefore, O Israel, and observe them diligently, so that it may go well with you, and so that you may multiply greatly in a land flowing with milk and honey, as the Lord, the God of your ancestors, has promised you. Hear, O Israel: The Lord is our God, the Lord alone. You shall love the Lord your God with all your heart, and with all your soul, and with all your might. Keep these words that I am commanding you today in your heart. Recite them to your children and talk about them when you are at home and when you are away, when you lie down and when you rise. Bind them as a sign on your hand, fix them as an emblem on your forehead, and write them on the doorposts of your house and on your gates. [Deuteronomy 6:1-9]

This emphasis on memory is integral to Jewish communal life, something very significant that the rest of humanity can learn from the Jewish people.

ANDRÉ

Tradition and memory are important in any religion. At the heart of the Christian liturgy stands the person of Jesus of Nazareth: Do this in memory of me! We see the bread and wine, and we recall, we remember, and in doing so we believe in the continuous process of transformation:

> We always hear of the life, person, work and teaching of Jesus, the full image and perfect servant. . . . In and through these readings, we recapture our identity: who we are, where we are from, where we are going, and how we are to get there. . . . The vision draws us ever forward. We are involved as individuals, as societies, and as a cosmos.[2]

The Second Vatican Council began and ended with a call to everyone: Go back to your roots! The Council felt it was crucial, at a time when reform was so necessary, to take a closer look at all of tradition. We cannot appreciate fully the quiet and patient historical research of Vatican II's many scholars, especially in the area of biblical study. They had a vitally important role to play in the renewal of Christian thought and life in the twentieth century and far beyond.

EXERCISES

• Take a pen and a large sheet of paper. Reflect on the word "Christmas" or "birthday" and jot down the memories that flow. Detail the memory by describing a certain gift or circumstance of that time. When you are through, look at the entire sheet and wonder! Close with a prayer of thanksgiving.

• Meditate on Psalm 136. Take a piece of paper and continue to meditate on the psalm, recalling specific events in your personal history and jotting them down on the paper. As you mention each event, embrace it with the refrain "God's love endures forever!"

NOTES

[1] Elie Wiesel, "Memory, Morality and Germany," *International Herald Tribune*, September 1992.

[2] Michael Guinan, O.F.M., *To Be Human Before God: Insights from Biblical Spirituality* (Collegeville, Minn.: The Liturgical Press, 1994), p. 87.

Tuesday

Do You Get It?

Bonaventure writes in chapters 3:1, 3:

1. Therefore, enter into yourself and recognize
that your mind loves itself most fervently.
But it cannot love itself if it does not know itself.
And it would not know itself unless it remembered itself,
for we do not grasp anything with our understanding
if it is not present to us in our memory.
From this you see,
not with the eye of the flesh but with the eye of reason,
that the soul possesses a threefold power.
Now consider the operation of these powers and their relation
to each other.
Here you can see God through yourself as through an image.
And this is to see *through a mirror in an obscure manner*
[1 Corinthians 13:12].

3. The function of the intellect is seen
in the intellect's understanding of terms, propositions, and
inferences.
The intellect understands the meaning of terms
when it comprehends what each thing is by means of a
definition.
But a definition is formulated by using broader terms;
and these, in turn, are defined by still broader terms.
Thus it goes until we arrive at the highest and most general
terms.
If these are not known,
it is impossible to understand the less general terms by means
of a definition. . . . For how can the intellect know that this
being is defective or incomplete

if it has no knowledge of that being which has no defect?. . .
Next, the intellect is said truly to comprehend the meaning of
propositions
when it knows with certainty that they are true.

Our intellect grasps the meaning of an inference in the truest
sense
when it sees that the conclusion follows necessarily from the
premises,
and when it sees this not only in necessary terms but in
contingent terms as well. For example: "If a person is running,
a person is moving."
It sees this necessary relation not only in existing things,
but even in non-existing things.
Thus, with respect to a person who exists in reality
it follows that "If a person is running, a person is moving."
But the conclusion is true even if such a person does not exist
in reality.
The necessity of this sort of inference does not come
from the real, material existence of a thing, because that is
contingent.
Neither does it come from the existence of the thing in the
mind
because that would be a fiction if the thing did not exist in
reality. . . .
So, as Augustine says in his book *On the True Religion,*
the light of anyone who reasons truly
is enlightened by that truth and seeks to return to it.
From this it is clear that our intellect is united with the eternal
truth itself.
And if that truth were not teaching our intellect,
it would be impossible to grasp anything with certitude.
So you are able to see within yourself that truth
which teaches you as long as unruly desires and sense images

do not stand as impediments becoming like clouds
between you and the ray of truth.

JOSEF

The human mind is fascinating! Even though humanity has
made great strides in discovering more of the immense
capacities and possibilities of our brains, we are just beginning to understand it. The virtual world and artificial intelligence are still very limited when compared with the complex
reality of our brain.

Setting aside modern hermeneutics, philosophy of
language or communication sciences, should you take for
granted that you are able to understand what someone else
says to you? We can read a book and understand the thought
of another person whom we do not know at all. We look at
the letters that form the word "blackbird" or "hammer" and
immediately we think we know what they mean. Ultimately,
everything can be traced back to the few basic elements that
we know, and even further. As we will see more clearly in
Bonaventure's fifth chapter, every definition ends with *being*
itself.

Considering *being* itself, everything that exists comes
together. The more we look into this *being*, the more differ-
entiated it becomes, but also the more limited. If you had to
describe your mother, there are many things you could
include—her personality, life, talents and accomplishments.
Ultimately, you would come to the broader terms: mother,
wife, human being, mammal, life-form, all the way back to a
cosmological understanding of her. Our understanding
quite surely and logically keeps taking us further and further.
In pushing our understanding further and further, the

development of Western culture has become heavily cerebral. Everything has to be sensible, comprehensible. It must all add up.

Intelligence is all too often disassociated from memory and imagination and occasionally from ethical considerations. Christianity, with its elaborate theological superstructure, has also fallen prey to this disassociation. Christian theology can certainly be numbered among the most logical and brilliant of teachings. Unfortunately, it gradually shifted increasingly to the word, to understanding and comprehension, to control and power. One cannot ignore the unhealthy consequences of this development. The praxis of the official church, for example, in the Inquisition cost the lives of many people.

However, I would like to return to more simple human experiences. In the first few years of its life, every child learns that some things are better than others. Each child develops a unique way of interpreting the world and begins to make connections for herself or himself.

Take the example of a five-year-old boy who sees his mother upset because her husband has left her and feels that in some way he is the cause of his mother's suffering. This interpretation can cause years of suffering and a great deal of disturbance. The opposite example is a girl who knows that she is loved and accepted by those in her world who delight in and treasure her. This interpretation opens up many possibilities in such a child that can evolve into a sense of basic trust in life and in people.

Truth

grasps the meaning of an inference (conclusion)

comprehends the meaning of propositions (sentence)

understands the meaning of terms (word)

Intellect

Illustration 6: Chapter 3.

From our limited experience Bonaventure leads us to the perfect fullness of the divine logic and art of interpretation. The illustration shows how our intellect in its three functions is an image of God, who is Truth.

ANDRÉ

Like memory, the intellect is something we human beings use daily. Our understanding is an essential part of human life, and should not be isolated. In its daily use, it mirrors the image of God, who is Truth itself. Our understanding mirrors the Word that expresses all things, understands all things and orders all things rightly.

Jesus says, "I am the Truth" [John 14:6]. In the opening verse of John's Gospel, he is called *Logos*: "In the beginning was the Word, and the Word was with God, and the Word was God" [John 1:1]. The Greek *logos* does not only signify "word," but also "meaning," "understanding" or "knowledge." With this all-important gift of human understanding, we are created in the image of God's Son, who bears within himself all meaning and interpretation of life.

Viktor Frankl (1905–1995), professor of neurology

and psychiatry, was imprisoned in a concentration camp during World War II. From that most inhuman situation, he developed his theory of logotherapy to cope with the events and experiences of life through meaning.[1] Frankl defines "the human person as one wrestling with concrete meaning for personal existence."[2] In his work, he echoes Bonaventure's emphasis on the value of understanding in *The Journey* of our lives.

EXERCISES

- Reflect on and pray your written personal history of yesterday. Just as the Israelites in Psalm 136 recalled some events of their history that they were not able to understand, similarly, you may find some items that only hindsight could reveal to you as the gift of a loving God. At the time these events occurred, it might have been very difficult for you. Choose one or two of these events for meditation!
- Play the following communication game with a partner of your choice. First, make a simple statement. Example: "The stairway is not clean." Then your partner is allowed to ask you ten questions beginning with: "Do you mean . . . ?" For example, "Do you mean I should clean it?" When you have answered your partner's questions affirmatively three times, switch roles. After playing this game for a while, ask yourself: what makes my words able to be understood? What do words mean? Try to summarize your observations when you finish.

NOTES

[1] See Viktor Frankl, *Man's Search for Meaning: An Introduction to Logotherapy* (New York: Simon and Schuster, 1963).

[2] Viktor Frankl, *Psychotherapy in Practice* (Munich: Piper Verlag, 1986), p. 9. Authors' translation.

Wednesday

I Do What I Want!

Bonaventure writes in chapter 3:1, 4:

1. The two preceding steps, which have led us to God by
means of the vestiges

through which God shines forth in every creature,

have brought us to a point where we can enter again into
ourselves,

that is, into the mind itself in which the divine image shines
forth.

4. The power of choice is seen in deliberation, judgment, and
desire.

Deliberation consists in inquiring whether this thing is better
than that thing.

But a thing is said to be better only because of its closeness to
the best.

But closeness to the best is measured in terms of likeness.

No one can know, therefore, whether one thing is better than
another

without knowing that this thing has a greater resemblance to
the best.

And no one knows whether something is more like another
without knowing that other.

For I do not know whether this person is like Peter
unless I know and recognize Peter.

Therefore, it is necessary that the notion of the highest good
be impressed on anyone who is engaged in deliberation.

Moreover, a sure judgment concerning matters that are the
object of deliberation takes place through some law.

And no one judges with certitude by virtue of a law
without being certain that the law is right

and that one should not make a judgment about the law itself.
But our mind does judge about itself.
Since it cannot judge about the law which it uses to judge,
that law is superior to our mind.
And our mind is able to judge by this law
in as far as the law has been impressed in the mind.
But nothing is superior to the human mind except God who
has created it. Therefore in making its judgments
our deliberative power is in contact with the divine laws
when it arrives at a full and complete analysis.

Finally, desire tends above all to that which moves it the most.
And that which moves it the most is that which is loved the
most.
And that which is loved the most is happiness.
But happiness is attained only by reaching the best and
ultimate goal.
Therefore, human desire is directed at nothing but the
supreme Good,
or that which leads to it or reflects that Good in a certain way.
The power of the supreme Good is so great
that nothing else can be loved by a creature
except through a desire for the supreme Good.
Therefore, anyone who takes the image or the copy for the
truth itself
is deceived and falls into error.
Behold, therefore, how close the soul is to God. . . .

JOSEF

What would human beings be without will power? Would we
simply be like compliant marionettes? Would we have our
own distinct character and drive? Would goodness really exist?

Between the ages of two and four children discover
their will. We have all heard—and perhaps experienced—

the "terrible twos," when a child stubbornly clings to his or her own will. Frequently conflicts arise between an individual and the immediate environment. The child is discovering herself and her own needs, finding it necessary to say, "I will," or "I will not," when demonstrating her own decision-making ability. Woe to you, Mom and Dad, if the dessert isn't exactly what your little one had in mind before the meal began! Alas for you if you do not tell or read the story exactly as your child knows or remembers it! Take courage in the thought that an immense power, a strong force is developing in your child in these early years, and that these eruptions of the will are necessary if the child is to learn to live.

Bonaventure sees this power as being in a direct line with God, who is the highest good human beings are able to reach. Even if he were to see my son in a toy shop, running from one end to another and screaming into my ears, "Daddy, I want that! Daddy, buy me this!," Bonaventure would see the beautiful and powerful image of God in us. He would describe this experience—so annoying, at least for parent and other customers wanting to shop in peace—as a demonstration of the powerful desire for the highest good, even better than we could imagine.

When we recently moved into a new house, my wife convinced me to go with her to the furniture store. We needed a sofa for our living room. For weeks she had been comparing information and prices. She had been careful to include me in her deliberations, although I was not all that excited about shopping for a sofa. We went from one store to the next until we finally found "our" sofa, one that fit our living room, our taste, our expectations and our family. As Bonaventure would say, it is a matter of proportion and numbers when considering whether something fits or not. All our human powers—the senses, memory, intellect and, of course, the will—are involved in this process of deliberation. This whole process of finding the right piece of furniture reflects the powerful reality of God in our limited, human way. Of course, in the future we may conclude that another sofa would have been better. We tried to find the best, but we realize our human limitations.

Highest Good

↑

desire

↑

judgment

↑

deliberation

↑

Will

Illustration 7: Chapter 3.

Through our use of the power of will in its three main functions, we reflect the image of God who is the Highest Good.

Every act of our will should be directed to the good, and everything should be compared to and measured against the good. What yardstick do I use? At times I adapt and give in when I should rise up in protest. And there are always some good reasons for doing so! What difference would my protest make? What will I get from it, besides an ulcer, perhaps? Or, how many people spend their lives keeping up with the Joneses, or even trying to outdo them? They constantly compare themselves with others. They always want to be first and sometimes even fight against someone who has more. As narrow-minded or perverted as the process of our power of will could be, Bonaventure still sees it as the image of God's love and tenderness.

All kinds of moral and ethical deliberations pertain to this step on *The Journey,* as do large-scale or small-scale political activities. We sometimes do not appreciate just how important the power of the human will is for being human, for living as individuals, or as part of a family, part of a group or society. It is impossible to overestimate this fact!

To demonstrate strength of will, we share the example of three remarkable men in Assisi during World War II. Colonel Valentin Müller (1891–1951) was the last German commander of the city. He protected and preserved Assisi from destruction, even by the German army itself, by declaring and making it a hospital city:

> Müller also had a barricade placed at Santa Maria degli Angeli . . . to make the last retreating German troops understand that they were not to go up to Assisi. . . . As night fell on 15 June 1944, Müller positioned himself outside the main gate of Assisi. From the valley he heard the sounds of demolition and could see the striking images of buildings set afire by the angry SS troops. The next day some of the SS troops came up to Assisi. Müller and they began a heated debate, but the verbal exchange did not last long. It was long enough, however, for him to convince the German rear guard to abandon the city. Assisi was safe! Shortly after midnight on 16 June, Col. Müller and his division set out on the road leading north.[1]

During this same time, Bishop Giuseppe Nicolini (d. 1973) and Don Aldo Brunacci were instrumental in hiding, protecting and saving many Jews. Don Aldo reports:

> The bishop's residence already hosted a center for aid to the refugees. . . . It was often necessary to hide, not only persons, but also the personal effects of those who were given refuge in the convents and private homes. . . . These items were placed in recesses in the basement of the bishop's residence and then walled over. The work was not done by workers, but by the bishop himself who used a trowel to build the walls while I held the lantern. When a wall had to be broken into to restore objects to those refugees leaving the city, I would wield the pick while the bishop held the light for me.[2]

Looking at the field of psychotherapy again, behavioral therapy would provide the best analogy to this discussion of the will. Behavioral therapists seek to effect change through the use of the power of will. One of the strengths of Buddhism and other Asian religions is their focus on the will. Some say that Buddhism is primarily, or even entirely, an ethical system. We Christians could learn how to balance theory with practice. Jesus gave us the theory of a three-fold commandment of love: genuine love of self, love of neighbor—even one's enemy—and love of God. Bonaventure encourages us to the practice of this love, deciding to love and always strive for the good.

EXERCISES

- Think of an important decision you made. What characterized the decision? How did your deliberation proceed? What was your point of orientation?
- What do you want to do with your life? Take a piece of paper and draw, paint or describe, what attracts or excites you.
- What do you want for today, for yesterday, for tomorrow? For someone close to you? For people of the earth and all of creation?

NOTES

[1] Francesco Santucci, *The Strategy That Saved Assisi*, edited and translated by Josef Raischl, s.f.o., (Assisi: Editrice Minerva Assisi, 1999), pp. 57–59.

[2] *Ibid.*, pp. 71–72.

Thursday

THE INNER CIRCLE

Bonaventure writes in chapter 3:5–7:

5. Furthermore, if one considers
the order, origin, and relation of these faculties to one
another,
one is led to the most blessed Trinity itself.
For intelligence emerges out of memory as its offspring,
because we come to understand only when a likeness
which lies in the memory emerges to the forefront of
consciousness.
And this is nothing other than a word.
From memory and intelligence,
love is breathed forth as the bond that unites them.
These three—namely, the mind that generates, the word,
and love—
are in the soul as memory, intelligence, and will. . . .
Therefore, when the soul reflects on itself and through itself
as through a mirror,
it rises to the consideration of the blessed Trinity of Father,
Word, and Love. . . .

6. For all of philosophy is either natural, rational, or moral.
The first deals with the cause of being
and therefore points to the power of the Father.
The second deals with the basis of understanding
and therefore leads to the wisdom of the Word.
And the third deals with the order of living
and therefore leads to the goodness of the Holy Spirit.
Furthermore, the first, or natural philosophy,
is divided into metaphysics, mathematics, and physics. . . .
The second, or rational philosophy is divided into

grammar which enables people to express themselves with
power;
logic, which makes people sharp in argumentation;
and rhetoric, which enables people to persuade and move
others.
Again, this points to the mystery of the most blessed Trinity.
The third, or moral philosophy
is divided into the monastic, the familial, and the political.
The first suggests the unbegottenness of the first Principle;
the second suggests the familial relation of the Son;
and the third suggests the liberality of the Holy Spirit.

7. All these sciences are governed by certain and infallible laws
that are like lights and beams coming down from that eternal
law into our mind. Therefore, our mind, enlightened and
filled with such splendors,
can be guided to reflect on this eternal light through itself
if it has not been blinded.
The radiation of this light and the reflection on it lifts up the
wise in admiration. On the other hand, the unwise
who reject faith as a way to understanding are led to
confusion
Thus the prophetic word is fulfilled:
You enlighten wonderfully from the everlasting hills.
All the foolish of heart were troubled [Psalms 75:5].

ANDRÉ

Bonaventure sees the powers of the human psyche not simply from the perspective of quality and function. Each of
these powers represents something of eternity, truth and the
total goodness of God. As we see in the following illustration,
Bonaventure also views memory, intellect and will from the
perspective of their collaboration with one another. In this

way our mental apparatus, together with our feelings, becomes an image of the Trinity itself, Father, Son and Holy Spirit. In chapter 3 we reach the fullness of how we Christians describe our God.

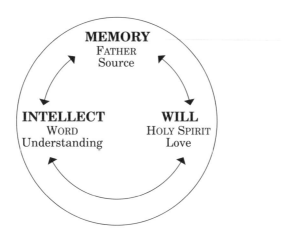

Illustration 8: Chapter 3.

The interrelationship of our three inner powers, experienced as limited by humanity, points to the perfect inner trinitarian exchange.

JOSEF

A member of our hospice team, an elderly lady, took it upon herself to keep track of the birthdays of all the team members. She searched our records—part of our institution's memory. She understood and appreciated the value of each person and expressed this by sending a birthday card to each one of them. This reminded the team members of their value and strengthened the bonds among us. This sign of thoughtfulness and special attention thus became a pleasant part of both the individual and the group memory experience. The circle, as illustrated above, closed, but repeated itself with each new birthday.

Rituals such as these birthday cards or the celebration of special feast days are crucial for the survival of a community. And it all comes back to remembering, a process that continually happens in all of us because this is part of our psyche, at least as Bonaventure perceived it when he was lecturing in Paris. And we function the same way all the time.

Are you really able to understand something if you cannot remember it? Certainly not! And if not, then the path toward reconciliation (understanding) and loving response (decision) is blocked, at least as far as this particular memory is concerned. In a healthy human psyche, memory should set free all its capacities, fantasies and dreams—even the dark shadows of early childhood—to lead one to greater awareness and articulation. And understanding should flow into more loving action and commitment, for that is the true aim of understanding anything. This would mean that the present and future, embraced in love and trust, could be fully lived and accepted. And this experience of reaching out with one's whole heart and soul toward the good is preserved in the memory. So the circular movement from memory to understanding to will is completed once again.

Bonaventure says that it is only in God, the perfect psyche, where one person gives all to the other. It is at this point on *The Journey* that Bonaventure introduces the Trinitarian God for the first time. Every second of our life this mechanism of our human psyche, memory/understanding/will, reproduces the mutual cooperation of the Father, Son and Holy Spirit. We are indeed created in the image and likeness of God! It is true that the more we allow this flow of giving to take place within us, the more closely we resemble God. And this image of God can be found in us every moment of our lives.

Let us consider the example of an elderly gentleman who lost his wife a few years ago. He keeps reliving her dreadful last days and can talk of nothing else. He is full of bitterness and accusations and has threatened many a doctor with a lawsuit. Every time I meet with him he repeats the same stories. Anger and hatred alternate in him. This dark memory dominates this man's life so much that he is no longer able to face the challenges in his own life, and fails to understand what has happened to him. The cyclical process has broken down because he stubbornly refuses to reconcile himself to his new life. Ultimately, this could become a deadly downward spiral for the man because he refuses to accept his new situation in life. Research has shown that many widows and widowers die within two years after their partners. One reason for this is that the cycle of life has not continued to flow. The memory of the death of a loved one must yield to some understanding of a new existence, a life that inspires a decision to move on with life.

In his *Testament*, composed shortly before his death on October 3, 1226, Francis of Assisi recalls a fundamental encounter of his early days. At that time leprosy was so dreaded that when people were diagnosed with the disease, funeral services were held for them and they were excluded from society. Their flesh had an offensive smell and it was difficult to look at them. Francis, always the aesthete, could not bear their sight, could not stand their smell. Whenever he came across one, he immediately fled. It was, in his very words, "bitter"[1] for him. He was not able to understand, and therefore, he could not change a thing. But one day something seized him when he met a leper on the road. He did not turn back, did not flee. He approached the figure that once would have repulsed him, and embraced and kissed him. Suddenly Francis knew that God was in this person! The way of the outcast was to become the way of Francis! Later, he taught all his followers to go and live for a time with lepers so that they would understand who God is and where God wanted to lead them. Living and working among the lepers eventually became the novitiate experience, the basic formative training of the friars minor.

When Christians celebrate the Eucharist (this analogy fits all types of rituals), they are remembering and trying to understand. They wish one another peace and decide to be peace-bearers. By repeating this ritual again and again they hope to be drawn into this most beautiful exchange from Father to Son to Holy Spirit. This is certainly not just a matter of mindless repetition but a process that is both life-giving and demanding.

This is precisely what the Second Vatican Council meant when it issued the call to all to return to their roots—to the Scriptures, to Tradition, to our mothers and fathers in faith—then to try to understand by articulating our own history. Only then can one make a decisive commitment to the future. One last point, this circle of memory, understanding, will can also be adapted by families, religious communities, groups, nations, the whole human race.

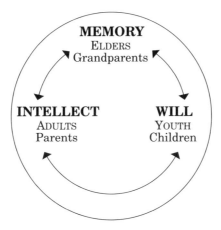

Illustration 9: Chapter 3

The chapter adapted to the interrelationship of the generations within a family or society

EXERCISES

In the light of Illustration 8 above:

• Focus on an important decision in your life. Ponder the process of your decision-making as you contemplate the interrelationship of memory, understanding and will. When doing this, listen to your memory, examine your understanding and follow the desire for the good in you.

• Reflect on John 15:9–17:

> "As the Father has loved me, so I have loved you; abide in my love. If you keep my commandments, you will abide in my love, just as I have kept my Father's commandments and abide in his love. I have said these things to you so that my joy may be in you, and that your joy may be complete.

"This is my commandment, that you love one another as I have loved you. No one has greater love than this, to lay down one's life for one's friends. You are my friends if you do what I command you. I do not call you servants any longer, because the servant does not know what the master is doing; but I have called you friends, because I have made known to you everything that I have heard from my Father. You did not choose me but I chose you. And I appointed you to go and bear fruit, fruit that will last, so that the Father will give you whatever you ask him in my name. I am giving you these commands so that you may love one another."

How is the above process seen in this Gospel passage? Conclude the meditation by praying to the Triune God, the circle of life and love.

NOTES

[1] See *The Testament* 3, in *Francis of Assisi: The Saint, op. cit.*, p. 124; *The Life of Saint Francis by Thomas of Celano* VII:17, *ibid.*, p. 195.

Friday

LISTEN TO ME!

Bonaventure writes in chapter 6:3, 6:

3. . . . For here we find the highest communicability
together with the property of the persons,
highest consubstantiality together with the plurality of
hypostases,[1]
highest conformability together with discrete personality,
highest co-equality together with order,
highest co-eternity together with emanation,
the highest intimacy together with mission.
Who would not be rapt in wonder at the thought of such
marvels?
But we know most certainly that all these things
are involved in the most blessed Trinity
if we raise our eyes to that super-excelling goodness.
If, therefore, there is supreme communication and true
diffusion,
then there is also true origin and true distinction.
And since it is the whole that is communicated and not just a
part,
it follows that whatever is possessed is given, and given totally.
Therefore, the one emanating and the one producing that
emanation
are distinguished by their properties but are one in essence. . . .
Since they are distinguished by their properties,
it follows that they have personal properties and a plurality of
hypostases.
They have emanation of origin.

6. . . . (A)nd if you are amazed to find
communicability together with property,

> consubstantiality with plurality,
> conformability with personality,
> co-equality with order,
> co-eternity with production,
> mutual intimacy with mission. . . .

JOSEF

For Francis, obedience meant belonging together. New brothers were "received to obedience,"[2] as Francis' Rule described acceptance into his Order. We would like to suggest using the circle of memory, understanding and will from Illustration 8 to consider a different concept of the evangelical counsel of obedience. We begin by remembering our story, reflecting on it in quiet, trying to grasp its meaning in our lives. Then we can make decisions with an eye focused on the Highest Good. This concept is valid whether we live alone or in a community.

Obedience must be more than just doing what some authority orders you to do. In his *Admonitions* Francis shows the difference between true and loving obedience on the one hand, and perfect obedience on the other:

> The Lord says in the Gospel: Whoever does not renounce all that he possesses cannot be my disciple (Luke 14:33); and: Whoever wishes to save his life must lose it (Luke 9:24). That person who offers himself totally to obedience in the hands of his prelate leaves all that he possesses and loses his body. And whatever he does and says which he knows is not contrary to his will is true obedience, provided that what he does is good.
>
> And should a subject see that some things

might be better and more useful for his soul
than what a prelate commands, let him will-
ingly offer such things to God as a sacrifice;
and, instead, let him earnestly strive to fulfill
the prelate's wishes. For this is loving obedience because it pleases God and neighbor (cf.
1 Peter 1:22).[3]

Where one member of a group gives totally and continually
to another, then there is no need for commands, decrees or
orders. There is total, mutual understanding. This is true
obedience for Francis because each member senses whether
she or he is connected to and in agreement with the others
This is the divine side of the coin. Humanity, however, repli-
cates this in spite of limitations, barriers or distortions.

Here is an example of true obedience. Remembering
that my wife wants our apartment clean and in order on week-
ends and understanding why, I do my housework on time.
We do not have to deal with one another on this issue every
week. Similarly, I can decide to give up some plan I had in
mind out of love and respect for my colleagues in work. The
latter would be loving obedience. Francis, however, takes an
additional step:

If the prelate, however, commands something
contrary to his conscience, even though he
may not obey him, let him not, however, abandon him. And if he then suffers persecution
from others, let him love them all the more
for the sake of God (cf. 1 John 3.15–16). For
whoever chooses to suffer persecution rather
than wish to be separated from his brothers
truly remains in perfect obedience because he

lays down his life for his brothers (cf. John
15:13).[4]

In the saint's mind everything depends upon adhering to
this process of memory, understanding and will flowing to
one another. What is fundamental is not to cut oneself off or
take flight from the process. He challenges us to integrate
even contrary and disturbing elements, because for Francis,
friction and opposition are important to the overall process.
It is clear that what is intended here is not some kind of
superficial, forced holiness, even though in some situations it
might be quite healing to separate and distance oneself. The
perfection of obedience, however, is to be found in the long-
term maintenance of this tension. What we speak of is not a
journey for those who want an easy way out. To withhold
one's involvement is treason; this is disobedience.

Francis' message is that we must take ourselves and
our consciences very seriously and distinguish one situation
from another. Would not many a religious Order be different today if its members had learned such a form of obedience? Would not many a couple, many a family—even business and society—be on sounder footing if their members
and leaders would find the courage for this kind of obedience? The disaster of the Nazi era and the suffering of countless men and women in countries of Latin America might
partially be blamed on an insidious type of humility,
preached for centuries, that taught people to be submissive,
acquiescent and resigned.

Humility, however, should not muzzle people when
a loud protest would better serve life. The Austrian poet
Erich Fried (1921–1988) once described this commonplace

deafness, this very common form of disobedience, in a poem called "Disturbance":

> They were speaking about their fight
> for freedom and love and human dignity.
>
> Suddenly a child came into the room
> and wanted to ask them something.
>
> They shooed the child away:
> "Leave us alone! Go and play!"
> The child looked at the father and the mother
> and went away.
>
> After that I was no longer able to concentrate.
> The two of them asked patiently and kindly:
> "Did the child disturb you?"[5]

In Francis' understanding of obedience, creativity and dynamism are essential. He would not encourage us to senseless rebellion and destructiveness. It is a question of ebb and flow, like the process we find in the Blessed Trinity. The Father, Son and Spirit give us the perfect example.

EXERCISES

- Compose your own prayer by recalling a concrete experience you had recently. Try to articulate this experience and the feelings linked to it. Ask for direction, for understanding and strength. Remain open to new meaning. Be silent.
- Try to find examples in your life of what Francis calls true, loving and perfect obedience. Try to recall as many details as possible and put them down on paper. Look at those situations in the light of Illustration 8.

NOTES

[1] The term "hypostatic union" speaks to the question of the union of the divine and human natures in Christ, the one person. For further explanation, see footnote 25 on page 404 in Part Four.

[2] *The Later Rule* II:11, in *Francis of Assisi: The Saint, op. cit.*, p. 101.

[3] *The Admonitions* III, *ibid.*, p. 130.

[4] *Ibid.*

[5] Erich Fried, *Gesammelte Werke (Works)*, vol. 3 (Berlin: Verlag Klaus Wagenbach, 1996), pp. 106–107. Authors' translation. Erich Fried, a Jew whose father was killed by the Gestapo, fled to England in 1938 where he served in the Resistance and helped refugees.

Saturday

Marry Me!

Bonaventure wrote in chapter 1:1 and 6:2:

1:1. *Blessed are those whose help comes from you.*
In their hearts they are disposed to ascend by steps in the valley of
tears,
in the place which they have set [Psalms 83:6 ff.].
Since happiness is nothing other than the enjoyment of the
highest good,
and since the highest good is above us,
we cannot find happiness without rising above ourselves,
not by a bodily ascent but by an ascent of the heart.

6:2. See and take note that the highest good in an unqualified
sense
is that than which nothing better can be thought.
And this is of such a sort that it cannot be thought of as not
existing,
since it is absolutely better to exist than not to exist.
And this is a good of such a sort that it cannot be thought of
unless it is thought of as three and one.
For "the good is said to be self-diffusive."
The supreme good, therefore, is supremely self-diffusive.
But the highest diffusion does not exist unless it is
actual and intrinsic,
substantial and personal,
natural and voluntary,
free and necessary,
lacking nothing and perfect.
In the supreme good there must be from eternity
a production that is actual and consubstantial,
and a hypostasis[1] as noble as the producer,

and this is the case in production by way of generation and
spiration.
This is understood to mean that what is of the eternal
principle
is eternally of the co-principle.
In this way there can be both a beloved and a co-beloved,
one generated and one spirated;
that is, Father, and Son, and Holy Spirit.
If this were not the case,
it would not be the supreme good
since it would not be supremely self-diffusive,
for that diffusion in time which is seen in creation is a mere
point or a center
in comparison to the immensity of the eternal goodness.
Therefore it is possible to think of another greater diffusion;
namely, that sort of diffusion in which the one diffusing itself
communicates the whole of its substance and nature to the
other.
Therefore, it would not be the highest good
if it lacked the ability to do this either in reality or in thought.

Therefore, if, with the eye of your mind
you are able to reflect on the purity of that goodness
which is the pure act of the principle
that in charity loves with a love that is free,
and a love that is due,
and a love that is a combination of both,
which would be the fullest diffusion by way of nature and will
and which is found in the diffusion of the Word in which all
things are spoken
and the diffusion of the Gift in which all goods are given,
you will be able to see
that the supreme communicability of the good demands
necessarily

that there be a Trinity of Father, Son and Holy Spirit.
And in these persons, because of supreme goodness
it is necessary that there be supreme communicability.
And because of supreme communicability, there must be
consubstantiality;
and from supreme consubstantiality there must be supreme
conformability;
and from these there must be supreme co-equality;
and because of this there must be supreme co-eternity;
and from all of the above, there must be supreme mutual
intimacy
by which each is necessarily in the others
by reason of their supreme interpenetration,
and one acts with the others in a total unity
of substance, power, and activity within the most blessed
Trinity itself.

ANDRÉ

Bonaventure subtitles *The Journey* he is proposing to us: *meditations of a poor person in the desert.* "To be poor before God" is a principal theme of religious life, at least since Jesus' Sermon on the Mount [cf. Matthew 5:3 ff.]. This idea flourished in the poverty movements of the Middle Ages. Francis and Clare of Assisi were crusading for this ideal within the church, for the "privilege of poverty," as Clare called it. At least in the beginning they maintained the practice that their followers would own no property.

We know several writings of Francis which concern Clare and her companions: a *Form of Life, The Canticle of Exhortation* and *The Last Will.*[2] Over and over again Clare makes reference to Francis' input:

As long as he lived he diligently fulfilled this and wished that it always be fulfilled by his brothers. Shortly before his death he once more wrote his last will for us that we or those, as well, who would come after us would never turn aside from the holy poverty we had embraced. He said:

> "I, little brother Francis, wish to follow the life and poverty of our most high Lord Jesus Christ and of His holy mother and to persevere in this until the end; and I ask and counsel you, my ladies, to live always in this most holy life and poverty. And keep most careful watch that you never depart from this by reason of the teaching or advice of anyone."

> As I, together with my sisters, have ever been solicitous to safeguard the holy poverty which we have promised the Lord God and blessed Francis, also, too, the Abbesses who shall succeed me in office and all the sisters are bound to observe it inviolably to the end: that is, by not receiving or having possession or ownership either of themselves or through an intermediary, or even anything that might reasonably be called property, except as much land as necessity requires for the integrity and proper seclusion of the monastery, and this land may not be cultivated except as a garden for the needs of the sisters.[3]

The focus of their life is found at the heart of their Rules. For Francis, we find it in chapter 6 of *The Later Rule*.

> Let the brothers not make anything their own,
> neither house, nor place, nor anything at all.
> As pilgrims and strangers in this world (cf. 1
> Peter 2:11), serving the Lord in poverty and
> humility, let them go seeking alms with confi-
> dence, and they should not be ashamed
> because, for our sakes, our Lord made
> Himself poor in this world (cf. 2 Corinthians
> 8:9). This is that sublime height of most exalt-
> ed poverty that has made you, my most
> beloved brothers, heirs and kings of the
> Kingdom of Heaven, poor in temporal things
> but exalted in virtue (cf. James 2:5). Let this
> be your portion that leads into the land of the
> living (cf. Psalms 142:6).[4]

"Lady Poverty" is the fascinating name Francis chooses for his bride. Just as happens when young people fall in love, this choice and decision is unmarred by bitterness, hurt or aggression. At a time when the institutional church had amassed more wealth and power than ever before, many people protested and revolted against this. However, in Clare and Francis, whose lifestyle was very similar to these other contemporary poverty groups,[5] we find an entirely positive attitude. Let us look at just how original their words are:

> Let everyone be struck with fear,
>   the whole world tremble,
>   and let the heavens exult
> when Christ, the Son of the living God,
> is present on the altar in the hands of a priest!
> O wonderful loftiness and stupendous dignity!
>   O sublime humility!
>   O humble sublimity!

The Lord of the universe,
God and the Son of God,
so humbles Himself
that for our salvation
He hides Himself
under an ordinary piece of bread!
Brothers, look at the humility of God,
and pour out your hearts before Him
(Psalms 62:8)!
Humble yourselves
that you may be exalted by Him
(cf. 1 Peter 5:6; James 4:10)!
Hold back nothing of yourselves for yourselves,
that He Who gives Himself totally to you
may receive you totally![6]

Franciscan poverty starts in the divine dynamic of boundless abundance. God gives everything, without prohibition or precaution! Therein is the mystery of the joy in poverty.[7]

Looking at the two last great meditations of Francis and Clare, their *Testaments*, we are struck by a leitmotiv that runs through them. We continually encounter the words *Dominus dedit mihi*, "the Lord gave me," in many variations. Francis and Clare know that they are gifted by the Lord of life as they witness:

The Lord gave me, Brother Francis, thus to begin doing penance in this way: for when I was in sin, it seemed too bitter for me to see lepers. And the Lord Himself led me among them. . . . And the Lord gave me such faith in churches. . . . Afterwards the Lord gave me, and gives me still, such faith in priests. . . . And after the Lord gave me some brothers, no one showed me what I had to do, but the Most High Himself revealed to me that I should live according to the pattern of the Holy Gospel. . . . [8]

Among the other gifts that we have received and do daily receive from our benefactor, the Father of mercies (2 Corinthians 1:3), and for which we must express the deepest thanks to the glorious Father of Christ, there is our vocation. . . . The Son of God has been made for us the Way (cf. John 14:6), which our blessed father Francis, his true lover and imitator, has shown and taught us by word and example. . . . Therefore, beloved sisters, we must consider the immense gifts that God has bestowed on us. . . . We can consider in this, therefore, the abundant kindness of God to us. Because of His mercy and love, He saw fit to speak these words through His saint about our vocation and choice [cf. 2 Peter 1:10] through His saint.[9]

JOSEF

If you are a person who is poor before God, you live with open and empty hands, and you know that you have nothing. You expect everything! You receive everything. You receive more than everything—the fullness of life and joy. Anyone who wants to hold on to anything remains blocked from such abundant generosity.

I meet many people who are in the process of bereavement. Mourning is the experience we have to undergo in order to cope with a loss. Without mourning we cannot survive. Mourning is an inner work that allows us to let go of the gift we had received, and let it continue flowing beyond us. This is wholesome. This process enables us to grow into new life. It is often very difficult to let go of someone we would like to continue to experience and enjoy. By refusing to let go, we no longer live; we are like the dead, walled up.

The art of walking with people in a mourning process means encouraging and supporting them as they bridge the gap between holding on to someone and letting the person flow away again, assuring them that they do not lose everything, and least of all themselves.

Creation in its rhythm of birthing and dying was precious to Francis. He lived in its embrace. Creation is the foremost teacher of poverty and the healing power for letting go and opening to new life again.

EXERCISES

• Once again, pray Psalm 136, the litany of thanksgiving of the people of God, looking back at their history. Try to get into some of the images mentioned in the psalm, such as the "outstretched arm," "heritage," "foes," "gives food," "low estate." Remain with one of these images that espe cially touches you today.

• Looking back on your personal history, or that of your family and life, write your own litany of thanksgiving. Do not exclude the difficult parts. Answer each part of your litany with one of the following refrains:

Your love is everlasting!

Thank you, for you, God, are always with me!

Thank you, for you were/are present there!

NOTES

[1] See Note 1 for Friday of Week Three on page 173.

[2] See *Clare: Early Documents, op. cit.,* p. iv.

[3] *Ibid.*, p. 72.

[4] *The Later Rule* VI:1–5, in *Francis of Assisi: The Saint, op. cit.*, p. 103.

[5] See *Writings of Jacques de Vitry, ibid.*, pp. 578–580. These authentic writings of the contemporary bishop, Jacques de Vitry (c. 1216) offer us a very precious insight from a source outside the Franciscan Order. He discovers strong similarities to the poverty movement in his own country.

[6] *A Letter to the Entire Order* 26-29, *ibid.*, p. 118.

[7] See *The Admonitions* XXVII, *ibid.*, p. 137.

[8] *The Testament, ibid.*, pp. 124–125.

[9] *Clare: Early Documents, op. cit.*, pp. 56–57.

SACRED ORDER WITHIN

Sunday

FULL OF GRACE

Bonaventure writes in chapter 4:1, 2, 8:

1. Since the first Principle can be contemplated
not only *through* ourselves while we are on the way, but also in
ourselves;
and since the latter is more excellent than the former,
this kind of consideration stands at the fourth stage of
contemplation.
After it has been shown that God is so close to our souls,
it is surprising that there are so few people
who are concerned with speculation on the first Principle
within themselves.
But an explanation for this is near at hand.
The human mind is distracted by many concerns,
and therefore does not enter into itself through memory.
It is obscured by images of sense objects,
and therefore does not enter into itself through intelligence.
And it is drawn away by disordered desires,
and therefore it does not return to itself
with a desire for internal sweetness and spiritual joy.
Totally immersed in matters of the senses,
the human person is unable to re-enter into itself as the image
of God.

2. Just as when a person falls,
it is necessary to remain lying there
until someone comes near to reach out and raise the fallen
person up [Isaiah 24:20],
so our soul could not be raised up perfectly from sensible
realities
to see itself and the eternal truth within itself

unless the truth, assuming a human form in Christ,
should become a ladder to repair the first ladder that had
been broken in Adam.

So it is that, no matter how enlightened one might be
with the light of natural and acquired knowledge,
one cannot enter into oneself to *delight in the Lord*
[Psalms 36:4]
except by means of the mediation of Christ who says:
I am the door.
Those who enter through me shall be saved;
they shall go in and out and find pasture [John 10:9].
But we do not draw near to this door
unless we believe in Christ,
hope in Christ,
and love Christ.
If we wish, therefore, to re-enter into the enjoyment of truth as
into a paradise,
we must do so through faith in, hope in, and love for
the mediator between God and humanity, Jesus Christ
[1 Timothy 2:5],
who is like the *tree of life in the middle of paradise*
[Genesis 2:9].

8. Flooded with all these intellectual lights,
our soul—like a house of God—is inhabited by the divine
Wisdom.
It is made to be a daughter of God,
a spouse and friend.
It is made to be a member, a sister, and a coheir of Christ the
Head.
It is made into the temple of the Holy Spirit,
grounded in faith,
elevated in hope

and dedicated to God through holiness of soul and body.
It is the most sincere love of Christ that brings this about,
a love which is
poured forth in our hearts through the Holy Spirit who is given to us
[Romans 5:5].
And without this Spirit we cannot know the secret things of
God.
Just as *no one can know a human person's innermost self*
except the spirit of that person which dwells within,
so no one knows the things of God but the Spirit of God
[1 Corinthians 2:11].
Therefore, let us be rooted and grounded in love,
so that we might comprehend with all the saints
what is the length of eternity,
the *breadth* of generosity,
the *height* of majesty,
and the *depth* of that discerning wisdom [Ephesians 3:18-19].

ANDRÉ

On the fourth step of *The Journey,* Bonaventure leads us into
the field of religious experience for the first time. This central chapter of *The Journey* offers the religious person a most
familiar language. Bonaventure alludes to sin, even if he
does not use the word itself. He stresses the helplessness and
powerlessness of the human person. We hear of God's direct
involvement in human affairs. God builds a bridge and crosses it in order to give humanity a helping hand. We arrive at
the fullness of life only by way of Christ, who opened the
door that was closed to us. This statement is the core of the
doctrine of original sin. Christians believe in Christ, who
brings peace and salvation to everyone. God's power has
been made so present and alive in Jesus that by following

him we find life. We are redeemed! And God's power is truly alive in us, not just figuratively.

This is the point at which God's presence and image are clearly obvious. It can only be God's work, not ours, for that which I experience and detect when I believe, hope and love is a direct encounter with the Spirit of God that is in me! Actually, this is where our human experience ends and God's initiative begins. Every human experience has its place in the first four chapters of *The Journey*. If we really are able to let it happen, then Someone will work in us. The work we have to do is to prepare a dwelling place. Francis reminds his brothers:

> Therefore, all my brothers, let us be very much on our guard that, under the guise of some reward or assistance, we do not lose or take our mind away from God. But, in the holy love which is God (cf. 1 John 4:16), I beg all my brothers, both the ministers and the others, after overcoming every impediment and putting aside every care and anxiety, to serve, love, honor and adore the Lord God with a clean heart and a pure mind in whatever way they are best able to do so, for that is what He wants above all else. Let us always make a home and a dwelling-place there (cf. John 14:23) for Him Who is the Lord God Almighty, Father, Son and Holy Spirit. . . . [1]

JOSEF

In Mary this experience was made flesh. She conceived Jesus physically. The Christian faith is thoroughly incarnational. It has hands and feet and affects human history. Mary is called "full of grace." Each and every one of us in our own way lives a life of grace.

Comparatively speaking, we are like some airless balloon just lying around until God personally picks us up and fills us with faith, hope and love—gifts of the Spirit. We are invited to accept these gifts, unwrap them and use them. And for us who do so, a dynamic power is released! Just blow up a balloon, and without sealing it, release it and you'll have a good image of this dynamism.

In his *Second Version of the Letter to the Faithful*, Francis writes:

> And the Spirit of the Lord will rest upon all those men and women who have done and persevered in these things (Isaiah 11:2; cf. Luke 4:18) and It will make a home and dwelling-place in them (cf. John 14:23). And they will be the children of the heavenly Father (cf. Matthew 5:45), Whose works they do. And they are spouses, brothers and mothers of our Lord Jesus Christ (cf. Matthew 12:50; Mark 3:35; Luke 8:21).
>
> We are spouses when the faithful soul is united by the Holy Spirit to our Lord Jesus Christ. We are brothers, moreover, when we do the will of His Father Who is in heaven (cf. Matthew 12:50; Mark 3:36); mothers when we carry Him in our heart and body (cf. 1 Corinthians 6:20) through love and a pure and sincere conscience; and give Him birth through a holy activity, which must shine before others by example (cf. Matthew 5:16).[2]

We are gifted with a variety of relationships in which we

experience grace, in which we become a temple of God's presence. The following metaphors come to my mind in response to the statement, "Grace is like. . .":

> rain that makes all things grow,
>
> a bridge over an abyss,
>
> the security a child feels when parents are near,
>
> water in the desert that saves my life,
>
> land for a sinking ship,
>
> a new beginning for a broken life,
>
> water that cleanses every impurity,
>
> peace after war and hatred,
>
> bread that strengthens our lives.

This grace-experience may be rare in our modern affluent society where everything has its price. The German Protestant theologian, Lothar Zenetti, sees the polarity very clearly: "What counts today is recognition-production-marketability-use. Grace doesn't fit here!"[3]

EXERCISES

• Play with a balloon. Try doing different things with it and observe yourself and the breath of God at play!

• Some areas for reflection or journaling: where do you experience the grace of God in your daily life, that is, where is there more happening in you than by just your own efforts? Compose a litany from these observations, responding to each entry with:

Breathe in me,

living Spirit of God,

and fill me

with faith, hope and love!

Notes

[1] *The Earlier Rule* XXII:25–27, in *Francis of Assisi: The Saint*, p. 80. Francis called his fraternity the friars minor and the leader he called the "minister," who literally serves the brothers. Francis repeatedly referred to himself as "lesser servant." The minister is responsible for a geographical region of the Order.

[2] *Second Version of the Letter to the Faithful* 48-53, *ibid.*, pp. 48-49.

[3] Lothar Zenetti, *Texte der Zuversicht (Hopeful Texts)* (Mainz, Germany: Grünewald Verlag, 1987), p. 140. Authors' translation.

Monday

WALKING ON WATER

Bonaventure writes in chapter 4:3:

Therefore the image that is our soul must be clothed over
with the three theological virtues
by which the soul is purified, illumined, and brought to
perfection.
In this way the image is reformed
and brought into conformity with the heavenly Jerusalem,
and it becomes a member of the church militant
which is the offspring of the heavenly Jerusalem,
according to the Apostle. For he says:
That Jerusalem which is above is free, and she is our mother
[Galatians 4:26].
The soul, therefore, believes in,
hopes in,
and loves Jesus Christ
who is the Word incarnate,
uncreated,
and inspired;
that is, *the way, the truth, and the life* [John 14:6].
When in faith the soul believes in Christ as in the uncreated
Word,
who is the Word and splendor of the Father,
it recovers its spiritual sense of hearing and of sight;
its hearing so that it might receive the words of Christ,
and its sight that it might consider the splendors of that light. . . .
With its spiritual senses restored,
the soul now sees, hears, smells, tastes, and embraces its
beloved.
It can now sing like the spouse in the *Canticle of Canticles*[1]
which was written for the exercise of contemplation on the

fourth level.

And this level

no one knows except one who receives it [Revelation 2:17],

for it consists more in the experience of affections

than in rational considerations.

ANDRÉ

So many people today think that there is a crisis of faith in others, while presupposing themselves to be believers with their two feet planted on solid ground. But just how fast somebody can sink was something that Peter himself painfully and shamefully experienced on Lake Genesareth. It must have been rather strange to see this well-known fisherman trying to do something that he should have known would not work. Matthew narrates this story about faith in chapter 14 of his Gospel. Jesus' friends are in a boat in the middle of the night in a storm and they begin to panic. Suddenly they think they see a ghost approaching them on the water who cries out: "Take heart, it is I; do not be afraid" (Matthew 14:27).

Jesus' invitation and encouragement fall on fertile ground in Peter. He is a fisherman, and from childhood learned how dangerous water can be. Yet, he risks stepping out on to the water from the boat. His eyes are fixed on Jesus, his trust placed squarely in Jesus. It is Jesus he is able to recognize. He cannot prove nor does he know for sure that the water will hold him up, but he leaves the safety of the boat and the refuge of its security. He is willing to take the risk, to set out on a path without knowing where it will lead. He has no escape plan. He merely knows that Jesus is calling him and he can feel Jesus' gaze on him. As long as he gazes at Jesus, the water supports him. But turning his attention to the storm, fear creeps in, he loses his footing, and he starts to sink. In this crisis of faith he throws himself again completely on Jesus: "Lord, save me!" [Matthew 14:30], cried Peter.

This well-known example of a story of faith demonstrates what we mean when we Christians speak about faith. Faith means walking toward Jesus Christ, filled with his Spirit. Christians believe that God's love is certain and true. Once this belief becomes imbedded, everything else flows freely because of the conviction that they are loved.

JOSEF

The Swiss priest-poet Kurt Marti once expressed this idea as follows: "God? So great, yet so crazy to still believe in people!"[2] This was similarly expressed by George Burns at the end of the movie *Oh God!* Burns, acting in the role of God, in baseball cap, enters the courtroom where John Denver is trying to prove God's existence. Burns takes the stand, and says at the end of his testimony, "You may not believe in me, but I still believe in you!"

Everything flows from faith in God. Blessed John XXIII (1881–1963) once noted that faith is the joy that comes from God. From the risk of such joyful faith, "good deeds" necessarily follow.

Can a person truly be walking the way of faith while never having experienced a crisis of faith? Of course, it is not always anything as spectacular as "walking on water"; it is more like the solid ground on which we journey day in and day out. Faith is like a beautifully wrapped gift just waiting for us to open and let it become a part of our life. The miracles of faith are all around us day after day: simply listening to another, trusting one another or not giving up when we feel alone or discouraged.

One day during the liturgy, a young mother from our parish offered thanks that everything was going so well. Her little daughter was sitting on her lap. Shortly after this child's birth, the mother began to experience progressive paralysis in her legs and was confined to a wheelchair. Her husband had been beating her for years and eventually left her. How could she possibly be grateful? Yet, she speaks like she is a believer. She manages to accept a truth that remains partially hidden by saying "yes" to God's path for her. Mary's *fiat* (Latin for "let it happen") is an example of the best faith-response. This is why she, of all believers, was given the title "Mother of the Church." She, too, surrendered herself totally. She listened and became pregnant! This is not something that happens instantly. The Latin word for "faith" is *fides*. Faith is linked to fidelity, which connotes more than loyalty. It implies a freedom that is exercised repeatedly, giving one the courage to say *fiat*, yes, let it happen.

ANDRÉ

In Paul's letter to the Romans we read: "So faith comes from what is heard, and what is heard comes through the word Christ" [Romans 10:17]. Bonaventure says that the person unwrapping the gift of faith "recovers (the) spiritual sense of hearing and of sight" [4:3]. The spiritual senses of hearing and seeing are revived and restored. A lived faith makes us more aware of what we see and hear, more attentive to the whole of life surrounding us. Moreover, the text from Romans states that belief is not simply some kind of inner feeling but rather a gift that unfolds by attentively listening to the Word. Just as in the story of Peter, it is a matter of maintaining the tension in our relationship with Jesus. The symbol of faith is the cross, which certainly is a good symbol for this tension. However, the cross also stands for courage. We might compare it with a sharp or flat symbol at the beginning of a piece of music, which symbol holds the power to change the value of every single note on the staff. The cross is more than a simple plus sign. It has the power to enlighten our lives.

The late Scripture scholar Carroll Stuhlmueller, C.P. (1923–1994), wrote:

> By faith we accept as real what we cannot prove nor see; we not only accept but we even risk our life and our eternity on the conviction that the purpose of our earthly life lies beyond the present form of our earthly existence.[3]

> Faith consists in doing our best, and then surrendering this best that God may take it beyond our power and dreams.[4]

Illustration 10:
Here we see the cross, the symbol of faith, by means of which we risk acceptance of a truth that is partly seen, partly unseen.

Zachary Hayes writes, "Bonaventure elaborates on faith as the guiding light of all virtues. . . . Faith is that habit by which our intellect voluntarily comes into the captivity of Christ."[5]

EXERCISES

- Concentrate on your breathing, inhaling and exhaling. Then repeat as follows: inhaling: *Lord, I believe*, exhaling: *help my unbelief!* Or simply pray *Amen*, your yes to the new risk God asks of you.

- Try to articulate your personal faith. What is important for you in life? On what do you base your life? What are the risks that you have crossed in your life?

Notes

[1] Song of Solomon

[2] Kurt Marti, *Zärtlichkeit und Schmerz (Tenderness and Pain)* (Zurich, Switzerland: Verlag Nagel und Kimche AG, 1974), p. 34. Authors' translation.

[3] Carroll Stuhlmueller, C.P., *Biblical Meditations for Ordinary Time—Weeks 1–9* (New York: Paulist Press, 1984), p. 39.

[4] Carroll Stuhlmueller, C.P., *Biblical Meditations for Ordinary Time—Weeks 10–22* (New York: Paulist Press, 1984), p. 248.

[5] Zachary Hayes, O.F.M., *Disputed Questions on the Mystery of the Trinity* (New York: Franciscan Institute Publications, 1979), p. 74, fn. 19.

Tuesday

HANG IN THERE!

Bonaventure writes in chapter 4:3:

The soul, therefore, believes in,

hopes in,

and loves Jesus Christ

who is the Word incarnate,

uncreated,

and inspired;

that is, *the way, the truth, and the life* [John 14:6]. . . .

When in hope the soul yearns to receive the inspired Word,

because of this desire and affection

it recovers its spiritual sense of smell. . . .

It is at this level where the interior senses have been restored

to see what is most beautiful,

to hear what is most harmonious,

to smell what is most fragrant,

to taste what is most sweet,

and to embrace what is most delightful. . . .

JOSEF

Life is hope. Can you imagine what your life would be like without hope? Perhaps you could recall some time in your life when hope eluded you, when you gave up on someone, something, or yourself. What sustains you now? Is hope something more than what you want for yourself or for others: good health, joy, satisfaction, success, progress, peace? Who or what do you hope in? What are your hopes for yourself?

I have met many people who think they can manufacture hope. Some claim that a loving encounter, a beautiful nature scene, an experience of rest or quiet and many other similar experiences can make one happy. I find strength and courage in these things. But is that hope?

Take the example of the medical doctor who tells a person with a terminal illness, "There is nothing more we can do for you!" Is that really true? Or isn't it rather a helpless, hopeless and, at the same time, dangerous illusion—a poor choice of words? "Abandon all hope, you who enter,"[1] Dante said was written over the gates of hell. But is it true that such a situation is hopeless? I have witnessed how a person's hope revives when he or she begins to accept a situation as it is. Take the diagnosis that medicine can no longer sustain your life. I think the deepest hope people have is that others will treat us honestly, warmly and stand by us when we are in need.

And how strong hope can be! Even in a desperate attempt to commit suicide there might be a last hope, a last cry, "Can't you hear me? Can't you see me? Please pay attention!"

I recently met a fifty-year-old man who had been living in total isolation in the middle of a large city. He has had cancer for the past five years and is fully aware that there is no cure for his disease. All his life he had lived with his mother, and she had protected and cared for him. After her death he found that he was completely isolated and helpless. He refused to go on with life. His apartment was a disaster. He had no energy to take on his mother's tasks and he had not cleaned the apartment for years. Yet, in the midst of this devastation, an extremely intelligent man sat there hopeless in the dust. In his mind, the thought kept coming back to him: should I kill myself? Is it permissible? He had read many books on the ethical discussion of suicide. And eventually he had the courage to let me in to see his pain. He literally opened the door to his apartment, and during the first visit we sat just inside the front entrance with all the other doors closed. Letting someone else look into his eyes without judging him or despising him, accepting the support of our team, to stand by him and treat his physical suffering for several months—all this in some way tapped into a part of that undying hope that someone would treat him like a human being.

ANDRÉ

The symbol for the virtue and the gift of hope is the anchor. The letter to the Hebrews speaks of "Abraham, having patiently endured, obtained the promise" [Hebrews 6:15]. The author suggests that we should "be strongly encouraged to seize the hope set before us. We have this hope, a sure and steadfast anchor of the soul" [Hebrews 6:18–19]. Hope invites us to ground ourselves in God and to hold on to God.

Bonaventure links the gift of hope with the sense of smell. Smell is a very important sense for our well-being, relaxation, even our sense of security. We can "smell" danger, and we find pleasure in things that smell good. We follow a fragrance, being drawn by it. In times of intense suffering, we may even say, "This stinks!"

As Saint Paul says in the Letter to the Romans:

> For in hope we were saved. Now hope that is seen is not hope. For who hopes for what is seen? But if we hope for what we do not see, we wait for it with patience. [Romans 8:24–25]

There are two aspects to hope from this description in Romans—waiting and patience. In today's society of instant communication and fast food, we try to annihilate waiting. Think of how you feel when you have aimed your supermarket cart full of groceries to the shortest cashier's line and, as you begin checking out, they change cashiers. Or, as your groceries are tallied, a price check is needed, halting the procedure until it is verified, and it gets worse if no one is available to respond to the request for verification. It is interesting that in Italian—the language of Francis, Clare and Bonaventure—the verbs meaning "to hope," *sperare,* and "to wait," *aspettare,* have the same root or stem. Carroll Stuhlmueller, C.P., writes, "Hope is identical with the virtue of waiting except that it adds a quality of optimism."[2]

As already noted, the word meaning "patience," *patientia,* comes from *pati,* meaning "to suffer." Don't we call a person who enters a hospital with an ailment a patient, one suffering from illness? Stuhlmueller also writes, "It is not suffering but patience which marks a person as a true disciple of Jesus. Very often, however, suffering is the school of patience. More people are attracted to religion by the patience and compassion of its religious leaders, than by any other virtue; and more are turned away from religion by anger and impatience than by all other sin or vice in religious leaders."[3]

Francis once looked upon suffering as meaningless or "bitter" with regard to lepers. Yet, this turned to "sweetness" and became meaningful for him in his embrace of the leper. In his *Prayer Before the Crucifix* of San Damiano, Francis asks for *speransa certa,* "certain hope."[4] In the book of Hebrews, hope's symbol, the anchor, is described as "sure and steadfast" [6:19]. Like an anchor that holds a boat stable in a storm, hope holds us in a balance during all of life's struggles, sorrows, sufferings.

In a sense, it is impossible to be "impatient," for that's like saying, "I refuse to suffer." "And we boast in our hope," wrote Paul, "of sharing the glory of God. And not only that, but we even boast in our sufferings, knowing that suffering produces endurance, and endurance produces character, and character produces hope, and this hope does not disappoint us" [Romans 5:3–5]. Our stance in life is "waiting in joyful hope," as we pray in every Eucharist, to enter Paradise.

EXERCISES

• Meditate on Isaiah 25.1–0, reflecting on the consoling images of shelter, shade, silence, festive meal. What are your personal images of hope? What images of hope keep you going in life? What images of hope attracted you earlier in life?

• The book of Numbers, chapter 13, tells us how the chosen messengers of Moses' people went to reconnoiter Canaan for forty days. When they returned, their words spread fear, although they reported that "It flows with milk and honey" [13:27].

Fear of the challenge and of what might happen means death for those who are without courage [see Numbers 14:37]. The people with Moses want to turn back, even if it means living without freedom and not in their own homeland.

Whenever you stand at a door that opens to something new, there is both something drawing you on and something holding you back. You are caught between hope and fear. Pick out a situation in your life when you had to make an important decision. Be as concrete as possible. Look at both your hopes and fears and situate them in the context of your whole life, keeping in mind that God wants to lead you home and to a land of peace.

• Read and meditate on Saint Francis' story of true joy as found in the *Little Flowers*.[5]

NOTES

[1] *The Inferno of Dante Alighieri*, Canto III, 9 (London: J. M. Dent & Sons, 1929), p. 26. Authors' translation.

[2] Carroll Stuhlmueller, C.P., *Biblical Meditations for Lent* (New York: Paulist Press, 1978), p. 138.

[3] Carroll Stuhlmueller, C.P., *Biblical Meditations for Ordinary Time—Weeks 10-22, op. cit.*, p. 10.

[4] Authors' translation.

[5] In *Omnibus of Sources, op. cit.*, p. 1501. See also *True and Perfect Joy*, in *Francis of Assisi: The Saint, op. cit.*, pp. 166–167.

Wednesday

THE TASTE AND TOUCH OF LOVE

Bonaventure writes in chapter 4:3:

The soul, therefore, believes in, hopes in, and loves Jesus
Christ
who is the Word incarnate, uncreated, and inspired;
that is, *the way, the truth, and the life* [John 14:6]. . . .
When in love the soul embraces the incarnate Word,
receiving delight from Him and passing over to Him in
ecstatic love,
it recovers its sense of taste and touch. . . .
the soul is disposed for spiritual ecstasies
through devotion, admiration, and exultation
in accordance with the three exclamations found in the
Canticle of Canticles.
The first of these comes from the abundance of devotion
through which the soul becomes like
*a column of smoke filled with the aroma of myrrh
and frankincense.*
The second comes from the overflowing sense of wonder
by which the soul becomes like the dawn, the moon, and the
sun
corresponding to the steps of illumination
that lift up the soul in wonder as it contemplates the
Bridegroom.
And the third comes through the superabundance of joy
through which the soul is brought
to *a fullness of delights*
and *rests totally upon her Beloved* [Canticle 3:6; 6:9; 8:5].

JOSEF

There is probably no other word that his been abused as much as the word *love*. What is love? What is it not? We have already begun to consider some of its essential elements, such as the experience of the eyes and the sense of touch. Erich Fromm (1904–1996), one of the great psychoanalysts from Vienna, wrote that we simply cannot live without love:

> Can you possess love?. . . In reality there is only the act of loving. . . . Loving is a productive activity; it implies caring for, knowing, sympathizing with, affirming, delighting in a person, a tree, an image, or an idea. It means awakening him/her to life and adding something to his/her/its liveliness. It is a process that renews someone and helps him/her renew.[1]

A second point is that love is not just a matter of a few romantic moments of hand-holding at sunset or being sexually united with another person, for these experiences are fleeting. The expression "making love" has lost all its meaning!

The foundation of love is a bond, a "yes" to another. It is a question of a communication that is vibrant. It involves being and remaining in an "eye-to-eye" relationship. It requires a vital fidelity that continually sees the other anew with eyes of love. This takes time, patience and silence!

Albert Camus (1913–1960), the French writer, journalist and playwright, claimed that love cannot exist in the midst of the shouting in which we live. Take a good long look at some of the signs and wonders the Gospels report about Jesus. With few words, with a calm, penetrating gaze, with the bodily touch of an outstretched hand Jesus worked miracles.

Bonaventure writes, "When in love the soul . . . recovers her sense of taste and touch" [4:3]; taste and touch are restored. There's an old saying that "the way to a person's heart is through the stomach," but that is only part of it. It really involves the whole process of "tasting" and "savoring." Equally important, however, are touching, sensing, feeling, caressing, fondling, embracing.

ANDRÉ

Many of the men who first came to join Francis in his movement were illiterate. Since they were unable to read or write, Francis could not tell them to go the Gospel book and there learn how to love. When walking through Assisi with the brothers, they occasionally encountered mothers with their children. This became the paradigm of love for Francis and Clare.[2] In *The Later Rule*, Francis wrote, "Wherever the brothers may be and meet one another, let them show that they are members of the same family. Let each one confidently make known his need to the other, for if a mother loves and cares for her son according to the flesh, how much more diligently must someone love and care for his brother according to the Spirit!"[3] When a baby is held, many powerful experiences well up within the holder—touching, sensing, feeling, caressing, fondling, embracing.

In the Middle Ages, Mary Magdalene was a significant figure, even for Francis. John writes in his Gospel, "Early on the first day of the week, while it was still dark, Mary Magdalene came to the tomb and . . . saw Jesus standing there . . . Jesus said to her, 'Mary!' . . . 'Do not hold on to me, because I have not yet ascended to the Father'" [20:1, 14, 16–17]. In her love for Jesus, she reaches out to touch him.

It is interesting to note that the artist who painted the crucifix of San Damiano situated the Magdalene beneath the right arm of Jesus directly next to his body. If you are familiar with Andrew Lloyd Weber's *Jesus Christ Superstar*, you will remember that the song that the Magdalene sings is entitled "I Don't Know How to Love Him."

When the Scriptures speak of the human person, the words used are "spirit, soul and body" [1 Thessalonians 5:23]. This is the person who loves. When our bodies, souls and spirits are in a balance, claims Richard Rohr, we are then biblical persons of the heart.[4]

The symbol of love, the heart, cannot continue to beat unless it is supported by a physical body. Love is not something hovering in the air high above our heads. It is a daily miracle, just like our heartbeat. Love is not anything we could grant ourselves, for love is a divine gift. Love bears us along and keeps us going, one breath after the next. Remember what Saint John says:

> In this is love, not that we loved God but that (God) loved us and sent the Son to be the atoning sacrifice for our sins. . . . God is love, and those who abide in love abide in God, and God abides in them. . . . We love because (God) first loved us. [1 John 4:10, 16, 19]

And this love is so strong, stronger even than death! Bonaventure writes, "And such is the power of your love, O soul, that, as Bernard writes, 'you live more truly where you love than where you breathe' [*De Praecepto*, 20:61]. This, dearest soul, is the kingdom of God within us. . . ."[5]

Sister Roselle Schaefer expressed this very beautifully in her poem, "A Divine Spark":

In the temple of the soul our God abides—
Waiting for the soul to awaken to love's call—
To hearken to the voice of the Beloved
To open the portals of the heart
And let love enter in
To cease the endless flight
And permit those pursuing feet to overtake it.

O divine spark,
I cherish you.
Live on in this Temple of my heart
Like a consuming fire
I long to be united to You
I long to fly away and be with you—
Consummate our union, Lord![6]

EXERCISES

• Read a part of Clare's *Fourth Letter to Agnes of Prague:*

> To the half of her soul and the special shrine
> of her heart's special love; to the illustrious
> queen, the bride of the Lamb of the eternal
> King; to the Lady Agnes, her dearest mother
> the daughter who is special among all the oth-
> ers. Clare, the unworthy family servant of
> Christ and unprofitable handmaid of his
> handmaids who abide in the monastery of San
> Damiano of Assisi, greetings; and with the rest
> of the most holy virgins, may she sing the new
> song before the throne of God and of the
> Lamb, and may she follow the Lamb wherever
> he goes.[7]

Then choose some special stationery to write a letter to
someone you love. Express your feelings honestly.
Later you can decide whether or not to send the letter.

- Read the *Song of Solomon* (the *Canticle of Canticles*), the great love song of the Old Testament. Clare of Assisi quoted that song. Let the text speak to you.

  (D)o not stir up or awaken love / until it is ready! [Song of Solomon 2:7]

NOTES

[1]Erich Fromm, *Haben oder Sein. Die Seelischen Grundlagen einer neuen Gesellschaft (To Have or to Be: The Psychical Foundation of a New Society)* (Stuttgart, Germany: Deutsche Verlags-Anstalt GmbH, 1976), p. 52. Authors' translation.

[2]See *The Form of Life of Clare of Assisi* VIII:15–16, in *Clare: Early Documents, op. cit.*, p. 74.

[3]*The Later Rule* VI:7–8, in *Francis of Assisi: The Saint, op. cit.*, p. 103.

[4]From workshop notes, "Mending the Breach," Richard Rohr, O.F.M., Franciscan Center, Tampa, Fla., February 7–11, 1993.

[5]*Soliloquy* IV, 4, in *The Works of Bonaventure*, Vol. III, José de Vinck, trans. (Paterson, N.J.: St. Anthony Guild Press, 1966), p. 109.

[6]Roselle Schaefer, O.S.F., *Mystical Expressions: A Book of Poetry* (Wheaton, Ill.: Our Lady of the Angels Motherhouse, P.O. Box 667, 1999), p. 47.

[7]Translation of Saint Clare's *Fourth Letter to Agnes of Prague*, 1–3, is that of Sister Frances Teresa Downing, O.S.C., *op. cit.*

Thursday

The Hierarchy within You

Bonaventure writes in chapter 4:4,6:

4. When these things have been accomplished,
and our spirit has been brought into conformity with the
heavenly Jerusalem,
it is ordered hierarchically so that it can ascend upward.
For no one enters into that city
unless that city has first descended into the person's heart by
means of grace,
as John sees in *Revelation.*
It descends into the heart
when our spirit has been made hierarchical
by the reformation of the image
and by the theological virtues,
the enjoyment of the spiritual senses,
and the ecstasy of rapture;
for then it has been purged, illumined and brought to
perfection.
In this way our spirit is adorned with nine levels
when within it the following are found in an appropriate
order:
announcing, dictating, leading,
ordering, strengthening, commanding,
receiving, revealing, and anointing.
These correspond to the nine choirs of angels.
The first three of the foregoing levels in the human mind
relate to nature;
the next three relate to work;
and the final three relate to grace.

When it has attained these, the soul, by entering into itself,

enters into the heavenly Jerusalem where,

as it considers the choirs of angels,

it sees in them the God who dwells in them

and who works in all their operations.

Therefore, Bernard says to Pope Eugene that

"God loves in the Seraphim as charity;

knows in the Cherubim as truth;

sits in the Thrones as justice;

reigns in the Dominations as majesty;

rules in the Principalities as a guiding principle;

protects in the Powers as salvation;

is at work in the Virtues as strength;

reveals in the Archangels as light;

assists in the Angels as kindness."

From all this, God is seen as *all in all* [1 Corinthians 15:28]

when we contemplate God in our minds

where God dwells through the gifts of the most generous love.

6. Therefore, all of sacred Scripture treats of this hierarch

and of the ecclesiastical hierarchy

through which we are taught how

to be purged, illumined and perfected

in terms of the threefold law

which has been handed down in the Scriptures:

namely, the law of nature,

the law of Scripture,

and the law of grace.

JOSEF

Earlier this week we used the image of a balloon. I'm sure everyone has blown up a balloon at some point in life. A balloon is simply a soft, limp membrane of rubber that really is no good until it is stretched and pulled. A balloon becomes what it is meant to be only when someone blows into it. The membrane stretches more and more, and slowly takes on the shape it was meant to have. Blowing up a balloon is also a liminal experience, as we try to arrive at its maximum tension, when all available space is filled with air just before the balloon might burst. What fun! What playfulness! What beautiful colors! What lofty flights, as it bobs along on the air currents! What energy there is in stretching, in exploding. Watch the children's faces as the balloon grows bigger and bigger. Let it fly through the room like a rocket and hear them laugh.

As you can see in Illustration 11 on page 216, we can compare chapter 4 of *The Journey* with a balloon. Just as the air streaming into the empty skin of a balloon brings the balloon to its intended shape, in a similar way the Spirit of God builds up a hierarchy, that is, a sacred order,[1] within a person. This inner order leads the person to her or his true shape, as God's Spirit is present within the person.

Bonaventure speaks of hierarchical operations and of the Supreme Hierarch, Jesus Christ. If we continue with the balloon imagery, the Supreme Hierarch is the one most expanded and filled. In this "balloon" all the divine gifts are brought to fulfillment. The gifts of the Spirit fill the empty space within the human person. As Spirit-filled people, our senses are awakened in a spiritual way. Hearing, sight, smell, taste and touch take on new depth and breadth. And ultimately—certainly with our last breath, so to speak—everything melts and fuses into a happiness of union with Jesus Christ, a happiness of adoration and joyful praise.

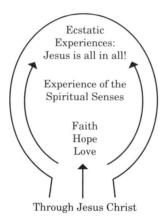

Illustration 11:

The sacred order within is here illustrated by a balloon. Jesus Christ
is the opening through which God blows life into us. Anyone who is
open to letting this fresh air in will be structured or ordered anew.
This person is made hierarchical.

This section also notes the place of angels along our *Journey.*
The hierarchies of angels, the nine choirs, stand for all the
powers of heaven and earth who support us along *The*
Journey. Three times three: the number nine stands for fullness, for all the arms outstretched, for all the wings unfold-
ed for us.

ANDRÉ

The angels represent the hierarchical cooperators who join
this spiritual work. They ceaselessly fan the flames of our
faith, our hope and our love and keep them burning. We are
not angels, but even in our brokenness and limitation, our
doubts and anxiety, we experience the power of God's loving
care. The angels represent this power, they stand for God's

constant offer to fill us up. A very powerful image, indeed, the well-structured choirs of the Almighty! Another related aspect is the power of the Word of God, which we shall return to later.

Jesus is the hierarch par excellence because he let Abba's Spirit, who is the God-with-us, fill him to the utmost. He let his angels lead him and thus he became the Son of God fully.[2]

If you follow Bonaventure's words more closely, there is even more to discover. He puts human nature on the lowest of the three levels of activity, which are "announcing, dictating, leading." Every human society needs these leadership characteristics, which are truly well ordered only if the person is able to be open to the Spirit of Jesus.

On the second level, we depend entirely on what we ourselves can create. The capacities linked to this level are "ordering, strengthening, commanding." Again, those are characteristics of leadership that distinguish a hierarchical person. These words certainly do not simply connote hierarchy as referring to the authorities of the church who can admonish us to accept responsibility for our own life or for those around us and to live in the spirit of Jesus' love.

On the third and highest level, Bonaventure speaks about what is given us. This level is marked by "receiving, revealing, and anointing." This highest level of this inner, sacred order that should be built up within us breathes the spirit of unconditional surrender and trustful waiting. We are living in a spirit of wonder, of ecstasy, of inner and outer joy.

From these few thoughts we could develop a model for Christian leadership, with the nine activities as a basic framework.

JOSEF

When I look a little more closely at these activities, my mind overflows with images of my family life and job. As a parent I am simply not on the same level as my children. I, too, live in a hierarchical structure with them and I can see myself in those words used by Bonaventure. It would be absolutely wonderful to have a perfect balance among all these activities in raising the children or even in collaboration with my colleagues at work. It is not a question of holding on to my own opinions or convictions or of choosing to head in a direction where the others refuse to go. It is basically a question of receptivity. The people entrusted to your care need direction, strengthening, encouragement, as well as some kind of anointing. They should be able to assume responsibility for themselves and search out their own way. This sacred, inner order makes us sure that our first, last and most important step is to listen intensely to the Spirit of Jesus Christ in us.

The heart of hierarchy in a Bonaventurian sense is this spiritual filling. This can best be expressed by a feminine image, where woman—in body and soul—is open to new life with all of her powers and capacities concentrated to serve that new life. Mary is certainly the model of the church, the foremost Christian, bearing Christ in her virginal body. That is hierarchy! As such this woman stands above all ecclesiastical hierarchies, a fact that even the hierarchy itself would not dispute. This is a deeply Franciscan thought.[3]

EXERCISES

• Reflect on Matthew 20:25–28:

But Jesus called them to him and said, "You know that the rulers of the gentiles lord it over them, and their great ones are tyrants over them. It will not be so among you; but whoever wishes to be great among you must be your servant, and whoever wishes to be first among you must be your slave."

How does Jesus handle power? How does Jesus deal with claims for leadership? How can you put this text into practice? Try to be specific.

- What connection can you find between love and the verbs Bonaventure uses: "receiving," "revealing" and "anointing"? What comes to mind? Jot down your ideas on paper. Perhaps you can attach a little story to each.

NOTES

[1] The Greek words *hiere arche* render the literal translation for the word "hierarchy."

[2] In Bonaventure's *The Triple Way*, he treats in detail the three traditional ways of the mystical, ascetical journey: the purgative, the illuminative and the unitive. This work offers a practical guide for living according to this fourth chapter. *De triplice via*, in *Doctoris Seraphici S. Bonaventurae opera omnia*, edita studio et cura Collegii a S. Bonaventura, 10 volumes, Quaracchi, 1882–1902, vol. 8, pp. 3–18. See *The Triple Way, or Love Enkindled*, in *The Works of Bonaventure*, op. cit., 1960, vol. 1, pp. 59–94.

[3] See Anton Rotzetter, O.F.M. CAP., Willibrord-Christian Van Dijk, O.F.M. CAP., Thaddée Matura, O.F.M., *Gospel Living: Francis of Assisi Yesterday and Today* (New York: Franciscan Institute Publications, 1996), pp. 126, 137: "Again we must turn our thoughts to Mary. She was the first to receive the Word of God. She bore him in her womb. It was through her that God was clothed in humility. She shared God's fate—God's poverty, God's homelessness. Mary is the mother who by hearing God's word conceived and bore him. She is and remains the archetypal figure of the Church, the virgin who is now church. What occurred in Mary historically must be mystically reenacted in every Christian. Every soul is the elect of God, the bride of the Spirit, the mother of the Son."

Friday

'But I Say to You. . .'

Bonaventure writes in chapter 4:5, 6:

5. At this level of contemplation
the divinely given sacred Scriptures are particularly helpful
just as philosophy was at the previous level.
For sacred Scripture is above all concerned with the work of
reparation.
Therefore, it deals mainly with faith, hope and charity;
that is, with the virtues by which the soul is to be reformed.
And most especially it deals with charity.
Concerning this the Apostle says that charity which arises
from *a heart that is pure and from a good conscience,*
and from genuine faith is the whole point of the Law.
As the same Apostle says, it is *the fulfillment of the Law*
[1 Timothy 1:5; Romans 13:10].
And our Savior says that the whole of the Law and the
Prophets
depends on two commandments;
namely, love of God and love of neighbor [Matthew 22:40].
These two are symbolized in Jesus Christ,
the one spouse of the church,
who is both our God and our neighbor,
both our lord and our brother,
both king and friend,
both the uncreated Word and the incarnate Word,
both our creator and our re-creator,
both the *alpha* and the *omega* [Revelation 1:8; 21:6; 22:13].
As the supreme hierarch,
it is He who purges, illumines and perfects His spouse,
namely the entire church and each sanctified soul.

6. . . . .Or rather, in accord with the three main parts of
Scripture:
the Mosaic law which purges,
the prophetic revelation which illumines,
and the teaching of the Gospel which perfects. . . .
All this is to be seen
in relation to the aforementioned three theological virtues,
the reformed spiritual senses,
the three spiritual ecstasies mentioned above,
and the three hierarchical acts of the soul
by which our soul returns to its interior
where it sees God in the *splendor of the Saints* [Psalms 109:3],
and in them as in her bed she *sleeps in peace* [Psalms 4:9]
while the bridegroom pleads that she should not be awakened
until it is her will to come forth [Canticle 2:7].

JOSEF

Language should be numbered among the milestones in the
history of human evolution. It separates us from all other
groups of living species. Words try to grasp something and to
give it a form that can be conveyed to another. Words both
express some kind of reality and create another kind of reality, as our modern communication sciences tell us.

For Christians the greatest word is the word that was
spoken and is constantly being spoken anew, namely the
unique person of Jesus of Nazareth. He is the *Word*, as the
beginning of John's Gospel tells us, that was with God from
the beginning. He is the most intimate Word or Thought
that God could have expressed.[1] This single Word contains
the whole of God's creativity and expressiveness. Therefore,
"word" is not to be understood merely in terms of speech. It
stands for all the various ways of expressing things, that is,

the forms of communication of God's power and love.

In the Second Vatican Council's document on divine revelation, *Dei Verbum*, this Word's meaning for our *Journey* is underscored quite impressively. The Council members expressed the desire that the "whole world may believe; by believing, it may hope; and by hoping, it may love."[2]

> Through . . . revelation . . . the invisible God out of the abundance of love, speaks to people as friends and lives among them, so that God may invite and take them into fellowship. . . . The deepest truth about God and the salvation of humanity is made clear to us in Christ, who is the Mediator and at the same time the fullness of all revelation. . . . He confirmed with divine testimony . . . that God is with us.[3]

For Francis and Clare, this Word of liberation, Jesus Christ himself, is the center of their lives. Thus "the form of life of the Order . . . is this: to observe the Holy Gospel of our Lord, Jesus Christ."[4]

In Thomas of Celano's biography of Francis we read:

> One day the Gospel was being read in that church (the Portiuncula), about how the Lord sent out his disciples to preach. The holy man of God, who was attending there, in order to understand better the words of the Gospel, humbly begged the priest after celebrating the solemnities of the Mass to explain the Gospel to him. When he heard that Christ's disciples should not possess gold or silver or money; or

carry on their journey a wallet or a sack, nor bread nor a staff, nor to have shoes nor two tunics, but that they should preach the kingdom of God and penance, the holy man, Francis, immediately exulted in the spirit of God. "This is what I want," he said, "this is what I seek, this is what I desire with all my heart"[5]

Such spontaneous decisions really sound great, but things like this don't often happen in everyday life. The biographer, it seems, has incorporated in this one scene what developed over a period of Francis' years of searching and questioning. For quite some time Francis had been looking for his way of life, and he never really completed the process. The institutional church and his brothers in the movement challenged him over and over again to come to a clearer definition of this form of life according to the holy gospel of Jesus Christ. Living a Franciscan life means bringing the Word and life of Jesus Christ into every situation of human life, in order to confront it with that same Word and life. This confrontation is quite challenging and never finished. It is only in the tensions of everyday life that the person who is looking for the way will find an answer, an answer that leads to deeper life and greater maturity.

Francis' encounter with the gospel, as described by Thomas of Celano, is related somewhat differently in the *Legend of the Three Companions.* Francis enters the church of St. Nicholas next to the Piazza Comune in Assisi, accompanied by Peter and Bernard. These three were certainly not Scripture scholars. Deep in their hearts they were looking for guidance and, praying, they opened the book of the

Gospels three times at random. They had already set out on a new way of life, already removed themselves from society. But now they had to come to a decision. "This is our life and rule and that of all who will want to join our company."[6] And the texts, which were opened at random, gave them direction. Francis' way of dealing with sacred Scripture might seem a little naive to us modern people, schooled in a historical-critical approach. A passage from his own writings can help us to understand his method, however:

> I, therefore, admonish all my brothers and encourage them in Christ to venerate, as best they can, the divine written words wherever they find them. If they are not well kept or are carelessly thrown around in some place, let them gather them up and preserve them, inasmuch as it concerns them, honoring in the words the Lord Who spoke them. For many things are made holy by the words of God and the sacrament of the altar is celebrated in the power of the words of Christ.[7]

In *The First Version of the Letter to the Faithful,* Saint Francis relates the *Word* to John 6:63, "It is the spirit that gives life; the flesh is useless. The words that I have spoken to you are spirit and life."

What is involved here is a very dynamic, tension-filled, dialogical confrontation with the Spirit of Jesus, which finds concrete expression in the words of sacred Scripture.

> In the love which is God, we beg all those whom these letters reach to accept with kindness and a divine love the fragrant words of our Lord Jesus Christ which are written above.

> And those who do not know how to read
> should have them read to them frequently.
> And since they are spirit and life (John 6:64),
> they should preserve them together with their
> holy manner of working even to the end.[8]

ANDRÉ

If you have a favorite food, you can recall what the aroma of this dish does to you. When I pick up the smell of garlic, my mouth begins to water and my legs start moving, almost by reflex action, toward the kitchen.

This is another connection that Francis makes when he speaks about "the fragrant words."[9] Clare, too, uses the same metaphor in her *Fourth Letter to Agnes of Prague*, when she speaks of the life-giving fragrance[10] of Jesus Christ. A fragrance can enchant me, seduce me and captivate me completely. Never forget, however, that this is a question of love! Studying the Scriptures is not so much a matter of dry analysis, intellectual research or historical explanations. All these things may help us deepen our understanding, but it is more than that—it is a matter of risk, wonder and falling in love.

In his biography of Francis, it is Bonaventure, the theologian, who tells us about another sensual experience in the context of the *Word*. When he prayed, Francis would lick his lips as he pronounced the name of Jesus. The very sweetness of this word made him "hungry"!

> He used to say the psalms with such attention
> of mind and spirit, as if he had God present.
> When the Lord's name occurred in the
> psalms, he seemed to lick his lips because of
> its sweetness.
>
> He wanted to honor with special rever-

ence the Lord's name not only when thought but also when spoken and written. He once persuaded the friars to gather all pieces of paper wherever they were found and to place them in a clean place so that if the sacred name happened to be written there, it would not be trodden underfoot. When he pronounced or heard the name Jesus, he was filled with an inner joy and seemed completely changed exteriorly as if some honey-sweet flavor had transformed his taste or some harmonious sound had transformed his hearing.[11]

For Francis and his sisters and brothers, Jesus Christ is the living center. He is the teacher. He is the *Word*. He is the form of life. He is the meditation book and the center of all creation, the perfect new creation, God's masterpiece. Everything that the Creator could have expressed was expressed in him. This encounter with Jesus is something far different from looking for him in some dry letters. It takes place amid the demands of love that daily come to us.

The story is told of a poor lady who came to the Portiuncula and asked Francis and his brothers for help. She was in dire need and wanted something to eat. However, the brothers did not have any food at hand. What should they do? Francis ordered them to give her the only copy of the Gospels they had. The brothers began to protest: How would they be able to hear the Word of God? Should they deny themselves that? But Francis replied that it was better to put into practice what is written in the book than merely to read it in a pious spirit.[12]

EXERCISES

- Jesus' friends are sitting all alone in the boat and the water starts to get very rough. They begin to panic; Jesus approaches them, and they think they are seeing a ghost. Use Jesus' reply to his frightened disciples as ruminating prayer[13]: "Take heart, it is I; do not be afraid." [Matthew 14:27].

- Look at John 15:11–12: "I have said these things to you so that my joy may be in you, and that your joy may be complete. This is my commandment, that you love one another as I have loved you." What is your rule of life? Look at the quote from John; which lines are most striking to you? Try to compose a personal rule of life.

NOTES

[1] John 1:1, 3: "In the beginning was the Word, and the Word was with God, and the Word was God. . . . All things came into being through him, and without him not one thing came into being."

[2] See *Dogmatic Constitution on Divine Revelation* VI:21, *Dei Verbum*, in *The Documents of Vatican II, op. cit.*, p. 111.

[3] *Dei Verbum* 1-4, *ibid.*, pp. 112–113.

[4] *The Form of Life of Clare of Assisi* I:1–2, in *Clare: Early Documents, op. cit.*, p. 64.

[5] *The Life of St. Francis* by Thomas of Celano IX:22, in *Francis of Assisi: The Saint, op. cit.*, pp. 201-202.

[6] *The Legend of the Three Companions* VIII:29, in *Francis of Assisi: The Founder, op. cit.*, p. 86.

[7] *A Letter to the Entire Order* 35–37, in *Francis of Assisi: The Saint, op. cit.*, p. 119.

[8] *The First Version of the Letter to the Faithful* 2:19–21, *ibid.*, p. 42.

[9] *Ibid.*

[10] See *Fourth Letter to Agnes of Prague* 13, in *Clare: Early Documents, op. cit.*, pp. 49–52.

[11] *The Major Legend of St. Francis* by Bonaventure of Bagnoregio 10:6, in *Francis of Assisi: The Founder, op. cit.*, p. 609.

[12] See *The Assisi Compilation* 118, in *Francis of Assisi: The Founder, op. cit.*, pp. 226–227; *The Remembrance of the Desire of a Soul* by Thomas of Celano (*The Second Life of Saint Francis*) LVIII:91, *ibid.*, p. 306.

[13] For rumination, see Sunday of Week Two.

Saturday

PRAISE GOD!

Bonaventure writes in chapter 4:8 and 5:1:

4:8. Therefore, let us be rooted and grounded in love,
so that we might comprehend with all the saints
what is the length of eternity,
the *breadth* of generosity,
the *height* of majesty,
and the *depth* of that discerning wisdom [Ephesians 3:18-19].

5:1. It is possible to contemplate God
not only outside ourselves and inside ourselves but also above
ourselves.
Outside ourselves this is done through the vestiges;
inside ourselves through the image;
and above ourselves through the light that shines on our
mind.
This is the light of the eternal truth,
since "the mind itself is formed immediately by truth itself."
Those who have become acquainted with the first way
have entered into the court before the tabernacle.
Those who are practiced in the second way have entered into
the holy place.
And those who are involved in the third way
enter together with the High Priest into the holy of holies
where the Cherubim of glory
stand above the ark and overshadow the Mercy Seat
[Exodus 25-28].
By the Cherubim we understand two modes or levels
of contemplating the invisible and eternal qualities of God.
The first of these concerns the essential attributes of God;
the second concerns the properties of the persons.

ANDRÉ

With the fifth chapter of *The Journey* we leave behind the realm of human and creaturely experience and turn our gaze to that which is, so to speak, the most that we can think of. We direct our attention to the limits of our imagination and ideas, to reach the greatest, the best, the most beautiful. We are switching our position. Thus far in chapters 1 through 4 of *The Journey,* Bonaventure has guided us to look at the realities of our world in order to show us from that perspective the greatness and perfection of God. Now in chapters 5 and 6, we look at perfection and divinity in itself, the Totally Other, the Transcendent One. In Bonaventure's Latin text, one is immediately struck by all the superlatives he uses, recognized by adjectives with the suffix *-issimus.* It is all one big superlative! We are entering into a philosophical-theological meditation on God that culminates in a wonderful hymn that sings of the unification of all the opposites in Jesus Christ.

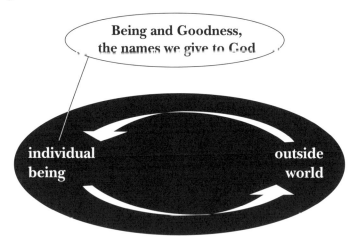

Illustration 12: Overview of chapters 1 to 6.

The lower dark circle contains all limited human experience. Here, all of creation is situated in chapters 1 to 4. In chapters 1 and 2, Bonaventure searches for God outside himself. In chapters 3 and 4, his search for God moves within the individual being, the human person. The circle above describes—like a voice in a cartoon—the world of our thought, that is, the most we can think of in terms of Being and Goodness itself.

This rather simple step leads to the questions: how do you pray? How do you address God? You must use words to express what is invincible. It seems that every possible word expressing magnitude has been used by believers to show God's greatness. Would you address or think of your God in terms that would admit that there might be anyone or anything greater? Of course not! And it is no accident that most prayers in the various religious traditions begin with the words "Almighty," "All knowing" or "Most High."

This, moreover, is also the language of philosophers, but Francis and Clare of Assisi and Bonaventure, as well, all focus on contemplation here. People of faith and prayer feel at home in chapters 5 and 6 of *The Journey*. Listen to Francis praying:

> Holy, Holy, Holy Lord, God Almighty,
> You who are, who were and who are to come:
> Let us praise and exalt God above all forever!

> You are worthy, O Lord our God,
> to receive praise and glory, honor and blessing:
> Let us praise and exalt God above all forever![1]

The prayer of this same hymn that concluded the praises showed just how important it was for Francis:

Almighty, most holy
most high and supreme God,
all good,
supreme good,
totally good,
You Who alone are good. . . .[2]

Francis' *Canticle of the Creatures* begins with the phrase "Most high, all powerful, good Lord."[3] In his texts Francis seems to be at the furthest limits of what is possible for him to express, happily juggling his words about. However, this is the language of our daily prayers, too. Once again listen to Francis as he meditates:

You are holy, Lord God, Who does wonderful things.
You are strong, You are great, You are the most high.
You are the almighty king.
You, holy Father, King of heaven and earth.
You are three and one, the Lord God of gods.
You are the good, all good, the highest good,
Lord God living and true.
You are love, charity; You are wisdom, You are humility,
You are patience, You are beauty, You are meekness,
You are security, You are rest,
You are gladness and joy, You are our hope, You are justice,
You are moderation, You are all our riches and sufficiency.
You are beauty, You are meekness,
You are the protector, You are our custodian and defender,
You are strength, You are refreshment. You are our hope,
You are our faith, You are our charity,
You are all our sweetness, You are our eternal life:
Great and wonderful Lord, Almighty God, Merciful Savior.[4]

JOSEF

In all these terms and images Francis always seems to be thinking in superlatives, the maximum, all he could possibly imagine. Anselm of Canterbury (1033–1109)[5] once said, "See and take note that the highest good in an unqualified sense is that than which nothing better can be thought of."[6] If you were able to think of something greater, that would be God.

The dimension and perspective of adoration, gratitude, praise and of a positive, joyful acceptance of goodness in itself may be Franciscan spirituality's most precious gift to humanity. Bonaventure notes that praying in this way, the seeker here is staring directly at the light and, as a consequence, sight is impeded! We are being blinded by this light.

It is an art to combine both perspectives—on the one hand, the concrete, broken story/history of our own experiences and human situations, and on the other hand, God's greatness and glory. For Bonaventure, both sides are different perspectives of the one and only Being. God's Being is mirrored in all that exists. In addressing God directly, using the language of prayer, the reflection of the divine reality grows clearer and foggier at the same time.

At the end of this reflection, let us join Francis in praise:

Wherever we are,
in every place,
at every hour,
at every time of day,
everyday and continually,
Let all of us truly and humbly believe,
and hold in our heart and love,
honor, adore, serve
praise and bless,

glorify and exalt,
magnify and give thanks
to the Most High and Supreme Eternal God
Trinity and Unity,
Father, Son and Holy Spirit,
Creator of all,
Savior of all
who believe and hope in Him,
and love Him, Who
without beginning and end,
is unchangeable, invisible,
indescribable, ineffable,
incomprehensible, unfathomable,
blessed, praiseworthy,
glorious, exalted,
sublime, most high,
gentle, lovable, delightful
and totally desirable above all else
for ever.
Amen.[7]

EXERCISES

• Write your own litany of praise, imitating Francis' *Praises of God* quoted above. Then slowly reread it, ruminating on what you have written.

• Sketch or paint an image of God, how you picture God. Without giving it too much thought, let the image flow from you.

• In a second sketch, try to be more abstract. Look at your pictures and try to begin a conversation with the God you have sketched.

NOTES

[1] *Praises to Be Said at All the Hours* 1–2, in Laurent Gallant, O.F.M., and André Cirino, O.F.M., *The Geste of the Great King: Office of the Passion of Francis of Assisi* (New York: Franciscan Institute Publications, 2001), p. 41. This is Murray Bodo's more literary translation of Francis' literal text.

[2] *Ibid.*, p. 42.

[3] *The Canticle of the Creatures*, in *Francis of Assisi: The Saint, op. cit.*, p. 113.

[4] *The Praises of God, ibid.*, p. 109.

[5] Anselm was a Benedictine abbot who became archbishop of Canterbury. He is known as a mystic and the father of medieval scholasticism.

[6] See *The Journey* 6:2.

[7] *The Earlier Rule* XXIII:11, in *Francis of Assisi: The Saint, op. cit.*, pp. 85–86.

BEING GOOD

Sunday

'I THINK THAT I SHALL NEVER SEE. . .'[1]

Bonaventure writes in chapter 5:2, 3:

2. The first method fixes our attention principally and first of
all on Being itself,
saying that *The One who is* [Exodus 3:14] is the first name of
God. . . .
The first looks above all at the Hebrew Scriptures
which are concerned to a great extent with the unity of the
divine essence.
For it was said to Moses: *I am who I am* [Exodus 3:14]. . . .

3. Anyone, therefore, who wishes to contemplate the invisible
qualities of God
that pertain to the unity of essence
looks first and principally at Being Itself,
and recognizes that Being Itself is so thoroughly certain
that it cannot be thought not to be,
for the most pure being does not exist
except in total opposition to non-being
just as *nothing* is the total opposite of *being*.
Therefore as total nothingness
possesses nothing of being nor of being's attributes,
so, on the contrary, being itself possesses nothing of non-
being,
neither in act nor in potency;
neither in reality nor in our understanding of it.
Now, since non-being is the privation of existence,
it does not enter into the intellect except through being.
Being, on the other hand, does not enter the intellect by
anything other than itself,
since everything that is known

is known either as non-being,
or as potential being,
or as actual being.
Therefore if non-being cannot be known except through
being,
and potential being cannot be known except through actual
being,
and if being names the pure actuality of being,
it follows that being is what first comes to the intellect;
and it is that being which is pure act.
But this is not a particular being,
which is limited because it is mixed with potentiality.
Nor is it analogous being which has the least actuality
because it has the least of existence.
It remains, therefore, that this being is the divine Being. . . .

JOSEF

When I try to think of being in itself, I find it is not easy to do so. Being is something that has been around a long time, something continuous and irreversible, something that is durable and imperishable. However, it is also very creative. Being must be absolutely here and now, and it must be powerful. It is something like water welling up from an underground spring. It can slake our thirst, even though we do not know where it comes from, where it is going, nor do we know much about its depth.

One image for being in itself is a tree. Trees touch us deeply. In fact, they enable and enhance our life. They are, so to speak, the lungs of planet earth. If they are cut down our land erodes, and we find ourselves in great danger. Yet we can take trees for granted, for they simply are there. They existed long before we appeared, and will be here when we are long gone. It is probable that trees are the oldest living creatures on earth. The California pine trees from the Sierra Nevadas, for example, have been around more than forty-six hundred years. What is our life span of sixty, eighty or even ninety years compared with that?

And what a lesson for us when we look at the way they live and survive! They can survive by clinging to places we couldn't even imagine possible. They penetrate walls and break stone or rock. Their roots follow the path of life, even in places where we think life would be impossible. What power it takes to keep those tall and mighty trunks erect! Anyone who goes hiking in the mountains is astonished by these marvelous creatures. We can only stand in speechless wonder with eyes raised taking it all in.

Trees invite us simply to rest in their shade, to be lulled by the soft and enchanting whisper of the leaves and branches swaying in the breeze. They offer us a gathering place and so create community, gifting us with strength and warmth. I remember from my childhood an old oak tree that stood in the middle of our village. It was the center around which we children played, the place where people would meet to talk. One day the tree was cut down because a new road was going through the village. Unfortunately, the village lost its focal point.

Many cultures or tribes, such as the Semites, the Greeks, the Druids, the Aztecs and the Normans, have a kind of sacred woods or trees. According to these groups, the gods lived in the sacred forests. Recall the example of Moses as he encountered God in the tree, the burning bush.

One reason trees touch us in this way is that they are similar in shape to us. Just stretch your arms out wide, root your legs to the ground and wave your hands gently with the wind! Trees have initiative, even imagination and hope. We cannot predict where they will grow. They seem to be so wise because they change what they can change and they accept what cannot be changed. If they encounter an obstacle, they simply grow around it. They grow out of the shadows reaching toward the light. Even when there seems no way for them to grow, they find new possibilities. And look at how steady they are! They offer us space under their branches for protection. They invite us simply to be, to breathe, to live!

What a message for our busy, restless and often insensitive world! What a message for people pummeled by stress and pressure on all sides and in danger of losing touch with their own roots, with the meaning of their life, with being itself.

Francis of Assisi was very fond of trees, as Thomas of Celano relates:

> He embraces all things with an intensity of unheard devotion, speaking to them about the Lord and exhorting them to praise Him. . . . When the brothers are cutting wood he forbids them to cut down the whole tree, so that it might have hope of sprouting again. He commands the gardener to leave the edges of the garden undisturbed so that in their season the green of herbs and the beauty of the flowers may proclaim the beautiful Father of all. He even orders that within the garden a smaller garden should be set aside for aromatic and flowering herbs so that those who see them may recall the memory of eternal savor. . . . He calls all animals by a fraternal name, although,

among all kinds of beasts he especially loves
the meek. Who is capable of describing all of
this? Truly, that fountain-like goodness, which
will be all in all, already shone clearly in all for
this saint.[2]

We have a lot to learn from our brothers and sisters the trees.

EXERCISES

- Contemplate a tree and, perhaps like Joyce Kilmer, salute
it through poetry.

- The cross has been called the "tree of life," and in his *Office
of the Passion*, we find Francis praying: "The Lord has
reigned from the wood" [Psalm of Francis 7:9].[3] As you
reflect on these expressions, what images emerge for you?

- Go for a walk in a forest or at least among some trees.
Maybe you can visit your favorite tree or go for a hike in the
mountains. As you walk, be aware of the trees; encounter
them. Try to understand and feel why a certain tree may
touch you more than others.

NOTES

[1] From Joyce Kilmer, "Trees," *One Hundred and One Famous Poems*, compiled
by Roy J. Cook (Chicago: Contemporary Books, Inc., 1958), p. 39.

[2] *The Remembrance of the Desire of a Soul* by Thomas of Celano CXXIV:165, in
Francis of Assisi: The Founder, op. cit., pp. 353–354.

[3] *Praises to Be Said at All the Hours*, in *The Geste of the Great King, op. cit.*, p. 289.

Monday

ALL IN ALL

Bonaventure writes in the chapter 5:6, 8:

6. These things are so certain that their opposites cannot be
conceived of
by anyone who understands what is meant by *being itself*.
And each one of these attributes necessarily implies the other.
For since it is being with no qualification,
it is first in an unqualified sense.
Since it is first in an unqualified sense,
it is not made by another, nor is it made by itself.
Therefore it is eternal.
And since it is first and eternal,
therefore it is not composed from others.
Therefore it is supremely simple.
Then, because it is first, eternal, and most simple,
therefore there is in it no potentiality mixed with act.
It is most actual.
Then, because it is first, eternal, most simple, and most actual,
it is also most perfect.
Such a being lacks absolutely nothing, and nothing can be
added to it.
Because it is first, eternal, most simple, most actual, and most
perfect, it is supremely one. . . .

8. Looking over the way we have come,
let us say that the most pure and absolute being,
because it is being in an unqualified sense,
is first and last;
and therefore it is the origin and consummating end of all things.
Because it is eternal and most present,
it embraces and enters into all things that endure in time,
simultaneously existing as their center and circumference.

Because it is most simple and greatest,
it is within all things and outside all things,
and hence "it is an intelligible sphere
whose center is everywhere
and whose circumference is nowhere."
Because it is most actual and immutable, therefore
"remaining unmoved, it imparts movement to all things."
Because it is most perfect and immense,
therefore it is within all things but is not contained by them;
and it is outside all things but is not excluded;
it is above all things but not distant;
and it is below all things, but not prostrate.
Because it is supremely one and all-embracing,
it is *all in all* [1 Corinthians 15:28],
even though all things are multiple and this is simply one.
And because this is most simple unity,
most peaceful truth,
and most sincere goodness,
it is all power, all exemplarity, and all communicability.
Therefore, *from him and through him and in him are all things*
[Romans 11:36],
for he is all-powerful, all-knowing, and all-good.
And to see him perfectly is to be blessed,
as it was said to Moses:
I will show you all good [Exodus 33:19].

ANDRÉ

In this fifth chapter, Bonaventure develops his teaching on
being itself, what is technically called "ontology." I do not
want to introduce you now to the details of his philosophical
viewpoint, but I want to guide you in reflecting on some
aspects of being. Our likeness to God, *similitudo* at this stage
of *The Journey,* is found in the human ability to consider what

my mind and my language create when I ask myself: What and how can I think about being in itself?

Bonaventure begins by naming six characteristics of being which are closely linked to one another:

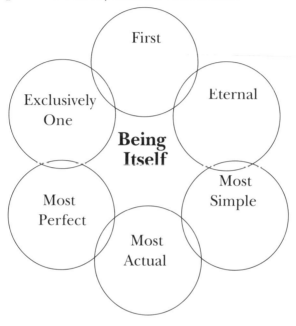

Illustration 13: Chapter 5:6.
Being Itself is shown as a chain consisting of six rings linked to one another. If you break one link, the chain is destroyed, that is, it no longer represents Being Itself.

That being that is the foundation for everything else must be absolutely first, with "no qualification," no reservation. It must be eternal, without beginning and end, timeless and always present. It cannot depend on anyone or anything and must not be subject to any limitations of time. From these two observations it follows that being must be utterly simple, that is, something that is not put together. Otherwise, it could be broken down or restored to something more original. The fourth link in Illustration 13 is most actual. Being in itself must be absolutely, and without limitations, realized. It does not stop at any stage of potentiality. Finally, therefore, it must be the most perfect of all, the superlative of the superlatives. Nothing can be added to it, nor can it be broken down into various parts. It is of necessity an absolute unity.

Of course, one can see how and why this being transcends our reality and our human situation, even our understanding. Our linguistic thinking allows us to construct an image like a beautiful symphony, with one note giving birth to the next, without any note replaced by another. One melody flows into the next in perfect harmony. Trying to change one note in this beautiful composition would destroy it. Just try changing the music of Mozart. George Bernard Shaw (1856–1950), the Anglo-Irish dramatist and music and theater critic, once said that Mozart's is the only music that would not sound out of place in the mouth of God. And Tchaikovsky (1840–1893), the Russian composer, loved Mozart as the musical Christ whose music is full of divine beauty.

Now, let us turn back to philosophy, which also can construct something like a wonderful, perfect harmony, one note after the other, one stone upon another.

In Segovia, Spain, there is an aqueduct that carries water through the valley and into the city. This aqueduct, more than two thousand years old, is composed of many stones, artistically arranged one on top of the other, but without any mortar to hold them together. The stones are held in place simply because they fit into and onto one another. If you were to push one or more stones out, the entire structure would collapse.

Supremely One	ALL IN ALL	All-Embracing
Most Perfect	Within all things but is not contained by them	Immense
Most Actual	Remaining unmoved, it imparts movement to all things	Immutable
Most Simple	Within all things and outside all things	Greatest
Eternal	Embraces and enters into all things that endure in time	Most Present
First	Origin and consummating end of all things	Last

Illustration 14: Chapter 5:7–8.

Being itself is compared here to an arch of an aqueduct.
The contrasts or extreme opposites maintain the tension needed to keep the arch standing.

So, like the arch, the Being who is "all in all" [1 Corinthians 15:28] is held together, so to speak, by contrasting tension. For entities like families, governments, nations, their goal of unity would then be reached by maintaining the contrasting tensions that could result in a lasting peace. Being in itself is the reason behind all that exists; it is "all in all" [1 Corinthians 15:28]. The closer we come to the goal of *The Journey*, the more we are entangled in contradictions, the more we wander aimlessly and blindly in the darkness. Philosophy is very closely related to real life, isn't it?

EXERCISES

• Select a piece of music—preferably classical music—and listen to it one or more times. Listen to the "arches of tension" which are most important for this piece, the tensions of the speed, the dynamic, the loudness, the melody and the interchange of the instruments. Try to be fully in the music.

• Draw an arch as we did in Illustration 14. Instead of using the words written there, write your own on the individual stones responding to the following questions: What is holding up, sustaining your life? Where are the contradictions, contrasts, tensions in you?

Tuesday

'To Be or Not to Be'

Bonaventure writes in chapters 5:5 and 6:2:

5.5 Therefore, think of the most pure being if you can,
and you will see that it cannot be thought of as something
received from another.
For this reason it is thought of as first in every sense
since it does not come into being from nothing,
nor does it come from some other being.
For what else could exist by itself
if pure being does not exist through and of itself?
Also you will understand this pure being to be totally lacking
in non-being,
and hence as having neither a beginning nor an ending,
but as eternal.
Also it appears to you to possess nothing else but being itself.
Hence it is in no sense composed, but is most simple.
It appears also to have nothing of potentiality
since whatever is potential in some way possesses something of
non-being.
Hence this being is supremely actual in the highest degree.
It appears also to have no defect, and therefore as most
perfect.
Finally it appears to have no diversity, and therefore it is
supremely one.
That being, therefore, which is pure being, simple being, and
absolute being
is the first, the eternal, the most simple, the most actual, the
most perfect,
and the supremely one being.

6.2. . . . (T)he supreme communicability of the good demands

necessarily that there be a Trinity of Father, Son
and Holy Spirit.

And in these persons, because of supreme goodness
it is necessary that there be supreme communicability.

And because of supreme communicability,
there must be consubstantiality;
and from supreme consubstantiality
there must be supreme conformability;
and from these there must be supreme co-equality;
and because of this there must be supreme co-eternity;
and from all of the above,
there must be supreme mutual intimacy
by which each is necessarily in the others
by reason of their supreme interpenetration,
and one acts with the others
in a total unity of substance, power, and activity
within the most blessed Trinity itself.

ANDRÉ

In this section, we are dealing with the convertibility of
being. If all the characteristics of the terms below were lined
up and set in contrast to each other, we would have to conclude that everything we can say about one word holds true
for the other. For example, "being" and "unity" are convertible or interchangeable. This holds true for the whole of the
sixth chapter. Everything that exists is good [Genesis 1:31]!
Everything that is must be good, true and beautiful, and vice
versa. Let us jot these ideas down in columns of opposites.

Being	↔	Non-being
↕		↕
Unity	↔	Division
↕		↕
Good	↔	Evil
↕		↕
Truth	↔	Lie
↕		↕
Beauty	↔	Deformity

Looking at the pairs of opposites, Bonaventure notes that it seems as if the left side is fleeing from the right side and vice versa. The terms and realities of the left column are interchangeable; they are *convertible*. So, too, the terms in the right column are *convertible* with each other. This is significant! The world is called into being, it is called to be one, in an ever closer union. And you, too, are called to be one, you as an individual. You are called to move from the right-hand column to the left. This movement, however, is not just a matter of your own energy and strength, but you can and must let yourself be drawn a bit.

The key to understanding how to cross the gap between the two columns is given to us by John the Baptist: "He must increase, but I must decrease" [John 3:30]. This sentence does more than simply mark the transition from the Old Testament to the New Testament. If the part of me that is a sinner, a liar, an evil person or a split personality can decrease, the divine can increase, start to grow and expand within me. Wherever I begin this process, the entire image and scene begins to turn upside down. Every potential within me is drawn toward realization or actualization of truth, toward the divine Being. Jesus' prayer remains valid, "that they may be one, as we are one" [John 17:11].

This process does not happen in some remote place, but in me and you, within each entire person. Seen in this manner, our desire for unity, goodness, love, truth and beauty is a fruit of the divine Being. Greater unity among people and races means that they are growing more into the divine Being. The English Franciscan Eric Doyle (1938–1984) saw the significance of the United Nations precisely in these terms and expressed this thought eloquently:

> Being and union are convertibles. In terms of this, the desire to create a planetary community through increased union among all people would be the product of evolution so far. The union achieved would be an increase of being. It is not too fanciful to suggest that the growing awareness of the oneness of humanity, the concern for others at the universal level, the peace movement and the longing for authentic community, are all in various ways the beginning of a planetary human community which, as an increase of union, is the product of evolution in the stage of humanization. This helps one to appreciate why Teilhard quoted the following words of J.B.S. Haldane with approval: "Now if the co-operation of some thousands of millions of cells in our brain can produce our consciousness, the idea becomes vastly more plausible that the co-operation of humanity, or some sections of it, may determine what Comte calls a Great Being."[1]

The evangelical counsels give us another example. Many

religious communities founded after the sixteenth century chose to live an active apostolic lifestyle. One might say that they were service-oriented. Action was given disproportionate priority. Today professional services have taken over some areas of ministry performed by these groups, and many of them are in a profound state of crisis. This approach was completely alien to Francis. For Francis, poverty meant he was in love with Lady Poverty (Christ); chastity meant he wanted to stand in solitude before God; obedience meant he wanted to be able to respond to God—to Being. These evangelical counsels as lived by men and women religious are meant to make visible and comprehensible what the divine Being means. Likewise, for couples living the sacrament of marriage, the invitation to being can be equally as healing and reconciling. Just to be, to be present to the other or to one's self is a blessing. From being-in-union can flow truth and beauty!

EXERCISES

• Choose one pair of opposites in the list above and look for images and scenes in your daily life that touch both sides. How did this situation develop? In which direction are you being drawn, and by what?

• Meditate on the ancient sequence for the mass of Pentecost, *Veni, Sancte Spiritus.* May the Spirit of God be with you and guide you more and more in the process of becoming more human and more divine.

NOTES

[1] Eric Doyle, *Song of Brotherhood and Sisterhood, op. cit.,* p. 141. J.B.S Haldane (1860–1936) was a British physiologist and philosophical writer.

Wednesday

OVERFLOWING GOODNESS

Bonaventure writes in chapter 6:1–3:

1. . . . Just as being itself is the foundational principle
and the name through which the essential attributes
of God and all other things come to be known,
so the good is the most basic foundation for our
contemplation of the emanations.

2. . . . For "the good is said to be self-diffusive."
The supreme good, therefore, is supremely self-diffusive.
But the highest diffusion does not exist
unless it is actual and intrinsic,
substantial and personal,
natural and voluntary,
free and necessary,
lacking nothing and perfect.
In the supreme good there must be from eternity
a production that is actual and consubstantial,
and a hypostasis[1] as noble as the producer,
and this is the case in production by way of generation and
spiration.
This is understood to mean that
what is of the eternal principle is eternally of the co-principle.
In this way there can be both a beloved and a co-beloved,
one generated and one spirated;
that is, Father, and Son, and Holy Spirit.
If this were not the case, it would not be the supreme good
since it would not be supremely self-diffusive,
for that diffusion in time which is seen in creation
is a mere point or a center
in comparison to the immensity of the eternal goodness.

Therefore it is possible to think of another greater diffusion;
namely, that sort of diffusion in which the one diffusing itself
communicates the whole of its substance and nature to the
other. . . .
Therefore, if, with the eye of your mind
you are able to reflect on the purity of that goodness
which is the pure act of the principle that in charity loves with
a love that is free,
and a love that is due,
and a love that is a combination of both,
which would be the fullest diffusion by way of nature and will
and which is found in the diffusion of the Word in which all
things are spoken
and the diffusion of the Gift in which all goods are given,
you will be able to see that the supreme communicability of
the good
demands necessarily that there be a Trinity of Father, Son and
Holy Spirit. . .
and from all of the above, there must be supreme mutual
intimacy
by which each is necessarily in the others
by reason of their supreme interpenetration,
and one acts with the others in a total unity of substance,
power, and activity
within the most blessed Trinity itself.

3. But as you contemplate these matters,
beware that you do not think that you can comprehend the
incomprehensible.
For you still have something to consider in these six
characteristics
that will lead the eye of our mind with great strength to a
stupor of admiration.
For here we find

the highest communicability together with the property of the
persons,
highest consubstantiality together with the plurality of
hypostases,[2]
highest conformability together with discrete personality,
highest co-equality together with order,
highest co-eternity together with emanation,
the highest intimacy together with mission.
Who would not be rapt in wonder at the thought of such
marvels?
But we know most certainly that all these things
are involved in the most blessed Trinity
if we raise our eyes to that super-excelling goodness.

ANDRÉ

That beyond which nothing greater can be thought continues to be the focus in chapter 6, which considers goodness
in itself. In this passage Bonaventure quotes Dionysius the
Areopagite who ultimately can find no better way of describing God than as goodness itself. Goodness must diffuse itself
and overflow. This is the fundamental divine principle.
Goodness cannot cut itself off nor can God be God in isolation. By its very nature goodness must flow beyond all limitations, much like a fountain pouring water from a higher
basin to a lower one, and so on. This is something that takes
place constantly, always in the present, here and now; it has
no beginning, nor will it ever end.

The most important times of our lives are marked by
some degree of flow and of letting go. In the beginning, a
mother shares everything with her child, from the flowing
waters of life to, after she has let go the child from her
womb, her nourishing milk. At the end of life, each of us has

to let flow from us all that we have been given—our loved
ones, our possessions, even life itself. We have to let go of it
and let it flow away. Our flowing tears also are part of this
process of letting go. And at times of crisis, we often waver,
weighing alternatives, in flux and unable to decide what to do.

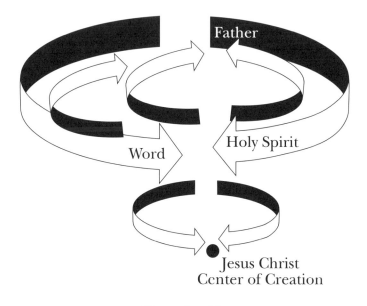

Illustration 15:
*The overflowing goodness of the Triune God. Everything flows
from the Father to the Word and to the Holy Spirit and vice versa.
This is a continuous process.*

Bonaventure uses the image of an overflowing fountain, continuously pouring out. He speaks of an eternal co-produc-
tion, a vibrant exchange, a cooperation between the Father,
Word and Holy Spirit within the Trinity. This image of God is
the greatest we humans can imagine. This philosophical-
theological concept of the Trinity belongs to the most mag-

nificent that the human mind could have produced.

Creation is not able to contain this great divine flow. Within this little dot—which represents the entire universe—there appears this even smaller point, the person of Jesus of Nazareth. In him the entire fullness of this process of overflowing goodness shines forth. In one person the entire mystery of life—its fullness in depth and height, length and breadth—is to be weighed and measured.[3]

This is the original gift, the inherited grace that the Catholic Church addresses in the mystery of Mary's Immaculate Conception. God's superabundance is without shame, precaution, limits, security and self-righteousness. With this as our point of departure, how positive everything would be. This is the message of another Franciscan, John of LaVerna (1259–1322).

John once addressed a numerous gathering of friars as follows:

> When I came to the Order, God favored me with this grace: to praise God for everyone and everything I saw therein. If I beheld large and beautiful churches belonging to the friars, or if in the friaries I saw spacious dormitories, refectories and infirmaries, I praised God. If I was aware that the friars were plentifully supplied with tunics and books and other alms from the divine mercy, in all this I praised God. And I was always at peace in my mind, judging that whatever good things had come to a religious or prelate or any secular person, they deserved them. And with this meditation I could keep silence and speak against no one.[4]

Francis believes that if in your zeal for what is good you are constantly upset and thinking the worst about everyone and everything, you are not living in peace. You are missing what is good and you are appropriating something that does not belong to you!

Peace is intimately linked to this experience of overflowing divine goodness. God's superabundance invites us to respond with an attitude of gratitude.

EXERCISES

• Go to your favorite place for meditation. Open your hands and place them with the palms up on your lap. Consciously breathe in and out; simply be aware of the coming and going of the breath of life.
• Sit beside a fountain, a spring or a river and silently watch the water flow.
• Go for a walk at night, if possible when the skies are clear and the stars fill the night. Look at the countless stars and let yourself be filled with wonder at the greatness of the universe.

NOTES

[1] See Note 1 for Friday of Week Three on page 173.

[2] *Ibid.*

[3] See Ephesians 3:16–19: "I pray that . . . Christ may dwell in your hearts through faith, as you are being rooted and grounded in love. I pray that you may have the power to comprehend, with all the saints, what is the breadth and length and height and depth, and to know the love of Christ that surpasses knowledge so that you may be filled with all the fullness of God."

[4] Thaddeus MacVicar, O.F.M. CAP., *Franciscan Spirituals and Capuchin Reform*, edited by Charles McCarron, O.F.M. CAP. (New York: Franciscan Institute Publications, 1986), pp. 16–17.

Thursday

'HOLD BACK NOTHING . . .'[1]

Bonaventure writes in chapter 6:2:

> . . . Therefore, if, with the eye of your mind you are able to reflect on the purity of that goodness which is the pure act of the principle that in charity loves with a love that is free, and a love that is due, and a love that is a combination of both, which would be the fullest diffusion by way of nature and will and which is found in the diffusion of the Word in which all things are spoken and the diffusion of the Gift in which all goods are given, you will be able to see that the supreme communicability of the good demands necessarily that there be a Trinity of Father, Son and Holy Spirit. . .

JOSEF

Francis and Clare were filled with this overflowing joy and gratitude. Several times Clare speaks of God, the "Father of mercies,"[2] "the Giver of grace" and "every good."[3] This spirited joy is a large reason for the attraction to the Franciscan lifestyle throughout the ages, even up to our own day. Life is not only a deadly serious business but also a blessing and part of the boundless, gratuitous gift of love. In this experience, the face of God is primarily that of mother. God is goodness, overflowing day after day, nourishing us and keeping us alive.

This experience is the foundation of what we can call Franciscan poverty. Francis and Clare wanted to live radically poorly, with no possessions. Our image of the overflowing fountain sheds light on the fact that this poor form of life was meant to proclaim and represent a principle of unlimited openness and receptivity. It should show the expropriation of everything that would block the divine flow of Being and Goodness. The sisters and brothers of Assisi were to have nothing of their own. This is what we find at the heart of *The Rule* each followed:

> Let the brothers not make anything their own, neither house nor place nor anything at all. As pilgrims and strangers in this world, serving the Lord in poverty and humility, let them go seeking alms with confidence, and they should not be ashamed because, for our sakes, our Lord made Himself poor in this world. This is that sublime height of most exalted poverty which has made you, my most beloved brothers, heirs and kings of the Kingdom of Heaven, poor in temporal things but exalted in virtue. Let this be your portion which leads into the land of the living.[4]

> Let the sisters not appropriate anything, neither a house nor a place nor anything at all; instead, as pilgrims and strangers in this world who serve the Lord in poverty and humility, let them confidently send for alms. . . . This is that summit of the highest poverty which has established you, my dearest sisters, heiresses and queens of the kingdom of heaven . . . Let this be your portion which leads into the land of the living. . . . Let each one confidently manifest her needs to the other. For if a mother loves and cherishes her child according to

the flesh, how much more diligently should a
sister love and cherish her sister according to
the Spirit. Those who are ill may lie on sacks
filled with straw and may use feather pillows
for their head; those who need woolen stock-
ings and quilts may use them.[5]

These central parts of these chapters at the heart of *The Rules*
of Francis and of Clare are identical. Each of them includes,
as well, the questions of communication among the sisters
and brothers and care of the sick.

If you want to hold something back for yourself, you
leave the mainstream of the All-Good and you become
bogged down! You end up isolated. In biblical terms, this
attitude of expropriation is best expressed in Paul's Letter to
the Philippians 2:1–11: "(Christ) who, though he was in the
form of God, / did not regard equality with God / as something to be exploited, / but emptied himself / taking the
form of a slave, / being born in human likeness" [2:6–7].

From the beginning of our lives it seems that avarice
and greed, envy and jealousy try to capture our heart, leaving us feeling disadvantaged or excluded. How often families
fight over inheritance! How many brothers and sisters have
become enemies because someone in the family feels they
have been treated unfairly. Do I ever feel that I am placed at
a disadvantage, injured by another?

The Franciscan view of sinfulness would focus more
on appropriation. We might say that for Francis and Clare
appropriation is sin at its worst.

The process of becoming whole and healthy proceeds through self-emptying, letting go, giving away. Against
this background I invite you to turn with me to what has

been called the Franciscan "sermon on the mount." In Francis' *Admonitions* we have a collection of twenty-eight brief sayings handed down through the centuries. Scholars say they are probably excerpts from talks Francis gave when the friars were gathered together. Almost all of them deal with the main theme of his life: expropriation, which begins where it seems to be the most difficult:

> For that person eats of the tree of the knowl-
> edge of good who makes his will his own and,
> in this way, exalts himself over the good things
> the Lord says and does in him.[6]

In regard to leadership in the fraternity Francis is very critical. He introduces a principle of rotation and strictly limited terms of office. The idea of not clinging to anything is very important to Francis:

> And if they are more upset at having their
> place over others taken away from them than
> at losing their position at their feet, the more
> they store up a money bag to the peril of their
> soul.[7]

In a self-critical way Francis warns us against appropriating the good:

> Therefore, it is a great shame for us, the ser-
> vants of God, that the saints have accom-
> plished great things and we want only to
> receive glory and honor by recounting them.[8]

Francis exhorts the theologians, preachers, scholars and all those who would like to be influential:

> Those people are put to death by the letter

who only wish to know the words alone, that they might be esteemed wiser than others and be able to acquire great riches to give to their relatives and friends.

And those religious are put to death by the letter who are not willing to follow the spirit of the divine letter but, instead, wish only to know the words and to interpret them for others.[9]

We can see quite clearly where Francis makes his point in the following admonition:

Therefore, whoever envies his brother the good that the Lord says or does in him incurs a sin of blasphemy because he envies the Most High Himself Who says and does every good thing.[10]

Nothing should displease a servant of God except sin. And no matter how another person may sin, if a servant of God becomes disturbed and angry because of this and not because of charity, he is storing up guilt for himself. That servant of God who does not become angry or disturbed at anyone lives correctly without anything of his own. Blessed is the one for whom nothing remains except for him *to return to Caesar what is Caesar's and to God what is God's*.[11]

A wonderful summary of Franciscan poverty can be found in *Admonitions*:

Blessed is that servant who no more exalts himself over the good the Lord says or does through him than over what He says or does through another. A person sins who wishes to receive more from his neighbor than what he wishes to give of himself to the Lord God.

Blessed is the servant who returns every good to the Lord God because whoever holds on to something for himself hides the money of his Lord God within himself.[12]

EXERCISES

• Reflect on the Letter to the Philippians 2:1-11. In the Greek original the word for "emptied himself" in verse 7 is ταπεινοσ (*tapeinos*). Try to find an image or picture—or create one for yourself—that expresses this word and the core of this Scripture passage. Looking at the first letter of the word in Greek above, perhaps Francis used the sign of the TAU to remember this idea.

• In the reflection above, seven of Saint Francis' *Admonitions* are cited regarding appropriation and expropriation. Read one, several or all of them slowly. What do these verses of wisdom say to you about appropriation in your own life? What do these verses of wisdom say to you about expropriation in your own life? Pray to the "Father of mercies," "the Giver of grace" and "every good" to teach you the wisdom of letting go.

NOTES

[1] *A Letter To the Entire Order*, in *Francis of Assisi: The Saint, op. cit.*, p. 118.

[2] Clare is fond of this expression for the Father taken from 2 Corinthians 1:3. See *The Testament* 58, in *Clare: Early Documents, op. cit.*, p. 60 and *The Blessing of Clare of Assisi* 12, *ibid.*, p. 82. Jean François Godet-Calogeras writes in *Clare of Assisi, op. cit.*, pp. 67–68: "Among the names that Clare uses for God, there is an expression that she borrowed from the Apostle Paul, which shows well how she came to recognize and to see God. God is 'the Father of mercies.' The father is the one who engenders life. But God, as

fully revealed by Jesus Christ, is a merciful God, a God full of mercy. What is mercy, *misericordia*? It means having a heart sensitive to suffering and sorrow. This, therefore, means that God is not a revenging or hostile God. But there is more, far more: the Latin word *misericordia*, corresponds in the Bible to a Hebrew notion of 'being a womb for someone.' To be merciful to someone means to be capable of taking that person into one's very entrails, having the entrails of a mother. The Father of mercies is a father-mother who, at one and the same time, engenders life and nourishes it, protects it, cares for it, helps it to grow. A masculine-feminine God who creates the Human in His/Her own image, male and female, at once strength and tenderness. Clare must have perceived all of that in the depths of her being."

[3] See *The Second Letter to Agnes of Prague* 3, in *Clare: Early Documents, op. cit.*, p. 40.

[4] *The Later Rule* VI:1–5, in *Francis of Assisi: The Saint, op. cit.*, p. 103.

[5] See *The Form of Life* VIII:15–17, in *Clare: Early Documents, op. cit.*, pp. 73-75.

[6] *The Admonitions* II:3, in *Francis of Assisi: The Saint, op. cit.*, p. 129.

[7] *The Admonitions* IV:3, *ibid.*, p. 130.

[8] *The Admonitions* VI:3, *ibid.*, p. 131.

[9] *The Admonitions* VII:2–3, *ibid.*, p. 132.

[10] *The Admonitions* VIII:3, *ibid.*, p. 132.

[11] *The Admonitions* XI:1–3, *ibid.*, p. 133.

[12] *The Admonitions* XVII:1-2 and XVIII:2, *ibid.*, p. 134.

Friday

A Balanced Life

Bonaventure writes in chapter 6:3, 6:

3. But as you contemplate these matters,
beware that you do not think that you can comprehend the
incomprehensible.
For you still have something to consider in these six
characteristics
that will lead the eye of our mind with great strength to a
stupor of admiration.
For here we find
the highest communicability together with the property of the
persons,
highest consubstantiality together with the plurality of
hypostases,[1]
highest conformability together with discrete personality,
highest co-equality together with order,
highest co-eternity together with emanation,
the highest intimacy together with mission. . . .

6. . . . (L)ook toward the Mercy Seat and be amazed
that in Christ there is personal union
together with a trinity of substances and a duality of natures.
And total harmony exists together with plurality of wills.
There is the mutual predication of God and humanity
together with a plurality of properties.
Co-adoration exists together with a plurality of rank;
co-exaltation over all things exists together with the plurality
of eminence;
and co-dominion exists together with a plurality of powers.

JOSEF

I would like to invite you to take a closer look at the possibilities and tensions of the way we humans live together. Franciscans throughout the ages have held that each member of a community—spouses, children, the young and the old, the sick and the well, the satisfied and the seekers—everyone is to be received as gift. We cannot look upon others as damaged goods, a burden or bother, or as a useless, superfluous crowd of people to be marginalized, locked up or cast aside. Each person, including you and me, emanates from the overflowing love of God, the All-good. I am able to accept myself because I am part of this immense mystery. I am gift to myself.

It sounds good, you're thinking, but something inside of you says that it is not so easy. There is so much brokenness within me and in my relationships with others. Just take a look at the family you live in now or the one in which you were raised.

What does it mean if a married couple constantly wants to be together? Will they be able to live like that for a long period of time? Isn't there the danger of their getting bogged down in some kind of symbiotic closeness? In my hospice work I meet couples who find it very difficult to face the death of their spouses. They never learned how to live apart from one another. They do not have any individual experience of joy and fulfillment. They have forgotten this freedom, and things begin to break down with the loss of their spouse. And how can the dying spouse leave in peace? A balance between being close and staying apart—Bonaventure speaks of "mission" here—is absolutely necessary for a balanced life. I believe that people occasionally try to escape such a confining relationship by developing a terminal illness. They see no other way out. There are psychologists who speak of the aim of illness or the advantage of dying. Is there no path other than death?

On the other hand, it frequently happens that people just separate. Each of them goes off to work and enjoys his or her own free time. But where is what Bonaventure calls their "mutual intimacy" or their unity? What are their common interests? How many families and couples separate because of this imbalance? They live as a kind of "dual solo."

From the example we have discussed above concerning mission and mutual intimacy, the fundamental ideas of the coincidence of opposites and the image of the overflowing goodness allow us to draw some conclusions about the ways we live together—whether in a family, in a religious congregation, in a circle of friends or even within the context of society. Through Illustration 16 (page 274) let us take a look at this wonderful image of God, the super-excellent All-good!

The poles or the opposite pairs need to be fully lived. When this or any wheel goes off balance, it is dangerous. Just as a wheel cannot function when either the spokes break or the tire is punctured, so, too, when one of the poles is ignored, imbalance is the result and the wheel cannot function as it should.

Another very interesting example emerges when we look at Illustration 16, at the opposite pair of Conformability-Distinct personality. How does a religious community or congregation appear to the public under these two opposites? How many problems there are simply concerning dress! In a religious community, "conformability" may support the value behind a community's decision to wear uniform religious garb. But the value of the "distinct personality" must be respected as well. For there are others who may struggle with such a decision but nevertheless accept it so that the "wheel may continue to function well, to turn."

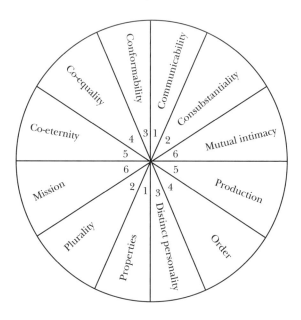

Illustration 16: Chapter 6:6.
Bonaventure brings together all the elements of the "wheel of Goodness itself." Each section supports the whole. If you diminish or take one away, you impair the whole. The numbered poles from the upper half are opposites of the numbered lower half.

Taking one final example, Bonaventure speaks of democratic ideas in the thirteenth century! For Bonaventure, "coequality" does not mean that everyone does the same thing or that everyone has the same say. "Order" implies that different areas of responsibility exist but, on the other hand, recognizes that they must not destroy the basic common level that exists. In a family, the parent is not the child. As human beings, they are equal, but from the viewpoint of order, their areas of responsibility differ. This is always a matter of a very sensitive balance.

Again, look at the poles of Communicability and Properties, which could be expressed as transparency and discretion. For Francis and Clare one expression is important in this context. The brothers and sisters should be more than brothers and sisters to one another; they should be caring mothers for one another.

> Let each one confidently make known his need to another that the other may discover what is needed and minister to him. Let each one love and care for his brother as a mother loves and cares for her son in those matters in which God has given him the grace. Let the one who does not eat not judge the one who does.[2]

Despite all the loving care and openness to one another, the free communication and the greatest transparency of thoughts and actions,[3] discretion and the protection of the personal sphere is always important. How much in our lives happens outside the awareness of others in our lives? Let us listen to Francis again:

> Blessed is the servant who loves and respects his brother as much when he is far away from him as when he is with him, and who would not say anything behind his back that he would not say with charity in his presence.[4]

Both freedom and commitment exist. Being and the All-good are the only axis around which everything can move, the only foundation upon which everything can be built. Of course, most of us will find it difficult to maintain the balance. However, there is no other way except through constant, patient and committed confrontation. So dare to accept the challenge with a grateful and joyful heart.

EXERCISES

• Look at Illustration 16 and try to find words or expressions to represent experiences in your life. Take a little time and try to note those situations. Where would you put yourself now on this wheel?

• Bring your whole life into a prayer of thanksgiving in the form of a litany. Think about your family and your friends and those who live around you. Try to thank God for all those who have gone before you and have accompanied you thus far. If you find it difficult to express gratitude for some of the people in your life, try harder to let the thanksgiving flow there as well.

NOTES

[1] See Note 1 for Friday of Week Three on page 173.

[2] *The Admonitions* IX:11–12, *ibid.*, p. 71.

[3] See *The Major Legend of St. Francis* 6:2, in *Francis of Assisi: The Founder, op. cit.,* pp. 570–571. Francis was not afraid to confess his own faults and mistakes, his own behavior in public. If he had enjoyed some leisure time or something good, he did not want to keep this to himself. He did not want to be looked upon as some kind of saint and give false impressions. Once he had his brothers drag him half naked and bound through the streets of the city of Assisi in order to confess his faults to the people.

[4] *The Admonitions* XXV, in *Francis of Assisi: The Saint, op. cit.*, p. 136.

Saturday

The Primacy of Christ

Bonaventure writes in chapters 4:2 and 6:5:

4:2. Just as when a person falls,
it is necessary to remain lying there
until someone comes near to reach out and raise the fallen
person up [Isaiah 24:20],
so our soul could not be raised up perfectly
from sensible realities to see itself and the eternal truth within
itself
unless the truth, assuming a human form in Christ,
should become a ladder to repair the first ladder that had
been broken in Adam.
So it is that, no matter how enlightened one might be
with the light of natural and acquired knowledge,
one cannot enter into oneself to *delight in the Lord*
[Psalms 36:4]
except by means of the mediation of Christ who says:
I am the door.
Those who enter through me shall be saved;
they shall go in and out and find pasture [John 10:9].
But we do not draw near to this door
unless we believe in Christ, hope in Christ, and love Christ.
If we wish, therefore, to re-enter into the enjoyment of truth as
into a paradise,
we must do so through faith in, hope in, and love for
the mediator between God and humanity, Jesus Christ
[1 Timothy 2:5],
who is like the *tree of life in the middle of paradise* [Genesis 2:9].

6:5. If you are that Cherub who contemplates the essential
attributes of God

and you marvel that the divine being is simultaneously
first and last,
eternal and most present,
most simple and greatest or uncircumscribed,
totally everywhere and contained nowhere,
most actual and never moved,
most perfect and having nothing superfluous nor deficient,
and nonetheless immense and infinite without end,
supremely one and yet all-embracing,
possessing in itself all things, all power, all truth, and all good,
then look toward the Mercy Seat and be astonished
that there the first principle is joined to the last,
God with humanity. . . .

JOSEF

I recently met a man and as I listened to him, I learned what was important to him. I realized that the most important value for him was his work as a craftsman. Secondly he prized his horse, and third on his list was his girlfriend. And, he added, that she was pregnant with his child.

What are your personal values? Your priorities? Risk putting this question to a person you know well. Try to make sure that the answers are not superficial confessions or the stately proclamation of high ideals. It should be rather a simple matter to state what is important in your life, to what do you devote your energy, what captivates you.

Are you familiar with the term "Christocentric"? What does it mean to you? Does it mean that everything revolves around Jesus Christ, or that everyone should be taken up with him? Is it a matter of more or less intense evangelization, like some preachers who will not let you go until you submit? Or does it mean that the whole world should be marked this way so that everyone would become a Christian?

All these interpretations can be associated with the word "Christocentric." However, it implies more that Jesus of Nazareth, the Christ, is at the center of life and at the center of the whole cosmos. He is life, as well as the way to life. This means that we should realize that he is alive, that we are alive in him, that we are saved through him and that we are at home in him. He is the energy of life; he is the powerful Word spoken by the creativity of a mighty God. Jesus Christ is creativity itself.

For theologians, "Christocentric" means that all thought, all analysis is focused on Jesus Christ, and from there everything else is enlightened and developed. He is the measure for everything. He is the turning point in time: B.C. (before Christ) and A.D. (*anno Domini*, or "in the year of our lord"). With him we start to count time in a new way. The world and all its mysteries are unwrapped in him. Pierre Teilhard de Chardin calls Christ the omega point toward which all things are moving, the whole of evolution, the history of our cosmos.[1] Christ is leading this world home—back to God! He is its inner stream, its balance and dynamism, its indestructible desire for growth and maturity. Against this backdrop the dramatic encounters between God and God's world can be seen in a new and different dimension.

The Bonaventurian scholar Ewert Cousins points out that this idea is expressed by the architecture of a Gothic cathedral:

> The movement of the stone as it reaches up toward heaven reflects the ascent through creation which Bonaventure describes in *The Soul's Journey,* and the light streaming through

the stained glass windows reflects the down-ward movement of God expressing himself in the variety of creatures and in his gifts of grace. The crossing of the axes of the design at the center, where the nave and the transepts intersect, suggests the cross of Christ, and together with the focus of the eye on the altar, suggests the convergence of all creation on Christ the center.[2]

Everything is gathered in Christ. Jesus Christ is the highest coincidence of opposites, the beginning and end, the alpha and omega, the masterpiece of all God's creation.

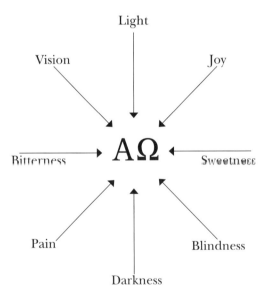

Illustration 17:
All contradictions and opposites within our life coincide in the very center, Jesus Christ, the Alpha and the Omega.

ANDRÉ

In his book *The Hidden Center,* Zachary Hayes, O.F.M., gives a detailed description of Bonaventure's Christology.[3] This is indeed Bonaventure's specialization. In *The Journey* and in his *Collations on the Six Days* he treats this topic at length. Each source has seven chapters and Christ is always dealt with in the central chapter because he is the center! Metaphysically, he is the second and middle person of the three divine persons. In terms of physics, he is the energetic center from which all power and grace flow. And this energy is never lost; it is only transformed.

Christ is the center of human history, too. He descends into the most profound depths of humiliation and despair in order to liberate creation. This is the measure and the center of a geometric circle. "For the center is lost in the circle, and it cannot be found except by two lines crossing each other at right angle."[4] The logic of the re-found center is the logic of love, of a love that is willing to share and give itself completely. This is the constructive divine love that counters the destructive diabolic logic, which says, according to Genesis 3:5, that our desire for happiness is fulfilled in rebellion against God's commandments. Ethically, we are invited to join Jesus in his descent and ascent, to imitate him and thereby become more and more like him. The juridical sciences deal with justice and reparation. Justice supports the beauty in our world because "it makes beautiful what had been deformed."[5] Christ, the archetype of all concrete forms of life found in this world and of all virtues, will make everything right, for he will judge the world in its final meeting with him. This means that in Christ all is seen in its true reality. And in this way we all will reach our eschatological goal through Christ Jesus.

I want to add an image from literature. Anna is a six-year-old girl living with her friend Fynn in London.[6] Anna thinks about God and the world in her own ways. One winter evening little Anna starts to play with a slide projector, with nothing but the beam of light. It takes her days to sort out her thoughts about this experience. When she puts her hand into the beam, she discovers a shadow on the wall. Then she asks Fynn for his help by holding a piece of paper near the wall to trace the shadow on to the paper and then cut it out. Again she reflects. Then she takes the cutout of the hand shadow and holds it horizontally into the beam of light. This time the shadow it casts on the wall is a line, and Fynn is asked to trace that line on a piece of paper and cut it out. Finally, Anna holds the thin line—the shadow of the shadow—into the projector's light lengthwise and, lo and behold, all that is left is the shadow of a dot on the wall. The result of Anna's long experiment is that everything—a hand, a dog, an elephant or a hat—can be reduced to this dot. Filled with excitement, she asks Fynn, "Now, can you see that everything is hidden in the dot? Can you see yourself? Can you see me?"

Christocentrism means that all of reality is concentrated and condensed in this one dot, Christ. In him all things find an explanation, in him all things are enlightened; they make sense and receive power.

EXERCISES

• Draw an empty circle on a piece of paper and put a dot in the middle of it. Continue to draw smaller concentric circles into the larger one and in those circles write what comes to mind when you ask yourself:

What is important in my life?

What are my priorities?

To what do I devote my energy?

Reflect on your value-picture in quiet and truth.

• Let the following words echo throughout your whole being: *Jesus Christ, Alpha and Omega, beginning and end*!

NOTES

[1] Teilhard de Chardin (1881–1955), a Jesuit priest and paleontologist, was concerned with the relationship between theology and the natural sciences. He succeeded especially in integrating the theory of evolution into a modern theological framework.

[2] Ewert Cousins, *Bonaventure, op. cit.*, pp. 16–18.

[3] Zachary Hayes, O.F.M., *The Hidden Center: Spirituality and Speculative Christology in St. Bonaventure* (New York: Franciscan Institute Publications, 1992).

[4] *The Works of Bonaventure, Collations on the Six Days* 1:24, *op. cit.*, 1970, Vol. V, p. 13.

[5] *Collations on the Six Days* 1:34, *ibid.*, p. 17.

[6] Fynn, *Mister God, This is Anna* (London: Collins Fount Paperbacks, 1987), pp. 126–131.

SUPERLUMINOUS
DARKNESS

Sunday

Diving into God's Darkness

Bonaventure writes in chapter 7:4-6:

4. . . . But this is mystical and very secret,
which *no one knows except one who receives it*
[Revelation 2:17].
And no one receives it except one who desires it.
And no one desires it but one who is penetrated to the very
marrow
with the fire of the Holy Spirit
whom Christ has sent into the world [Luke 12:49]. . . .

5. . . . (W)ith Dionysius we cry out to the Triune God:
"O Trinity,
essence beyond essence and God beyond all deities,
and supremely good Protector of the wisdom of Christians,
lead us to that which is supremely unknown,
to the light beyond lights and to the most sublime height of
mystical knowledge.
There new mysteries—
the new, absolute, and unchangeable mysteries of theology—
lie hidden in a superluminous darkness of a silence
that teaches secretly in the total obscurity
that is manifest above all manifestations
and a darkness in which all things shine forth;
a darkness which fills invisible intellects
with a full superabundance and splendor of invisible goods
that are above all good."

6. . . . Only one who loves this death can see God,
for it is absolutely true that
no one can see me and live [Exodus 33:20].
Let us die, then, and enter into this darkness.

Let us silence all our cares, our desires, and our imaginings.
Let us pass over with the crucified Christ *from this world to the Father*,
so that when the Father has been shown to us,
we may say with Philip: *It is enough for us. . . .*

ANDRÉ

Bonaventure at last is leading us to the place where all the opposites and contradictions suddenly and forcefully come together. In his original Latin text the language also expresses this idea by its very sound: the dominant grammatical form used throughout is the superlative of superlatives. An incredible tension builds up—the tension between the brightest brightness and the darkest abyss, paralyzed expectancy and most intimate encounter.

The summit of mystical communication, the peak of our *Journey* is reached. The pilgrims are entering a world of silence where everything is at rest, where direction and clarity are gone. And yet, these pilgrims are not lost. Their imagination and fantasy, as well as their desire and memories, are all eclipsed in this one instant. Their minds stop struggling. Logical and illogical conclusions are shut down. Feelings yield to transformation. Is this peace? Is darkness the goal of *The Journey*?

In scriptural imagery, darkness ordinarily connotes chaos, evil and death. Its other side would be light, order and the life of God who is good. Bonaventure uses two Latin terms for darkness—*tenebra* and *caligo*. *Tenebra* indicates the threatening and negative aspect of darkness as evil, while *caligo* represents the positive aspect, the summit where the contemplative person hangs with Christ on the cross. And with Christ the contemplative person then leaves this world to go to the Father.

JOSEF

When lights are turned out, we become confused because we are not able to see. Years ago I was hitchhiking in Scotland. Being a child of the mountains, I had to climb the highest peak in Scotland, Ben Nevis. However, my enthusiasm evaporated quickly. First of all, my backpack was extremely heavy. So, before long I hid it under some stones along the way. I found the path rather boring. There were stones, stones and more stones. The view was not spectacular, for I could neither see much above me nor below. And as I climbed, the clouds became thicker and thicker, until suddenly I noticed the path disappeared. I had reached the top, and was I ever disappointed. I could see almost nothing because of the dense fog. Having lost sight of the path, I roamed about on the top for almost an hour trying to find my way down. Anxiety was creeping in. The "cloud of unknowing"[1] had spread out over me.

It is precisely in the experience of the hiddenness and indescribability of God that we experience God. In the highest forms of contemplation, the light blinds a person to such a degree that the person is unable to see anything. The closer one gets to the peak, the less of the peak one can see. And yet, this is precisely when one is closer than ever to the truth. In one section of his *Collations on the Six Days,* Bonaventure reflects on why God's radiation, these "super-essential rays of divine darkness,"[2] blind us. Should they not rather enlighten us? He comes up with the following response:

This blinding, in fact, is supreme illumination, because it occurs in the loftiest part of the mind, beyond the range of investigation of the human intellect. Here, the intellect is in darkness, unable to seek since the matter transcends every power of search. There is inaccessible obscurity which yet enlightens those minds that have rid themselves of idle research.[3]

The late Eric Doyle makes a very helpful observation on this point:

When the moon is directly opposite the sun and at the furthest distance from it, it receives the least light, though it appears to receive the most, and we call it a full moon. Whereas during an eclipse the moon is as close to the sun as it can be and it receives more light then than at any other time, though it appears to receive none at all because we cannot see it. When the Church is engaged in contemplation it is enlightened to the highest degree by God's brilliance, and can be compared to the moon during an eclipse. In ecstasy a person is outside himself and lost in contemplation and at times can appear dead, whereas there is an abundance of life and grace present.[4]

JOSEF

Arnaldo, the confessor of Blessed Angela of Foligno, reported what she experienced on Holy Saturday, in the year 1294:

She was rapt in spirit and found herself in the sepulchre together with Christ. She saw Him, eyes closed, lying there dead . . . a most wonderful and indescribable odor emanated from His mouth as she kissed it . . . she then placed her cheek against Christ's own and He in turn placed His hand against her other cheek and pressed her closely to Him. And He then told her: "This is how I held you before I was laid in the tomb."[5]

Clare was in a trance-like state one Good Friday. The third witness at the hearings for the canonization process of Clare made the following statement:

The said witness also said the Lady Clare was so caught up in her contemplation that during the day of Good Friday, while thinking about the Passion of the Lord, she was almost insensible throughout that entire day and a large part of the following day.[6]

Is it so far from our experience? I don't think so. Neither did our thirteenth-century forebear, Jacopone da Todi:

In his last meditation on total self-surrender, the experience that in proto-baroque language he called self-annihilation, the charity of Jacopone opened like rose petals when the sun is high. When humanity lost all, all things became humanity's; in disowning all things one shared in their possession. In such moments the images and music that had previously played such a modest part in the lauds flowered, and Jacopone sang of "stone (that) will liquefy before Love lets me go," and of the transformation of the soul:

Just as a red-hot iron
Or forms touched by burning colors of dawn
Lose their original contours,
So does the soul immersed in You,
O Love.[7]

EXERCISES

• Start with Psalm 22:2–22. Think of a personal experience of darkness in your life. With each question below, pause to reflect for a few moments.

What feelings were linked to this darkness?
What were you thinking? Imagining?
What finally led you out of the darkness?

At the end of the exercise pray Psalm 22.

• Retire to a secluded place. Concentrate on your breathing. Light a candle or a fire, if possible in a dark place. Try to absorb this light as much as possible.

• If you are familiar with *The Phantom of the Opera* by Andrew Lloyd Webber, listen to the song "Music of the Night" that expresses so much of what we find in chapter 7.

NOTES

[1] This is the title of a book written originally by an anonymous author in the fourteenth century in England. It is a masterpiece in the Western contemplative-mystical tradition.

[2] "Super-essential" is translated here literally. It is one of many expressions beginning with the prefix "super" in chapter 7. Bonaventure is using the most extreme limits of language in order to express what God means to him. God's light cannot be exceeded in intensity, strength, brightness and warmth.

[3] *Collations on the Six Days* 20:11, *The Works of Bonaventure, op. cit.*, 1970, vol. V, p. 17.

[4] Doyle, *Song of Brotherhood and Sisterhood, op. cit.*, p. 93.

[5] Lachance, *op. cit.*, p. 227.

[6] The acts of the process of canonization are a valuable historical source for Clare's life. On November 24 and 28 in 1253, Bishop Bartholomew of Spoleto interviewed fifteen sisters at San Damiano, as well as some citizens of Assisi who knew Clare, who died on August 11, 1253. This excerpt is taken from *Clare: Early Documents, op. cit.*, p. 151.

[7] Jacopone da Todi, *The Lauds, op. cit.*, p. 61.

Monday

THE GOD OF SILENCE

Bonaventure writes in chapter 7:4, 5:

4. If this passing over is to be perfect,
all intellectual activities must be given up,
and our deepest and total affection must be directed to God
and transformed into God. . . .

5. Therefore since nature is helpless in this matter,
and even personal effort does not help much,
little importance should be given to investigation and
much to unction;
little to speech but much to interior joy;
little to words or writing and all to the gift of God,
namely the Holy Spirit;
little or no importance should be given to the creature
but all to the creative essence,
the Father and the Son and the Holy Spirit. . . .

ANDRÉ

In this last chapter of Bonaventure's *Journey*, I want to speak about a type of theology that offers a way to talk about God considering the limitations of our thought, expression and language. I want to consider what has been called apophatic or negative theology. Doing so is a bit awkward because the only part we really can express is that which we cannot express.

The theological language of the mystics was frequently an attempt to describe unspeakable encounters. Can one really find words to express the mysteries of our life? The German philosopher Ludwig Wittgenstein (1889–1951)

put it this way: "One must be silent concerning that which
you cannot talk about."[1] This silence is a different kind of
silence than we experience when we try to explain, for
instance, how a just and loving God could allow the immense
suffering following the attack on the World Trade Center of
September 11, 2001, in New York. In apophatic theology,
however, we are dealing with a God who is entirely different,
who is far beyond our verbal possibilities of expression. This
God completely escapes our grasp and our attempts to
understand. What can we mortal beings in time say about
that which is beyond time? We can only make the statement
that this Being is not time.

JOSEF

Theology, therefore, in its proper meaning is not only that
which we know or are able to affirm about God, but also is a
knowledge of God by means of sharing life, of communion
and contemplation. Dionysius said that cataphatic or symbolic theology deals with what we can affirm about God.
Karl-Dieter Ulke, a professor of philosophy in Munich, says:

> God is clear and final. God is expressionless
> and naked. However, we have accepted God
> and made of God something that can be
> shown and demonstrated. For centuries and
> millennia we have been forcing God into well-
> tailored but ill-fitting layers of clothing of
> words and thoughts. With those costumes we
> tried to cover God's nakedness rather than
> accepting it. We have dressed God up,
> wrapped God up in choice fabric of excellent
> design. Then like connoisseurs of clothing, we
> look at the many layers of the unknown and

> unknowable God. An incredible feat of the
> theological clothing designers of the ages![2]

Within the theological tradition we also find the other side
of the coin. Apophatic theology deals with theologians'
growing deficiency of answers and clear insights. It leads us
into the silence that spreads in and around us the closer we
draw near to God. Max Picard (1888–1965), German medical doctor and writer, used eloquent images in writing about
silence:

> Speech came out of silence, out of the fullness
> of silence. The fullness of silence would have
> exploded if it had not been able to flow out
> into speech. . . . Silence reveals itself in a thou-
> sand inexpressible forms: in the quiet of
> dawn, in the noiseless aspiration of trees
> towards the sky, in the stealthy descent of
> night, in the silent changing of the seasons, in
> the falling moonlight, trickling down into the
> night like a rain of silence, but above all in the
> silence of the inward soul—all these forms of
> silence are nameless. . . . Speech is therefore
> opposed to silence, but not as an enemy; it is
> only the other side, the reverse of silence. . . .
> Real speech is in fact nothing but the reso-
> nance of silence.[3]

Are we able to express anything at all without this silence?
What do we really know?

> Eric Doyle writes:

> Without some imaginative power and a touch
> of artistic talent, it is difficult to grasp even
> vaguely the significance and to appreciate

even remotely the beauty of these staggering figures about our galaxy: it is 80,000 to 100,000 light years across and our solar system is 27,000 light years from its center. To get something of the impact of these figures we need only recall that light travels in a vacuum at a speed of 186,000 miles per second. A distance therefore of 186,000 miles = 1 light second; so 186,000 x 60 x 60 x 24 x 365 = 1 light year (= nearly 6 million million miles). Our galaxy is about 16,000 light years thick at the center and 3,000 light years thick at the position of our sun.[4]

When looking at the immensity of God, how ridiculous are our scientific expressions of the immensity of the cosmos! God's reality is endlessly ungraspable and yet always perceivable.

Again Max Picard writes:

What many preachers say about the Mystery of God is often lifeless and therefore ineffectual. What they say comes only from words jumbled up with many thousands of other words. It does not come from silence. But it is in silence that the first meeting between (humanity) and the Mystery of God is accomplished, and from silence the word also receives the power to become extraordinary as the Mystery of God is extraordinary. . . . Word and silence are one in God. Just as language constitutes the nature of (humanity), so silence is the nature of God.[5]

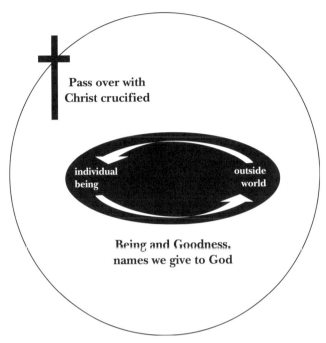

Illustration 18: Summary of chapters 1 to 7.

The inner circle describes chapters 1 to 4—all our limited experience in creation. The outer circle symbolizes the realm of our thoughts (the most we can think of) and imagination (the most beautiful, powerful and wholesome that we can imagine). This is how we name our God. The blank paper beyond the two circles represents the summit of mystical communication. Bonaventure describes this space of "transformed affection" with expressions such as "death," "silence," "the height of mystical knowledge," "desert," "superluminous darkness," "Sabbath of rest" [7:5–6].

There is a necessity for us to become silent in order to be able to hear the God of silence. Meister Eckhart (c. 1260–1327), the great Dominican philosopher and spiritual master of Western mysticism, states, "Mark that anyone who wishes to hear God speaking must become deaf and inattentive to others . . . . Therefore, be deaf that you may hear."[6]

A final note from Karl Rahner (1904–1984) on this unspeakable divine mystery. Although he had published hundreds of scientific papers and theological discussions, in his later years he became very simple and unassuming:

> Satan: the one who does not love. This definition is correct and reveals the essence of damnation. In this state a person does not love, and wants to go on not loving forever. This person seeks happiness in the dispensation from being lovingly drawn into the incomprehensibility of God. . . . For the one who loves and knows what love is, the one who lives without love is damned . . . . More and more we notice that all our knowledge is nothing more than the path into incomprehensibility. The true essence of knowledge is love. In love knowledge becomes ecstatic, and (the human person) freely lets (him/herself) be lost in this incomprehensibility.[7]

EXERCISES

• Choose a painting of a crucifixion scene or stand in front of a crucifix. Simply try to look Jesus in the eye and remain silent.

• Choose a song you like to sing or listen to. Let the melody run through you for a while. Forget the words as you hum, dance or play with the tune.

NOTES

[1] Ludwig Wittgenstein, *Tractatus Logico-philosophicus* (London: 1960), p. 188.

[2] Karl-Dieter Ulke, *Das Fragment. Meditationen über Mensch und Sprache (The Fragment. Meditations on Humanity and Language)* (Wien: Passagen Verlag, 1997), p. 186. Authors' translation.

[3] Max Picard, *The World of Silence* (Washington, D.C.: Regnery Gateway, Inc., 1988), pp. 24–27.

[4] Doyle, *Song of Brotherhood and Sisterhood, op.cit.*, p. 95.

[5] Picard, *op. cit.*, pp. 228–229.

[6] *Meister Eckhart: The Essential Sermons, Commentaries, Treatises, and Defense*, translation and introduction by E. Colledge and B. McGinn (New York: Paulist Press, 1981), p. 114.

[7] Karl Rahner, *Wagnis des Christen (The Risk of Being a Christian)* (Freiburg, Germany: Herder Verlag, 1975), p. 79. Authors' translation.

Tuesday

PASS OVER

Bonaventure writes in chapter 7:1, 5:

1. We have covered these six meditations,
comparing them to the six steps
by which one ascends to the throne of the true Solomon
where we arrive at peace.
It is here that the true person of peace rests
in the quiet of the mind as in an interior Jerusalem.
They are also compared to the six wings of the Seraphim
by which the mind of the truly contemplative person
is filled with the light of heavenly wisdom and can come to
soar on high.
They are also like the first six days
during which the mind needed to be trained
so as to finally arrive at the Sabbath of rest. . . .

5. . . . But to the friend to whom this was written we can say
with Dionysius:
"In this matter of mystical visions, my friend, being
strengthened for your journey,
leave behind the world of the senses and of intellectual
operations,
all visible and all invisible things,
and everything that exists or does not exist,
and in this state of unknowing,
allow yourself to be drawn back into unity with that One
who is above all essence and knowledge in as far as that is
possible.
Thus, leaving all things and freed from all things,
in a total and absolute ecstasy of a mind that has been
liberated,

transcending your self and all things,
you shall rise up beyond to the superessential radiance of the
divine darkness."

JOSEF

From the very moment of our birth we are faced with the fact of life's central task, namely, that of letting go. Life itself is marked by a continuous waxing and waning, receiving and giving, birthing and dying. The one who does not let go of what cannot be kept becomes bogged down and cannot keep pace with life. Life's contradiction, therefore, does not lie in death, but in this desire to hold on to what is passing away. Just as the sands of the hourglass flow without interruption unless the hourglass is broken or turned on its side, there is no life without the experience of loss. Even the very process of birth requires letting go, losing the warm, sheltered, familiar environment and being literally thrust into a world which we know only through the muffled sounds that have reached our ears. Why does this have to happen? It seems like such a nice place to be, so why would we ever want to leave the womb? Yet, we all know that it is a matter of our vival for both the mother and child. Holding on could mean death for both!

The end of life is no different. Once again we must go through life's normal process of transition, of letting go. However, we must ask ourselves a simple question about the place to which we are heading: are we any more capable of imagining the afterlife than the unborn child can picture what living in this world will be like? Don't we have only vague ideas about this next life? Wouldn't we rather stay right where we are, where everything is familiar and we are surrounded by the things and people we love?

One central task and challenge of life from beginning to end seems to be letting go, although creating, accepting and receiving have their place as well! Only by letting go can a person receive totally what is coming to them. Only in letting go are we able trustingly to open our hearts wide to the gift of the new moment.

ANDRÉ

If the experience of peace is your goal, you will achieve it only by accepting this complex, emotional and challenging truth of life. Bonaventure does not come up with a simple, superficial solution. Peace still is, and always will be, a goal for which we reach out and pray. Peace will never be something like a simple fairy-tale ending, where everyone lives happily ever after.

The last chapter of this *Journey* is actually a prayer of acceptance of our human condition. The author, who accepted life as it was, was filled with peace, and peace in the real sense of the word. Nothing had changed for Bonaventure; neither his external situation, his personality, his religious family, nor his individual and social setting. All were exactly the same as before, yet he was able to experience peace.

Anthony de Mello tells the following story:

> The Master was known to side with the revolutionaries, even at the risk of incurring the displeasure of the government. When someone asked him why he himself did not actively plunge into social revolution, he replied with this enigmatic proverb:
>
> "Sitting quietly
> doing nothing.

> Spring comes
> and the grass grows."[1]

JOSEF

Once again we have come full-circle. The person who truly knows that everything flows from God who holds nothing back is able to move beyond even the most meaningful and most basic needs, plans and projects. Each of us continues to experience fear of missing something or failing to do something or feeling guilty about something. But isn't this some kind of heresy and not in conformity with what we believe? If each of us could let go of not only all that is behind us, but also of all that still lies before us, then we truly would be able to live! Oh, if only we could let go of all because the One has taught us to let go!

Again the philosopher Karl-Dieter Ulke writes:

> Reality itself, that is being itself, is both time-less and image-less. Therefore it is inaccessi-ble. Let us sever the illusion of reaching being itself! But what kind of knife do we need to make the necessary cut? And what does it take to once again make time the most important boundary? What courage does one need to let silence flow into this wound, into this torn, open abyss? What strength, what concentra-tion, and endurance does it take to bear the total soundlessness of this silence? And even more: to increase this silence in a stance of expectancy justified by nothing, grounded on nothing, reasoned by nothing?[2]

The philosopher is leading us to a radical way of letting go. Even that which we expect or hope for is situated in the midst of emptiness, kenosis. Bonaventure knows what he is talking about by urging the reader to leave everything behind and just to be there in total openness, ready to pass over with Christ, fully trusting his guidance.

EXERCISES

- Read Mark 6:45–52. The setting for this narrative is the archetype of anxiety: darkness, in the middle of a huge lake, a small boat, a storm brewing and even a ghost appearing! And the ghost addresses the fearful disciples in verse 50:

  Take heart, it is I; do not be afraid!

  Are we any different from Jesus' friends in the boat?

  Mark depicts them as stubborn and full of fear.

  What makes you anxious?

  What is it you do not want to lose?

- Take some time in solitude with the words of the Swiss hermit and peace-maker, Nicholas of Flue (1417–1487):

  God, take from me everything that hinders
  me from reaching you.
  God, give me everything that supports my
  reaching you.
  God, strip me of myself and hand me over
  completely to you.[3]

NOTES

[1] De Mello, *op. cit.*, p. 85.

[2] Ulke, *op. cit.*, p. 183. Authors' translation.

[3] *Das Enneagramm der Weisheit: Spirituelle Schätze aus drei Jahrtausenden (The Enneagram's Wisdom: Spiritual Treasures from Three Millennia)*, edited by Marion Küstenmacher (Munich, Germany: Claudius Verlag, 1996), p. 272. Authors' translation.

Wednesday

SURRENDER

Bonaventure writes in chapter 7:6:

Now if you ask how all these things are to come about,

ask grace, not doctrine;

desire, not intellect;

the groaning of prayer and not studious reading;

the Spouse not the teacher;

God, not a human being;

darkness not clarity;

not light, but the fire that inflames totally and carries one
into God

through spiritual fervor and with the most burning affections.

It is God alone who is this fire,

and God's *furnace is in Jerusalem* [Isaiah 31:9].

And it is Christ who starts the fire with the white flame of his
most intense passion.

Only that person who says:

My soul chooses hanging, and my bones, death [Job 7:15]

can truly embrace this fire.

Only one who loves this death can see God,

for it is absolutely true that *no one can see me and live*
[Exodus 33:20].

Let us die, then, and enter into this darkness.

Let us silence all our cares, our desires, and our imaginings.

Let us pass over with the crucified Christ *from this world to the
Father,*

so that when the Father has been shown to us,

we may say with Philip:

It is enough for us.

Let us hear with Paul:

My grace is sufficient for you

[John 13:1; 14:8; 2 Corinthians 12:9];
and let us exult with David, saying:
My flesh and my heart waste away;
you are the God of my heart,
and the God that is my portion forever.
Blessed be the Lord forever,
and let all the people say:
let it be, let it be.
Amen
[Psalms 73:26; 106:48].

ANDRÉ

Have you ever climbed up to a high-diving board to jump into a swimming pool? Have you ever leaped off a rock or swung on a vine from the shore into the middle of a river? Perhaps you did so to impress your friends or prove to them—and to yourself—just how brave you are! With a combination of courage and desperation, you took that plunge or let go of the vine, entrusting your body to the air. Surrendering yourself to the air? Yes, letting yourself fall into the arms of the wind, falling, falling, falling! And who is there to catch you? How much courage does it take for you to do this? Just enough, it seems, to jump off solid ground and let yourself sail. This is the power, the strength of surrender. If you really look at the process, you are surrendering yourself to an air current, to another power that draws and leads you.

How can you even dare to surrender? Who is drawing you? Where are you going?

Did you ever try to make bread? All it takes is some milk, salt, flour, yeast, water and much kneading. All the individual ingredients have to surrender to the whole, to the new creation. They have to let themselves go. They have to die and let go of everything they have. What a miracle flows from that process! The individual elements fuse together, letting go of their own form and thus, are transformed into a new creation. They meld into one another. If the ingredients did not yield to one another, nothing would happen. Everything would remain the same. And the miracle of bread would not happen!

Surrendering is not easy, not something we sing and dance about. It is usually accompanied by anxiety, insecurity, disorientation, sometimes even by panic. It is a question of losing control, of letting go of our plans, and all our ways of understanding. Darkness and silence take over. A deep abyss looms before us.

JOSEF

Unfortunately the term "surrender" has been misused frequently because a significant dimension of this issue is letting go of power and control. How many religious fanatics have surrendered—and still do—to their distorted ideas of God, church and religion and blindly followed their leaders? Critical reflection and responsible action were and are left behind.

Looking at the entire *Journey* Bonaventure shares with us, I would like to emphasize that surrender must always be examined carefully.[1] Blind trust and surrender have their time. For Bonaventure they are the summit of a long, arduous climb, the final lesson of the school of spiritual life. The first surrender we are challenged to make is to surrender to our very human condition and existence—the way we are and the way we live with our limitations and complexities.

This is how we were created! If you stand up and spread your arms out wide, you realize we were created cruciform! This cross—ourselves—first must be embraced, and other crosses as well. The various forms of injustice and poverty, misery and anxiety, confusion and violence all demand our surrender before we can soar to other levels. Surrender, as it is explained in chapter 7, has to be integrated into the ups and downs of all the chapters. This *Journey* is not simply a one-way road leading us ultimately to a heaven devoid of people and Mother Earth!

In this last chapter, Bonaventure also uses the language of death. The image he uses is that of the tomb in which you lie next to the crucified Christ. Quite often in our desperate attempts to avoid death, we walk the most sure way toward death itself. Whereas by learning to die by stripping ourselves through surrender, we wait with Christ in the tomb. You lie there in waiting, waiting to be awakened, to rise to new life.

In conclusion, I would like to recall Francis of Assisi and his dramatic death. Francis sees death as an encounter with his "sister" who wants to teach him about the ultimate letting go and surrender. Are we, too, able to respond to Sister Death's invitation?

> . . . Knowing that *the time* of his death was *close at hand,* (Francis) called to him two brothers, his special sons, and told them to sing *The Praises of the Lord* with a loud voice and joyful spirit, rejoicing at his approaching death, or rather at the life that was so near. He himself, as best he could, broke into that psalm of David: *With a loud voice I cried to the Lord; with a*

loud voice I beseeched the Lord.

There was a brother there whom the holy man loved with great affection. Seeing what was happening and realizing the saint was nearing the end, he grew very concerned about all the brothers and said: "Oh, kind father, your sons will now be *without a father*, and will be deprived *of the true light* of their eyes! Remember the orphans you are leaving behind; forgive all their faults, and gladden them all, whether present or absent, with your holy blessing." The holy man answered: "See, my son, I am being called by God. I forgive all my brothers, present and absent, all their faults and offenses, and I absolve them insofar as I am able. When you give them this message, bless them all for me."

Then he ordered the book of the Gospels to be brought in. He asked that the Gospel according to John be read to him, starting with the passage that begins: *Six days before the Passover*, Jesus, knowing that the hour had come for him to pass from this world to the Father. . . . Then he told them to cover him with sackcloth and to sprinkle him with ashes, as he was soon to become *dust and ashes. Many* brothers *gathered* there, for whom *he* was both father and *leader*. They stood there reverently, all awaiting his blessed *departure* and happy *end*. And then that most holy soul was released from the flesh, and as it was absorbed into the abyss of light, his body *fell asleep in the Lord.* One of his brothers and followers, a man of some fame . . . saw the soul of the most holy

> father *rise straight to heaven over many waters.* It
> was *like a star* but as big as the moon, with *the*
> *brilliance of the sun,* and *carried up* upon *a small*
> *white cloud.*[2]

EXERCISES

- The next time you prepare a meal, when you have gathered together and prepared the ingredients needed, pause
  to reflect on the individual ingredients yielding to one
  another. Enjoy the new creation that emerges from the surrender of all the ingredients.

- Try to do something wholeheartedly, surrendering yourself
  entirely to it. Be conscious of what you are doing, and concentrate on it. This, too, is a form of surrender. It is not
  important what you choose to do, but that you devote your
  entire self to it.

NOTES

[1] See Tuesday of Week Three, "Do You Get It?" pp. 147–152.

[2] *The Life of Saint Francis* by Thomas of Celano VIII:109–110, in *Francis of Assisi: The Saint, op. cit.,* pp. 277–278.

Thursday

The Burning Love of the Crucified

Bonaventure writes in the Prologue 3 and in chapter 7:1, 2:

P:3. For those six wings can well be understood as symbols
of six levels of uplifting illuminations
through which the soul is prepared, as it were by certain stages
or steps,
to pass over to peace through the ecstatic rapture of Christian
wisdom.
There is no other way but through the most burning love of
the Crucified.
It was that sort of love which lifted Paul into the *third heaven*
and transformed him into Christ to such a degree that he
could say:
With Christ I am nailed to the cross.
It is now no longer I that live,
but Christ lives in me [2 Corinthians 12:2; Galatians 2:20].
This sort of love so absorbed the mind of Francis also
that his spirit became apparent in his flesh;
and for two years prior to his death,
he carried the holy marks of the passion in his body.
The image of the six wings of the Seraph, therefore,
is a symbol of six stages of illumination
which begin with creatures and lead to God
to whom no one has access properly except through the
Crucified.
For anyone *who does not enter by that door, but climbs up another*
way, is a thief and a robber.
But anyone who enters by that door will go in and out,
and will find pastures [John 10:1; 10:9].
For this reason, in Revelation John writes:
Blessed are those who wash their robes in the blood of the Lamb

for they are nourished at the tree of life
and they may enter the city through the gates [Revelation 22:14].
This means that no one can enter into the heavenly Jerusalem
by means of contemplation
without entering through the blood of the Lamb as through a
door. . . .

7:1. . . . And in this passage, Christ is the way and the door
[John 14:6; 10:7].
Christ is the ladder and the vehicle,
like the Mercy Seat placed above the ark of God
and *the mystery that has been hidden from all eternity*
[Exodus 25:20; Ephesians 3:9].

7:2. Anyone who turns fully to face this Mercy-Seat
with faith, hope, and love, devotion, admiration, joy,
appreciation, praise and rejoicing, will behold Christ hanging
on the Cross.
Such a person celebrates the Pasch, that is, the Passover, with
Christ.
So, using the rod of the Cross this person can pass over the
Red Sea [Exodus 14:16],
moving from Egypt into the desert
where the *hidden manna* [Exodus 16; Revelation 2:17]
will be tasted.
This person may then rest with Christ in the tomb,
as one dead to the outer world,
yet experiencing, in as far as possible in this pilgrim state,
what was said on the cross to the thief who was hanging there
with Christ:
This day you will be with me in Paradise [Luke 23:43].

JOSEF

Bonaventure knows of what he writes when he mentions

burning and the cross. Burning is not a pleasant experience. Although a discomfort, it is, nevertheless, also a glowing passion. Burning in this latter sense is totally different from scientific objectivity, critical observation, objective knowledge.

Bonaventure was a theologian and university professor by trade, and yet he loved with all his might. He fell in love, was deeply touched by and fascinated with the person of Francis of Assisi. He was so thoroughly captivated that his glowing passion and energy compelled him to address publicly some serious problems threatening the young Franciscan movement. He wanted to solve these problems immediately. His first two years as minister of the whole fraternity almost led him to burnout. He paid the price with his life's blood; he seemed deeply hurt. In spite of a heavy spirit, he did not run away, resign his office, or become proud, cynical or stubborn. He entered into himself and confronted the enormous tension in his life. He reached out to embrace the cross that was placed before him. He delved deeper into his ongoing passionate search for how to live the Franciscan life. The written witness of Bonaventure's withdrawal to LaVerna we find in this very book of *The Journey of the Human Person into God.*

Now, at the end of our *Journey* we have come full circle back to the reality we noted as key to understanding the Prologue, namely, deep restlessness and the desire for peace. And the way to peace is not so much like a stroll through a garden, but more like a difficult trek. It is a journey that demands a great deal of endurance and patience, but reveals itself as filled with surprise and tension.

How many crosses are there in human lives? A brief excerpt from my hospice diary may serve as an illustration: I am visiting an eighty-four-year-old man, unconscious and restless in his bed, constantly turning from side to side. The doctor tells me the end is near. His cancer has metastasized throughout his body. The neighbors, who opened the door to let me in, tell me a bit about the patient's life. For fifty years he and his wife had lived together in this same place. This man had treated his wife terribly, especially when he was drunk. He had beaten her frequently and their son often ran to the neighbors' apartment seeking refuge. He became like a son to them. And when suddenly the ailing man's wife had died the previous year, the bereaved widower fell into a deep depression, accusing himself of all kinds of mistreatment of his wife, ultimately losing his mind. The neighbors found him on the stairs, sobbing and shouting that he wanted to go home, that he wanted his wife!

I was touched by the many unresolved issues in the dying man's life. And yet, he wanted peace and reconciliation. Unfortunately, it was impossible to engage him in conversation. And he was alone since his only son had left on a five-hundred-mile holiday journey to Sweden just a few days before. He obviously had a very poor relationship with his father.

Then the neighbor took me to his own apartment and pointed to the cross in his living room. In his younger days, he says, he had one consuming dream: he wanted to buy a large, powerful motorboat. He worked hard, at least sixteen hours a day. Finally, at the age of forty he was able to buy the dream boat, but got to use it only once. A heart attack awakened him from his dream, and he had to live with the threat of death. I saw very clearly how this man, confronted with his dying neighbor, was struggling with the meaning of his own life. It didn't make any sense to him. Does God really love him? Is God really good? I planned to return the next day, but the patient had died.

ANDRÉ

Yes, there are many meaningless and desperate situations in our lives. Bonaventure says: "There is no other way but through the most burning love of the Crucified." The path to peace and happiness in my life does not lead me away from tension and darkness of my heart, my life. This path leads me right into those very situations where I am torn and burned. This path leads me into the valley of death and right up to the walls of an impenetrable fog. Walking this journey, I try to hang on to Jesus in the confusion of my love and in my great desire. I cling to the Jesus who traveled this way before me, and serves as my model. This is what makes me a Christian. This is the *ars vivendi et moriendi*, the art of Christian living and Christian dying.

Reading the signposts Bonaventure has given us these past forty days all along *The Journey*, we are left at the juncture of the passing over. It is here that we pass over into "super-luminous darkness, the silence, the desert, death, the Sabbath of rest, the height of mystical knowledge." We make this pass over burning intensely with love for the Crucified who completed *The Journey*. We conclude with Bonaventure's haunting appeal (7:6):

> Let us pass over with the crucified Christ *from this world to the Father*, so that when the Father has been shown to us, we may say: . . . *It is enough for us*. Let us hear: . . . *My grace is sufficient for you*; and let us exult . . . saying: *My*

flesh and my heart waste away; you are the God of
my heart, and the God that is my portion forever.
Blessed be the Lord forever, and let all . . . say:
let it be, let it be. Amen.

EXERCISES

• Describe the Stations of the Cross of your own life. When or how did someone or something nail you to a cross? When were you stretched out on the cross, torn between life and death? Where did you sweat blood in your life?

• Meditate on the Book of Revelation 22:1–2:

> Then the angel showed me the river of the
> water of life, bright as crystal, flowing from the
> throne of God and of the Lamb through the
> middle of the street of the city. On either side
> of the river, is the tree of life with its twelve
> kinds of fruit, producing its fruit each month;
> and the leaves of the tree are for the healing
> of the nations.

Has the cross in your life become a "tree of life"? Or did you break down beneath your cross?

Part Three

JOURNEYING WITH OTHERS

Guide for Group Meetings

INTRODUCTION

Like Francis and Clare, who did not want to be alone when withdrawing into solitude,[1] we recommend making *The Journey* together with others, engaging in these reflections and exercises in home groups, church groups or community groups.

We suggest that the leader or team prepare by reading beforehand the section under consideration. An overall plan could be:

- an introductory meeting
- four weekly meetings
- one final meeting

Each participant would need a copy of the original text of *The Journey* as found at the back of this book, as well as the daily reflections and exercises. In addition a common songbook would enhance each session.

For a regular rhythm of the group gatherings, we suggest the following structure:

Welcome

A. Introduction
- Song or physical exercise or dance.
- Prayer (formal and/or spontaneous).
- Begin by asking:
    Any comments or questions regarding the content of last week's meeting?

B. Reflection
- Leader introduces the theme of the day.
- Reading (from the original text of *The Journey*).
- Silence (3 minutes).

C. Exercise
 • Leader explains the exercise (1–2 minutes).
 • Participants do the exercise (20 minutes).
 • Brief pause and/or a song.

D. Group Sharing (15–20 minutes)
> If the gathering is small enough, sharing could be done by the whole group together. Larger groups could be split into smaller sub-groups, and the leader may facilitate feedback from each of them. In group sharing, participants should be free to speak or to listen, focusing on personal experience rather than theoretical discussion, avoiding domination by any one person.

E. Closing
 • Leader gives an overview on the daily reflections and exercises for the coming week.
 • Response to logistical questions concerning the next meeting.
 • Closing song and/or prayer and/or dance.

Each meeting should last about ninety minutes. The third meeting and the final meeting (the meal) may require more time.

A suggested schedule for Lent might be:
> 1. Introductory meeting on the first Saturday of Lent;
> 2. Four meetings on each of the following Saturdays;
> 3. Final celebration on Wednesday of Holy Week.

OUTLINE
Introductory Meeting
Desire for Peace

A. Introduction
- Song
- Prayer *The Journey* P:1:

> To begin our reflections I call upon that First
> Beginning from whom flows every
> illumination as from the God of lights.
> Through God's Son, our Lord Jesus Christ, I
> call upon God from whom comes every good
> and perfect gift that through the intercession
> of the most holy virgin Mary, the mother of
> our God and Lord, Jesus Christ, and through
> the intercession of blessed Francis, our
> leader and father, God might grant
> enlightenment to the eyes of our mind and
> guidance to our feet on the path of peace—
> that peace which surpasses all
> understanding.

- Leader invites participants to introduce themselves.
- Leader introduces method to be used for the retreat with some historical background to *The Journey* (see Life of Saint Bonaventure, pages 3-10), and, if necessary, for Francis and Clare of Assisi (see Thursday and Friday of Week One).
- Song

B. Reflection: See Tuesday of Week One.
- Leader introduces the theme of the day.
- Reading: Anthony de Mello's text (see Tuesday, Week One, page 36)
- Silence (3 minutes)

C. Exercise

- Leader asks the following questions:

  Where do you sense a desire for peace in your life now?

  What areas of your life lack inner or outer peace?

- In silence, participants respond in writing. For each of the answers, use another small sheet of paper. Place each paper into a container, then burn them, lighting a candle from this flame.

- During this time a mantra may be sung, such as the Taizé chant *Da pacem Domine.*

- Brief pause.

D. Group Sharing

E. Closing

- Leader presents an outline of the retreat, perhaps using Illustration 1.

  For planning the following week's assignments see How to Use This Book, pages 11-13.

- Closing text: *The Journey* 1:8:

  The natural powers of the soul . . . must be brought under the power of reforming grace; and this is done through prayer. These powers must also be brought to the knowledge which illumines, and this happens in meditation. And they must be brought to the wisdom that perfects, and this takes place in contemplation. For just as no one arrives at wisdom except through grace, justice, and knowledge, so no one arrives at contemplation except by means of penetrating meditation, a holy lifestyle, and devout prayer. Therefore, as grace is the foundation of the righteousness of the will and the clear enlightenment of reason, so it is necessary first of all to pray. Then we must live in a holy way. And third, we must attend to the reflections of truth, and gazing on them, rise gradually, until we arrive at the high mountain, where the God of gods is seen in Zion.

- Song

OUTLINE
Second Meeting
Let Flowers Speak!

A. Song

- Leader invites participants to spontaneous prayer concluding with the psalm texts you find in *The Journey* 1:1.

Happy are those whose strength is in you,
in whose heart are the highways to Zion. . . .
They go from strength to strength;
the God of gods will be seen in Zion. [Psalm 84:5–7]

Teach me your way, O LORD,
that I may walk in your truth;
give me an undivided heart to
revere your name. [Psalm 86:11]

B. Reflection: See Monday, Week Two.

- Song: Any version of *The Canticle of the Creatures*
- Text: *The Canticle of the Creatures* (pages 103-104 in Week Two) or the following:

Song of Sister Energy[2]

Transcendent, limitless, Immortal God of the universe.
Yours are wisdom, intelligence, order, method and logic.
In you alone is their origin
and no one is able to know your mind.
Be praised, Lord God, through the brotherhood of creation,
and especially Lady Sister Energy,
who is throughout the universe and equivalent to mass by the
equation:
$E - mc^2.$
She is awe-inspiring and alluring,
of you, the Invisible God, she is the image.
Be praised, Lord God, through Sisters Quasars, Novae and

Supernovae,
in distant Galaxies you formed them brilliant, majestic and
breath-taking.
Be praised, Lord God, through Sister Light,
traveling at a speed of 186,000 miles per second,
by whom the beauty of all creatures is revealed.
Be praised, Lord God, through Brother Quark discovered among
elementary Particles by the light of the electron.
Be praised, Lord God, through brother DNA, a double helix,
who carries coded genetic information in the cell nucleus.
Be praised, Lord God, through Brother Ocean,
who is wide and deep and teeming with varied fauna and flora.
Be praised, Lord God, through Brothers Coal, Oil and Gas,
and Sisters Nuclear Fusion, Solar and Tidal Power,
by whom you give us light and warmth;
they are strong and vigorous, dependable and attractive.
Be praised, Lord God, through our Sister Mother Earth,
who has a modest though radiant place
in the splendor and vastness of the expanding universe;
from her evolved the intricate and lovely network of matter,
life and mind.
Be praised, Lord God, through those who work for justice and
peace.
Blessed are they who serve and support the United Nations
organization,
for by you, Source of Peace, they shall be honored.
Be praised, Lord God, through our Sister Bodily Death,
who takes us to the next stage of our existence.
Woe to those who drive out love and destroy the brotherhood
of creation.
Blessed are they who love all creatures according to your will,
for they are building the new heaven and earth.
Praise and bless the Lord of the universe,
and give him thanks and serve him with great humility.

C. Exercise

- Form small groups for each one of the verses of *The Canticle*. On separate pieces of poster paper the leader writes the names of each element in the verses of *The Canticle*, such as the sun. Participants should join whatever group they wish.

    The groups may proceed as follows:

    1. Share ideas and experiences regarding the verse, for example, about the stars.

    2. On a large poster board participants may paint their impressions for this verse or the group may express their impressions through pantomime.

- Song

D. Group Sharing

- Group reports are made according to the sequence of the verses of *The Canticle*.

- Song

E. Closing

- Allow some time to discuss the experience of the participants doing this retreat at home.

- Closing text: *The Journey* 1:15:

    Therefore, any person who is not illumined by such great splendors in created things is blind. Anyone who is not awakened by such great outcries is deaf. Anyone who is not led from such effects to give praise to God is mute. Anyone who does not turn to the first principle as a result of such signs is a fool. Therefore open your eyes, alert your spiritual ears, unlock your lips, and apply your heart so that in all creation you may see, hear, praise, love and adore, magnify and honor your God lest the entire world rise up against you. For because of this the entire world will fight against the fools. On the other hand, it will be a cause of glory for the wise who can say in the words of the prophet: You have given me delight, O Lord, in your deeds, and I shall rejoice in the work of your hands. How wonderful are your works, O Lord. You have made all things in wisdom, the earth is filled with your richness.

• Song

OUTLINE
Third Meeting
Drink It All In!

A. Song or dance

- Create a spontaneous litany of praise:

  The leader could begin with: *Praise to you, my God, through creation.*

  Response: *We sense your power, wisdom and goodness.*

  Participants could continue the litany by adding their own verses, such as:

  Praise to you, my God, through rivers and streams.

  Response: *We sense your power, wisdom and goodness.*

  Praise to you, my God, through . . .

  Response: *We sense your power, wisdom and goodness.*

B. Reflection: See Tuesday of Week Two.

- Text by Jacopone da Todi (see Tuesday, Week Two, pages 97-99)
- Song

C. Exercise

- Sit in a comfortable chair and listen to a favorite musical selection, such as "Morning" by Edvard Grieg (from *Peer Gynt*), or *New World Symphony*, second movement, by Antonín Dvořák, or *Piano Concerto No. 2*, Larghetto, by Frédéric Chopin.
- Silence (2 minutes)
- Listen again to this musical selection.
- Alternative exercise:

  Participants see, smell, touch and taste bread, wine and water. As they do so, they are invited to share their thoughts and prayers about each item.

- Song

- Then share the bread, wine and water in silence. Enjoy the sensual experience.

D. Group sharing

- What did you hear and what did it evoke in you?
- For alternative exercise:

  Which senses did you engage in sharing the food?

- Song

E. Closing

- Leader summarizes the first two steps: see Illustration 1.
- Closing Text: *The Journey* 2:13:

  . . . (W)e may conclude that *from the creation of the world the invisible things of God are seen, being understood through those things that are made* so that *they are without excuse* who do not wish to pay attention to these things, or to know, bless, and love God in all things, since such people do not wish to be lifted from darkness to the marvelous light of God. But *thanks be to God through Jesus Christ our Lord who has lifted us out of the darkness into his marvelous light,* since because of the lights that come to us from outside we might be disposed to reenter the mirror of our mind in which divine realities shine forth.

- Song or repetition of the dance or blessing.

OUTLINE
Fourth Meeting
The Inner Circle

A. Song

- Pray Psalm 136 in this manner:
  1. Have each person read one verse, going through the entire group, verse by verse.
  2. Invite participants to review the psalm silently and repeat any phrase or verse they wish.
  3. Invite participants to continue the psalm by adding a verse of their own creation, recalling an event from their personal salvation history, to which all respond: *For your love endures forever!*
  4. All conclude with: *Glory to the Father . . .*

B. Reflection: Thursday of Week Three (see pages 161-168)

- Text: Chapter 3:1:

  The two preceding steps, which have led us to God by means of the vestiges through which God shines forth in every creature, have brought us to a point where we can enter again into ourselves, that is, into the mind itself in which the divine image shines forth. Therefore, in this third stage, as we leave the outer court and enter into ourselves, we should try to see God through a mirror . . . It is here that the light of truth shines like the light of a candelabrum upon the face of our mind in which the image of the most blessed Trinity shines in splendor. Therefore, enter into yourself and recognize that your mind loves itself most fervently. But it cannot love itself if it does not know itself. And it would not know itself unless it remembered itself, for we do not grasp anything with our understanding if it is not present to us in our memory. From this you see, not with the eye of the flesh but with the eye of reason, that the soul possesses a three-fold power. Now consider the operation of these powers and their relation to each other. Here you can see God through yourself as through an image. And this is to see *through a mirror in an obscure manner.*

C. Exercise

• For Memory

1. The leader writes one word on the board or newsprint, such as: vacation, snow, birthday.

2. All participants are invited to share memories on the word chosen.

3. The leader writes their responses on board or newsprint.

• For Intellect: Definition

1. The leader asks the participants to define a well-known person, such as an actor, politician, athlete or religious leader.

2. Participants are invited to define this person by single-word descriptions, such as generous, open-minded, immature, etc.

3. The leader writes responses on a board or on newsprint and indicates the movement from the specific to the more universal.

• For Will: Deliberation Process

1. Have two participants role-play an interview for a job, one being the employer and the other the prospective employee.

2. Leader can later note how the employer deliberates with the good of the company in mind.

• Reading of chapter 3:4:

The function of the elective faculty is seen in deliberation, judgment, and desire. Deliberation consists in inquiring whether this thing is better than that thing. But a thing is said to be better only because of its closeness to the best. But closeness to the best is measured in terms of likeness. No one can know, therefore, whether one thing is better than another without knowing that this thing bears a greater resemblance to the best. And no one knows whether something is more like another without knowing that other. For I do not know whether this person is like Peter unless I know and recognize Peter. Therefore, it is necessary that the notion of the highest good be impressed on anyone who is engaged in deliberation.

- Reflection: See Illustration 8.
- Song

D. Group sharing in small groups.

- Song

E. Closing

- Invite participants to bring their Bibles to the next meeting.
- Song

OUTLINE
Fifth Meeting
Full of Grace

A. Song

B. Reflection: See Sunday of Week Four (pages 187-194)

- Text: Chapter 4:3:

  > Therefore the image that is our soul must be clothed over with the three theological virtues by which the soul is purified, illumined, and brought to perfection. In this way the image is reformed and brought into conformity with the heavenly Jerusalem and becomes a member of the church militant which is the offspring of the heavenly Jerusalem, according to the Apostle. For he says: *That Jerusalem which is above is free, and she is our mother.* The soul, therefore, believes in, hopes in, and loves Jesus Christ who is the Word incarnate, uncreated, and inspired; that is, *the way, the truth, and the life.* When in faith the soul believes in Christ as in the uncreated Word, which is the Word and splendor of the Father, it recovers its spiritual sense of hearing and of sight; its hearing so that it might receive the words of Christ, and its sight that it might consider the splendors of that light. . . . With her spiritual senses restored, the soul now sees, hears, smells, tastes, and embraces her beloved. She can now sing like the spouse in the *Canticle of Canticles* which was written for the exercise of contemplation on the fourth level, and which *no one knows except one who receives it;* for it consists more in the experience of affections than in rational considerations.

- Silence
- Song

C./D. Exercise and group sharing

- Invite participants to open their Bibles to Matthew 14:22–32.
  1. Ask someone to read the passage. Follow this by another reading of the same passage in a different translation.
  2. Silence
  3. Break into small groups of two or three to share responses to the reading.
  4. Reassemble the entire group to answer these questions:
     What does this story say about faith, belief?
     What is faith?
     Can you see any connection to your daily life?
- Song

E. Closing

- Prepare the group for the last full week of the retreat, raising final logistical questions.
- Song or dance

OUTLINE
Final Meeting
Praise God!

A. Song: *Magnificat* or *Adoramus te Domine*

- Both could be accompanied by spontaneous bodily gestures.

- Prayer: Praises of God (Saturday, Week Four, pages 229-236)

B. Reflection: See Saturday of Week Four (pages 229-236) and Wednesday of Week Five (pages 257-262)

- Text: Chapter 5:2:

> The first method fixes our attention primarily and first of all on Being itself, saying that *The one who is* is the first name of God. The second method fixes our attention on the reality of the Good, saying that this is the first name of God. The first looks above all at the Hebrew Scriptures which are concerned to a great extent with the unity of the divine essence. For it was said to Moses: *I am who I am.* And according to the Christian Scriptures, which determine the plurality of persons, we are to baptize *In the name of the Father, and of the Son, and of the Holy Spirit.* Therefore Christ, our Master, wishing to raise to evangelical perfection the young man who had observed the Law, attributed to God principally and precisely the name of *Goodness* saying: *No one is good but God alone.* So Damascene, following Moses, says that *The one who is* is the first name of God. And Dionysius, following Christ, says that *Good* is the first name of God.

- Song

C. Exercise

- As Francis and Clare wrote a *Testament*, we will compose

a testament. See Thursday of Week One.

1. Each participant receives the same symbol copied on paper, a line drawing such as a treasure box, a bouquet of flowers, a bird.

2. Sitting in a circle, each member prints her or his name in the upper right-hand corner of the paper and passes the paper to the person on the right.

3. On each paper received, write a word or a phrase that characterizes some precious gift, virtue or talent of the person.

4. Supply background music, such as Pachelbel's *Canon.*

5. When the papers return to the person to whom they belong, give participants a few minutes to read the entries.

6. The leader asks:

   Which entry surprised you most?

   Each person chooses one entry that is most precious to him or her, writes it on an index card, inserting it into a sentence such as: *The Lord granted me_____. I cherish this gift and wish to pass it on to future generations of Christians.*

7. The index cards are collected by the leader and pasted to a large posterboard. The word *Testament* is printed large at the top of the poster and the place and date recorded on the bottom, such as: *Given at_____ on_____.*

8. To conclude the exercise the complete testament is presented and read aloud.

• Song

D. For the last group sharing, include the entire retreat experience. If possible, conclude by sharing a meal together.

E. Song

- Closing text: Chapter 7:1:

    We have covered these six considerations, comparing them to the six steps by which one ascends to the throne of the true Solomon where the mind finds peace. It is here that the true person of peace rests in the quiet of the mind as in an interior Jerusalem. They are also compared to the six wings of the Seraphim by which the mind of the truly contemplative person is filled with the light of heavenly wisdom and can come to soar on high. They are also like the first six days during which the mind needed to be trained so as to finally arrive at the Sabbath of rest. After our mind has contemplated God outside itself through and in the vestiges, within itself through and in the image, and above itself through the similitude of the divine light shining on us from above in as far as that is possible in our pilgrim state and by the exercise of our mind, and when finally the mind has come to the sixth step where it can find in the first and highest principle and in the mediator between God and humanity—Jesus Christ—mysteries which have no likeness among creatures and which surpass the penetrating power of the human intellect, there remains for the mind, when it has come to contemplate all these things, to pass over and thus to transcend not only the sensible world but the soul itself. And in this passage, Christ is *the way and the door,* Christ is the ladder and the vehicle, like the Mercy Seat placed above the ark of God and *the mystery that has been hidden from all eternity.*

NOTES

[1] See Francis' *Document on Solitude*, where he suggests that there should be four brothers in solitude. Two should be mothers caring for their sons' needs, so that the sons are free simply to be, that is to sit at the feet of Jesus. See *Franciscan Solitude*, edited by André Cirino, O.F.M., and Josef Raischl, S.F.O. (New York: Franciscan Institute Publications, 1995).

[2] Doyle, *The Song of Brotherhood and Sisterhood, op. cit.*, p. 215.

Part Four

THE JOURNEY OF THE HUMAN PERSON INTO GOD

Prologue

The Journey of the Human Person into God
(Itinerarium mentis in deum)[1]
of Saint Bonaventure
Translated by Zachary Hayes, O.F.M.

1. To begin my reflections, I call upon that First Beginning from whom all illumination flows as from the *God of lights* and from whom comes *every good and perfect gift* (James 1:17). I call upon God through the divine Son, our lord Jesus Christ, that through the intercession of the most holy virgin Mary, the mother of the same Lord, Jesus Christ, and through that of blessed Francis, our leader and father, God might grant *enlightenment to the eyes* of our mind and *guidance to our feet on the path of peace*—that peace *which surpasses all understanding*. It is that peace which our Lord Jesus Christ proclaimed and granted to us (Ephesians 1:17; Luke 1:79; Phillippians 4:7). It was this message of peace which our father Francis announced over and over, proclaiming it at the beginning and the end of his sermons. Every greeting of his became a wish for peace; and in every experience of contemplation he sighed for an ecstatic peace. He was like a citizen of that Jerusalem about which the man of peace—*who was peaceable even with those who despised peace*—says: *Pray for those things that are for the peace of Jerusalem.* For he knew that it is only in peace that the throne of Solomon exists, since it is written: *His place is in peace, and his dwelling is in Zion* (Psalms 119:7; 121:6; 75:3).

2. Moved by the example of our most blessed father, Francis,

I eagerly desired this peace—I a sinner who, unworthy as I am, had become the seventh general minister of the brothers after the death of the most blessed father. It happened around the time of the thirty-third anniversary of the death of the saint that I was moved by a divine inspiration and withdrew to Mount LaVerna since it was a place of quiet. There I wished to satisfy the desire of my spirit for peace. And while I was there reflecting on certain ways in which the human person might ascend to God, I recalled, among other things, that miracle which the blessed Francis himself had experienced in this very place, namely the vision of the winged Seraph[2] in the form of the Crucified. As I reflected on this, I saw immediately that this vision pointed not only to the uplifting of our father himself in contemplation but also to the road by which one might arrive at this experience.

3. For those six wings can well be understood as symbols of six levels of uplifting illuminations through which the soul is prepared, as it were by certain stages or steps, to pass over to peace through the ecstatic rapture of Christian wisdom. There is no other way but through the most burning love of the Crucified. It was that sort of love which lifted Paul into the *third heaven* and transformed him into Christ to such a degree that he could say: *With Christ I am nailed to the cross. It is now no longer I that live, but Christ lives in me* (2 Corinthians 12:2; Galatians 2:20). This sort of love so absorbed the mind of Francis also that his spirit became apparent in his flesh; and for two years prior to his death, he carried the holy marks of the passion in his body.

The image of the six wings of the Seraph, therefore, is a symbol of six stages of illumination which begin with creatures and lead to God to whom no one has access properly except through the Crucified. For anyone *who does not enter by that door, but climbs up another way, is a thief and a robber. But anyone who enters by that door will go in and out, and will find pastures* (John 10:1; 10:9). For this reason, in *Revelation* John writes: *Blessed are those who wash their robes in the blood of the Lamb for they are nourished at the tree of life and they may enter the city through the gates* (Revelation 22:14). This means that no one can enter into the heavenly Jerusalem by means of contemplation without entering through the blood of the Lamb as through a door. For no one is disposed in any way for those divine contemplations which lead to spiritual ecstasies without being, like Daniel, *a person of desires* (Daniel 9:23). But desires of this type are enkindled in us in two ways, namely through the *cry of prayer* which makes us cry aloud with *groaning of the heart* (Psalms 37:9), and through the *brightness of speculation* by which we turn our attention most directly and intently to the rays of light.

4. Therefore, I first of all invite the reader to groans of prayer through Christ crucified, through whose blood we are purged from the stain of our sins (Hebrews 1:3). Do not think that reading is sufficient without unction, reflection without devotion, investigation without admiration, observation without exultation, industry without piety, knowledge without charity, intelligence without humility, study without divine grace, or the reflecting power of a mirror without the inspiration of divine wisdom. To those who are already disposed by divine grace—to the humble and pious; to those who are devout and sorrowful for their sins; to those anointed with the *oil of gladness* (Psalms 44:8); to those who are lovers of divine wisdom and are inflamed with desire for it;

and to those who wish to give themselves to glorifying, admiring, and even savoring God, I propose the following reflections. At the same time I ask them to keep in mind that the mirror of the external world is of little significance unless our interior mirror is cleansed and polished. Therefore, O child of God, awaken yourself first to the remorseful sting of conscience before you raise your eyes to those rays of wisdom that are reflected in its mirrors. Otherwise it might happen that the very act of looking on these rays might cause you to fall into an even more treacherous pit of darkness.

5. It seemed good to me to divide this tract into seven chapters with a title prefixed to each chapter. This will make the content easier to understand. I ask, therefore, that you give more attention to the intent of the writer than to the work itself, more to the things said than to the uncultivated language, more to the truth than to attractiveness, more to the stimulation of affect than to intellectual enrichment. So that this might happen, it is important that you not run through these reflections in a hurry, but that you take your time and ruminate over them slowly.

The end of the Prologue.

Chapter Headings

Chapter One: The Steps of the Ascent into God and the Reflection on God through the Vestiges in the Universe

Chapter Two: The Reflection on God in the Vestiges in This Sensible World

Chapter Three: The Reflection on God through the Image Imprinted on Our Natural Powers

Chapter Four: The Reflection on God in the Image Reformed by the Gifts of Grace

Chapter Five: The Reflection on the Divine Unity through God's Primary Name, Which Is Being

Chapter Six: The Reflection on the Most Blessed Trinity in Its Name, Which Is the Good

Chapter Seven: The Mental and Mystical Transport in Which Rest Is Given to Our Understanding and through Ecstasy Our Affection Passes over Totally into God

Here begins the contemplation of the poor one in the desert.

Chapter One

THE STEPS OF THE ASCENT INTO GOD AND THE REFLECTION ON
GOD THROUGH THE VESTIGES IN THE UNIVERSE

1. *Blessed are those whose help comes from you. In their hearts they
are disposed to ascend by steps in the valley of tears, in the place
which they have set* (Psalms 83:6 ff.). Since happiness is nothing other than the enjoyment of the highest good, and since
the highest good is above us, we cannot find happiness without rising above ourselves, not by a bodily ascent but by an
ascent of the heart. But we cannot be elevated above ourselves unless a superior power lifts us up. No matter how
well-ordered the steps of our interior life may be, nothing
will happen if divine aid does not accompany us. But divine
aid comes to those who pray from their heart humbly and
devoutly. We must sigh for it through fervent prayer in this
valley of tears. Therefore prayer is the mother and the well-
spring of the upward movement of the soul. It is for this reason that Dionysius, at the beginning of his book, *Mystical
Theology,*[3] wishing to instruct us on the matter of spiritual
ecstasy, offers a prayer: Let us, therefore, pray and say to the
Lord our God: *Lead me, O Lord, in your way so that I might enter
into your truth. Let my heart rejoice that it may be in awe of your
name* (Psalms 86:11).

2. When we pray in this way we are given the light to recognize the steps of the ascent to God. For it is in harmony with
our created condition that the universe itself may serve as a
ladder by which we can ascend to God. Among created
things, some are vestiges, others are images; some are bodily, others are spiritual; some are temporal, others are ever-

lasting; some are outside us, others are within us. In order to arrive at that first principle which is most spiritual and eternal, and above us, it is necessary that we move through the vestiges which are bodily and temporal and outside us. And this is to be led in the way of God. Next we must enter into our inner reality which is the image of God, an image which is everlasting, spiritual, and within us. And this will enable us to enter into the truth of God. Finally we must pass beyond to that which is eternal, most spiritual, and above us by raising our eyes to the First Principle. And this will bring us to rejoice in the knowledge of God and to stand in awe before God's majesty.

3. This, therefore, is the three-day journey in the solitude of the desert (Exodus 3:18); this is the triple illumination of a single day; the first is like evening, the second like morning, and the third like noon. This relates to the three-fold existence of things, namely in matter, in understanding, and in the eternal art, according to which it is written: *Let it be, God made it,* and *it was made* (Genesis 1:3). This also relates to the triple substance in Christ who is our ladder, namely the corporal, the spiritual, and the divine.

4. In harmony with this three-fold progression, we have three principal ways of seeing things. One way relates to the corporal beings outside ourselves, and this is known as our animal or sense power. The second way relates to what is interior and within the person; and this is called spirit. In the third way, the person is drawn to what is above itself; and this is called soul. In the ascent to God, all three of these ought to be used so that God will be loved *with the whole mind, the whole heart, and the whole soul* (Mark 12:30; Matthew 22:37; Luke

10:27). In this we see perfect fidelity to the Law together with Christian wisdom.

5. Each of these foregoing ways may be doubled depending on whether we consider God as the *Alpha and the Omega* (Revelation 1:8), or whether in each of the above-mentioned ways we consider God as *through* a mirror or as *in* a mirror. Or we may consider each of these ways as related to another with which it is connected, or simply in itself in its purity. Thus, it is necessary that these three principal levels of ascent be increased to six. Just as God completed the entire world in six days and rested on the seventh, so the micro-cosm (i.e. humanity) ought to be led in a most orderly way through six levels of illumination to the quiet of contemplation. This was symbolized by the *six steps* with which one ascended to the throne of Solomon (2 Chronicles 10:18). Similarly, the Seraphim which Isaiah saw had *six wings* (Isaiah 6:2); the Lord called Moses from the midst of the cloud *after six days* (Exodus 24:16); and, as Matthew writes, *after six days Christ led the disciples to the mountain and was transfigured before them* (Matthew 17:1 ff.).

6. Corresponding to the six steps of the ascent to God there are six levels of the powers of the soul by which we ascend from the depths to the heights, from the external to the internal, and from the temporal to the eternal. These six levels are: sense, imagination, reason, understanding, intelligence, and the high point of the mind, or the spark of conscience. These powers are implanted in us by nature. They are deformed through sin and reformed through grace. They must be cleansed by justice, developed by knowledge, and brought to perfection by wisdom.

7. According to the way nature was originally instituted, the human being was created with the capability of experiencing the quiet of contemplation. Therefore, *God placed the first human being in a paradise of pleasures* (Genesis 2:15). But turning from the true light to a changeable good, the first human was bent over through a personal fault, and the entire human race became bent over by original sin which infected human nature in two ways. It infects the mind with ignorance, and the flesh with concupiscence. The result is that humans, blind and bent over, sit in darkness and do not see the light of heaven without the aid of grace together with justice to fight concupiscence, and knowledge together with wisdom to fight ignorance. All this comes about through Jesus Christ, who by God *has been made wisdom and justice and sanctification and redemption.* For since He is the power of God and the wisdom of God (1 Corinthians 1:30), and the incarnate Word of God *full of grace and truth* (John 1:14; 1:17), He is the source of grace and truth. He pours into us the grace of charity which, since it arises from *a pure heart and a good conscience and unfeigned faith* (1 Timothy 1:5), rectifies the entire soul according to the triple power mentioned above. He has taught the knowledge of truth according to three modes of theology, namely symbolic, proper, and mystical, so that through symbolic theology we might use sensible things properly, through theology in the proper sense we might deal with intelligible things correctly, and through mystical theology we might be drawn up to ecstasy beyond the intellect.

8. Therefore, a person who wishes to ascend to God must avoid sin which deforms nature. The natural powers of the soul described above must be brought under the power of reforming grace; and this is done through prayer. These

powers must also be influenced by justice which purifies; and this is carried out in everyday actions. They must also be brought to that knowledge which illumines, and this happens in meditation. And they must be brought to the wisdom that perfects, and this takes place in contemplation. For just as no one arrives at wisdom except through grace, justice, and knowledge, so no one arrives at contemplation except by means of penetrating meditation, a holy lifestyle, and devout prayer. Therefore, as grace is the foundation of the righteousness of the will and the clear enlightenment of reason, so it is necessary first of all to pray. Then we must live in a holy way. And third, we must concentrate on the reflections of truth; and gazing on these, we must rise gradually, until we arrive at the peak of the mountain, *where the God of gods is seen in Zion* (Psalms 84:8).

9. Now since we must ascend before we can descend on Jacob's ladder (Genesis 28:12), let us place the first step of our ascent at the bottom, putting the whole of the sensible world before us as a mirror through which we may pass to God, the highest creative Artist. In this way we may become true Hebrews, passing from Egypt to the land promised to the Fathers (Genesis 28:13 ff.; Exodus 13:3 ff.). And we shall be Christians passing over with Christ from this world to the Father (John 13:1). We shall be lovers of that wisdom which calls and says: *Pass over to me, all you who desire me, and be filled with my fruits. For in the greatness and beauty of created things their Creator can be seen and known* (Wisdom 11:21).

10. The supreme power, wisdom, and goodness of the Creator shines forth in created things as the bodily senses make this known to the interior senses in a three-fold way.

For the bodily senses assist the intellect as it investigates rationally, or believes faithfully, or contemplates intellectually. When it contemplates, the intellect considers the actual existence of things; when it believes, it sees the habitual flow of events; and when it investigates with reason, it is concerned with the potential excellence of things.

11. In the first way of seeing, as we contemplate, we view things as they are in themselves, seeing them in terms of weight, number, and measure. Weight refers to the place toward which they are inclined; number is that by which things are distinguished; and measure is that by which things are limited. Thus we see things in terms of mode, species, and order and in terms of substance, power, and operation. From these perspectives, we can rise as from the vestige to an understanding of the immense power, wisdom, and goodness of the Creator.

12. In the second way of seeing, namely, that of faith, we consider this world by attending to its origin, development, and end. For it is *by faith* that *we believe that the world was fashioned by the Word of life* (Hebrews 11.3). By faith we believe that the periods of the three laws followed each other in a most orderly way; namely, the law of nature, the law of Scripture, and the law of grace. By faith we believe that the world is to come to an end in the final judgment. In terms of the first we consider the power of the highest Principle; in terms of the second we consider the providence of that Principle; and in terms of the third we consider the justice of that same Principle.

13. In the third way of seeing, as we investigate by means of reason, we see that some things merely exist; others exist and

live; and yet others exist, live, and discern. Here we recognize that the first of these are the less perfect ones; the second are the intermediate ones; and the third are the more perfect ones. Again, we see that some are merely corporal; some are partly corporal and partly spiritual; and from this we conclude that some are wholly spiritual and hence are better and of greater dignity than the first two types of being. We see also that some things are mutable and corruptible, such as terrestrial things; some are changeable but incorruptible, such as heavenly beings; and from this it can be concluded that some are immutable and incorruptible, such as those things that transcend the earth.

Therefore, from visible realities, we rise to the consideration of the power, wisdom and goodness of God in as far as God is existing, living, and intelligent, purely spiritual, incorruptible and immutable.

14. This consideration can be extended to the sevenfold properties of creatures which offer a sevenfold witness to the power, wisdom, and goodness of God if we consider the origin, greatness, multitude, beauty, fullness, activity, and order of all things. For the origin of things in terms of their creation and in terms of their distinction and adornment as the work of the six days proclaims the power that produces all things from nothing, the wisdom that clearly distinguishes all things, and the goodness that richly adorns all things. The greatness of things viewed in terms of their length, width, and depth; or seen in terms of the immense energy which extends in length, width, and depth as is clear in the way light is diffused; or seen in terms of the efficiency of their operations which are internal, continuous, and diffuse, as

appears in the action of fire—all this clearly points to the immensity of the power, wisdom, and goodness of the triune God who, though uncircumscribed, exists in all things by virtue of power, presence, and essence. And the multitude of things in the diversity of their general, particular, and individual substance, form or figure, and activity which is beyond human estimation manifestly points to and demonstrates the immensity of the three attributes in God mentioned above. The beauty of things in terms of the diversity of light, shape, and color in bodies that are simple, inorganic, and organic, as in the heavenly bodies and in minerals, in stones and in metals, in plants and in animals clearly proclaims the three attributes mentioned above. Moreover, the fact that matter is full of forms because of the seminal reasons;[4] and form is full of power in terms of active potency; and power is full of effects by reason of its efficiency, shows that the fullness of things clearly proclaims the same attributes. Likewise, the many forms of activity, whether natural, artistic, or moral, show by their very great variety the immensity of that power, art, and goodness which is for all things "the cause of being, the basis of understanding, and the rule of life."[5] Finally, order when viewed in terms of duration, position, and influence, namely, in terms of prior and posterior, higher and lower, more noble and less noble, clearly shows in the book of creation the primacy, sublimity, and dignity of the First Principle with respect to the infinity of its power. The order of the divine laws, precepts and judgments in the book of the Scriptures shows the immensity of God's wisdom; the order of the divine sacraments, graces, and rewards in the body of the church shows the immensity of God's goodness. So in this way order leads us most manifestly to that which is first and highest, most powerful, most wise, and best.

15. Therefore, any person who is not illumined by such great splendors in created things is blind. Anyone who is not awakened by such great outcries is deaf. Anyone who is not led from such effects to give praise to God is mute. Anyone who does not turn to the First Principle as a result of such signs is a fool. Therefore open your eyes, alert your spiritual ears, unlock your lips, and apply your heart (Proverbs 22:17) so that in all creation you may see, hear, praise, love and adore, magnify and honor your God lest the entire world rise up against you. For because of this *the entire world will fight against the fools* (Wisdom 5:21). On the other hand, it will be a cause of glory for the wise who can say in the words of the prophet: *You have given me delight, O Lord, in your deeds, and I shall rejoice in the work of your hands. How wonderful are your works, O Lord. You have made all things in wisdom, the earth is filled with your richness* (Psalms 92:4; 104:24).

Chapter Two

THE REFLECTION ON GOD IN THE VESTIGES IN THIS SENSIBLE
WORLD

1. With respect to the mirror of things perceptible to the
senses, it is possible that God might be contemplated not
only *through* them, but also *in* them in as far as God is present in them by essence, power, and presence. This way of
reflecting is higher than the previous one. Therefore it follows as the second level of contemplation by which we ought
to be led to contemplate God in all those creatures that
enter into our consciousness through our bodily senses.

2. It should be noted that this world which is called the
macrocosm enters the human person, which is said to be a
microcosm, through the doorways of the five senses by which
we become aware of, enjoy, and judge concerning the
objects of sense experience. This can be clarified as follows.
In the world of sense objects, some things generate, some
are generated, and some govern both of these. Those that
generate are simple bodies such as the heavenly bodies and
the four elements. For anything that is generated or produced through the operation of a natural power must be
generated or produced from these elements by means of the
power of light that harmonizes the contrary qualities of the
elements in mixed things. Those things that are generated
are bodies composed of the elements. This includes minerals, plants, animals, and human bodies. Those things that
govern both the former and the latter are spiritual substances, either completely bound to matter as are the souls
of the non-human animals, or separably joined to matter, as

are the rational spirits, or totally separated, as are the heavenly spirits which the philosophers call Intelligences, but we call angels. According to the philosophers, it is the task of these latter beings to move the heavenly bodies. Because of this, the administration of the universe is attributed to them in as far as they receive from the first cause, namely God, an infusion of power which they then use in the work of administration. This sustains the natural stability of creation. But according to the theologians, the ruling of the universe that is attributed to the angels is grounded in a command of the most high God that relates to the works of reparation. For this reason they are called *ministering spirits sent for the sake of those who are to inherit salvation* (Hebrews 1:14).

3. The human being, therefore, who is said to be a *microcosm*, has five senses which are like five doorways through which the knowledge of all things in the sensible world enters into the interior world. For the sublime and luminous bodies and all other colored things enter through sight; solid and terrestrial bodies enter through touch; and the intermediary things enter through the intermediate senses; liquid things through taste, sounds through hearing, and vapors through smell. Vapors contain something of the nature of water, air, and fire or heat, as is clear from the pleasant smell produced by incense.

Therefore, it is through these doorways that simple and composite or mixed bodies enter into the soul. In a true sense we perceive not only particular sense objects such as light, sound, smell, taste, and the four primary qualities which the sense of touch notices, but also the common sense objects such as number, size, shape, rest, and motion. Now "whatever is moved is moved by another." And even though certain things such as animals move and come to rest by themselves,[6] when we take note of their bodily movement through these five senses we are led to the knowledge of spiritual movers, as from an effect to the knowledge of its cause.

4. Therefore, the whole sensible world in its three categories of beings enters into our interior through our basic sense experience. These external, sensible beings are the first to enter into us through the doors of the five senses. It is not the substance of such an object that enters in, but rather a likeness of the object. And that likeness is generated in a medium. And from the medium this likeness passes into the organ, and from the external organ it moves to the internal organ, and from here it moves to the faculty of awareness. So the generation of the likeness in the medium and its movement from the medium to the organ, and the turning of the faculty of awareness to it leads to the knowledge of all those things which we come to know as external to ourselves.

5. Now pleasure follows from the awareness of a suitable object. For the senses delight in an object that is perceived by means of the likeness that has been abstracted. This delight comes either from its beauty, as in the case of vision, or sweetness, as in the case of smell and hearing, or from its healthful quality as in the case of taste and touch, to speak in terms of appropriation. For all pleasure flows from proportion. Now the species contains the principle of form, of power, and of activity depending on whether it is viewed in terms of the principle from which it comes, the medium through which it passes, or the object toward which it moves. Therefore proportion is seen in the likeness in as far as it

contains the principle of the species or the form, and then it is called beauty, because "beauty is nothing else but numerical equality," or "a certain arrangement of parts together with pleasing color."[7] Or proportion can be viewed as possessing the quality of power or strength, and then it is called sweetness when the power that is acting is not out of proportion to the recipient, for the senses are pained by extremes but take delight in moderation. Finally, proportion can be viewed in as far as it is active and impressive. In this case proportionality is found when the impression of the agent fulfills a need in the recipient and thus preserves and nourishes it. This is most apparent in the case of taste and touch. Thus it is through pleasure that external delights enter into us by means of a likeness and in terms of three kinds of pleasure.

6. Awareness and delight are followed by judgment through which one judges not only whether a thing is white or black—for this pertains to a particular sense; and not only whether it is healthful or harmful—for this pertains to the interior sense; but one judges and explains why this object gives pleasure. And in this act, one asks about the cause of the enjoyment which the senses derive from the object. When we ask why an object is beautiful, sweet, or wholesome, the cause for this is found in a proportion of equality. Now the nature of equality is the same in large things or in small things; it is not extended in dimensions nor is it changed by movements through successive stages, nor does it pass away with transitory things. It is independent of place, time and motion, and hence it is unchangeable, unlimited, endless; and it is entirely spiritual. Judgment, therefore, is an action which takes the sense species received from the sense organ,

purifies it, abstracts it, and causes it to enter into the intellective faculty. And in this way the entire world enters into us through the doorways of the senses in accord with the three operations cited above.

7. Now these actions are vestiges in which we can see our God. For the species of which we become aware is a likeness generated in the medium and then impressed on the organ itself; and through that impression it leads to its source as to the object to be known. This clearly suggests that the eternal light generates a likeness of itself, or a splendor that is coequal, consubstantial, and coeternal. It suggests that the one who is *the invisible image of God and the splendor of God's glory and the figure of God's substance* (Collosians 1:15; Hebrews 1:3), exists everywhere by virtue of an original generation just as an object generates its likeness in the entire medium. It suggests also that this one is united to an individual rational nature by the grace of union as the species is united to the bodily organ so that through this union He might lead us back to the Father as to the fontal principle and object. If, therefore, it is in the nature of all knowable things to generate a likeness of themselves, they clearly proclaim that in them as in mirrors we can see the eternal generation of the Word, the Image, and the Son eternally emanating from God the Father.

8. In like manner, the likeness that gives delight in its beauty, sweetness, and wholesomeness suggests that in that first likeness there is a first beauty, sweetness, and wholesomeness in which is found the highest proportionality and equality in relation to the one that generates it. And there is power suggested not by means of the phantasm, but by means of the

truth that floods our awareness. It suggests also an impression that nourishes and is sufficient to fulfill all the needs of the knower. Therefore, if "delight is the union of two beings that are proportionate to each other,"[8] and if it is only in the likeness of God that one finds that which is by nature supremely beautiful, sweet and wholesome; and if that likeness is united in truth, and intimacy, and in a fullness that transcends our every need, it can be seen clearly that it is in God alone that the true fountain of delight is to be found. So it is that from all other delights we are led to seek this one delight.

9. Moreover, in a way that is more excellent and more immediate, judgment leads us to see the eternal truth with greater certainty. If a judgment has to be made by means of reason that abstracts from place, time, and change, and hence from dimension, succession, and change, it takes place through a reason that is immutable, unlimited, and unending. But nothing is entirely unchangeable, unlimited, and unending except that which is eternal. But whatever is eternal is either God or in God. Therefore, if all our more certain judgments are made by virtue of such a reality, then it is clear that this reality itself is the reason for all things and the infallible rule and light of truth in which all things shine forth in a way that is infallible, indelible, beyond doubt and beyond questioning or argumentation, unchangeable, having no limits in space and no ending in time, in a way that is indivisible and intellectual. Therefore those laws by which we judge with certitude concerning all sense objects that come to our consideration, since they are infallible and beyond doubt to the intellect of the one who is aware of them; and since they cannot be removed from the memory of one who recalls, for

they are always present; and since they are beyond question and beyond the judgment of the intellect of the one who judges because as Augustine says:[9] *no one judges about them, but by means of them*, it follows that these laws must be changeless and incorruptible because they are necessary. They are without limits in space since they are not circumscribed. They are endless in time since they are eternal. They are indivisible because they are intellectual and incorporeal. They are not made but are uncreated, existing eternally in the eternal Art from which, and through which, and in accordance with which all beautiful things are formed. Therefore they cannot be judged with certainty except through that eternal Art which is the form that not only produces all things, but also conserves and distinguishes them; for this is the Being that sustains the form in all things and the rule that directs all things. And it is through this that our mind comes to judge about all those things which enter into it through the senses.

10. This speculation can be developed further by a consideration of the seven kinds of numbers by which, as by seven steps, we ascend to God, as Augustine shows in his book, *On the True Religion*, and in his *On Music*, book 6. In these texts he shows the differences of numbers that ascend gradually from all these sensible beings to the Maker of all, so that in all things God may be seen.

He says that numbers are in bodies, and especially in sounds and voices. And these he calls "sounding numbers." Then there are numbers abstracted from these and received in our sense organs. These he calls "occurring numbers." There are numbers that proceed from the soul into the body as is clear in gestures and in dancing. These he calls "expressive numbers." There are numbers involved in the pleasures of the senses. This comes when the attention is turned to the species that has been received. These he calls "sensual numbers." There are numbers retained in the memory. These he calls "remembered numbers." There are numbers through which we make judgments about all these others. These he calls "judicial numbers." As has been said above, these are necessarily above the mind and are infallible and beyond any judgment of ours. And from this last category of numbers, the "artistic numbers" are impressed in our minds. Augustine does not mention these in his classification since they are connected with the "judicial numbers." And the "expressive numbers" also flow from the "judicial numbers." It is from the "expressive numbers" that the numerous forms in works of art are created. Thus from the highest numbers to the intermediate to the lowest numbers there is an orderly descent. And we ascend to the highest numbers step by step, moving from the "sounding numbers" through the "occurring numbers" to the "sensuous numbers" and then to the "remembered numbers."

Therefore, since all things are beautiful and in some way delightful; and since there is no beauty or delight without proportion; and since proportion resides first of all in numbers; it is necessary that all things involve number. From this we conclude that "number is the principal exemplar in the mind of the Creator,"[10] and in creatures it is the principal vestige leading to wisdom. Since number is most evident to all and is closest to God, it leads us very close to God by its sevenfold distinction; and it makes God known in all bodily and sensible things when we become aware of numerical realities, when we take delight in numerical proportions, and when we come to make irrefutable judgments by means of the laws of numerical proportions.

11. From these first two steps by which we are led to behold God in vestiges like the two wings covering the feet (of the Seraph), we can conclude that all creatures in this world of sensible realities lead the spirit of the contemplative and wise person to the eternal God. For creatures are shadows, echoes, and pictures of that first, most powerful, most wise, and most perfect Principle, of that eternal source, light, and fullness; of that efficient, exemplary, and ordering Art. They are vestiges, images, and spectacles proposed to us for the contemplation of God.[11] They are divinely given signs. These creatures are copies or rather illustrations proposed to those who are still untrained and immersed in things of the senses, so that through sensible objects which they do see they may be lifted to the intelligible realities which they do not see, moving from signs to that which is signified.

12. For the created beings of this sensible world signify the invisible things of God (Romans 1:20) partly because God is the origin, exemplar, and goal of all creation, and every effect is a sign of its cause; every copy is a sign of its exemplar; and the road is a sign of the goal to which it leads. They function this way partly by reason of natural representation, partly by reason of prophetic prefiguration, partly by reason of angelic operation, and partly by reason of additional institution. For every creature is by nature a kind of copy and likeness of that eternal Wisdom. But those which, according to the book of Scripture, have been raised up by the spirit of prophecy to prefigure spiritual realities do this in a special way. And in an even more special way, those creatures do this

in whose image it has pleased God to appear in angelic ministry. And in a most special way this is done by those which it has pleased God to institute as a sign but which are signs not only in the ordinary sense but also are known as sacraments.

13. From all that has been said above we may conclude that *from the creation of the world the invisible things of God are seen, being understood through those things that are made so that they are without excuse* (Romans 1:20) who do not wish to pay attention to these things, or to know, bless, and love God in all things, since such people do not wish to be lifted from darkness to the marvelous light of God. But *thanks be to God through Jesus Christ our Lord who has lifted us out of the darkness into his marvelous light* (1 Corinthians 15:57; 1 Peter 2:9), since because of the lights that come to us from outside we might be disposed to reenter the mirror of our mind in which divine realities shine forth.

Chapter Three

The Reflection on God through the Image Imprinted on Our Natural Powers

1. The two preceding steps, which have led us to God by means of the vestiges through which God shines forth in every creature, have brought us to a point where we can enter again into ourselves, that is, into the mind itself in which the divine image shines forth. Therefore, in this third stage, as we leave the outer court[12] and enter into ourselves, we should try to see God through a mirror, as it were, in the holy place—namely in the area in front of the tabernacle. It is here that the light of truth shines like the light of a candelabrum upon the face of our mind in which the image of the most blessed Trinity shines in splendor.

Therefore, enter into yourself and recognize that your mind loves itself most fervently. But it cannot love itself if it does not know itself. And it would not know itself unless it remembered itself, for we do not grasp anything with our understanding if it is not present to us in our memory. From this you see, not with the eye of the flesh but with the eye of reason, that the soul possesses a threefold power. Now consider the operation of these powers and their relation to each other. Here you can see God through yourself as through an image. And this is to see *through a mirror in an obscure manner* (1 Corinthians 13:12).

2. The function of the memory is to retain and to represent not only things that are present, corporal, and temporal, but also things that are successive, simple, and everlasting.

Memory holds past things by recall, present things by reception, and future things by means of anticipation. It retains simple things such as the principles of continuous and discrete quantities like the point, the instant, and unit. Without these it would be impossible to recall or to know those things which are derived from them. It also retains in a lasting way the principles and axioms of the sciences which are enduring; for as long as one uses reason, it is impossible to forget them. So it is that when one hears them one approves and gives one's assent to them. But it is not as though one were hearing them for the first time. Rather, it is as though one recognizes them as innate and familiar. This becomes clear when the following principle is proposed to a person: "Concerning any particular matter, one must say either true or false," or "Every whole is greater than its part," or any other principle which cannot be contradicted "by our inner reason."[13]

In its first function, the actual retention of all temporal things past, present, and future, the memory is similar to eternity whose undivided presentness extends to all times. In its second function, it is clear that memory is formed not only by phantasms from external objects, but also from above by receiving and holding within itself simple forms which cannot enter through the doorways of the senses or by means of sensible phantasms. In its third function, we hold that memory has present within itself a changeless light by which it remembers changeless truths. So through the operations of memory, it becomes clear that the soul itself is an image of God and a similitude so present to itself and having God so present to it that it actually grasps God and potentially "has the capacity for God and the ability to participate in God."[14]

3. The function of the intellect is seen in the intellect's understanding of terms, propositions, and inferences. The intellect understands the meaning of terms when it comprehends what each thing is by means of a definition. But a definition is formulated by using broader terms; and these, in turn, are defined by still broader terms. Thus it goes until we arrive at the highest and most general terms. If these are not known, it is impossible to understand the less general terms by means of a definition. Therefore, if we do not know the meaning of being per se, we cannot fully know the definition of any particular substance. And we do not know the meaning of being per se unless we know it together with all its properties such as: unity, truth, and goodness. But since being can be thought of as diminished or complete, as imperfect or perfect, as being in potency or being in act, as being in a qualified sense or as being in an unqualified sense, as being in part or as being totally, as transient being or as permanent being, as being through another or as being through itself, as being mixed with non-being or as pure being, as dependent being or as absolute being, as posterior being or prior being, as mutable being or as immutable being, as simple being or as composite being; and since "privations and defects cannot be known except through affirmations,"[15] our intellect does not come to a full analysis of any particular created being unless it is aided by an understanding of the most pure, most actual, most complete, and absolute being, which is being simply and eternally, in which the principles of all creatures are found in their purity. For how can the intellect know that this being is defective or incomplete if it has no knowledge of that being which has no defect? The same line of argument can be made concerning

the other qualities cited above.

Next, the intellect is said truly to comprehend the meaning of propositions when it knows with certainty that they are true. And this is genuine knowledge, for the intellect cannot be deceived in such a comprehension. Since the intellect knows that this truth cannot be other than it is, it knows also that this is an unchangeable truth. But since our mind itself is changeable, it would not see this truth shining unchangeably except by reason of the illumination of some other entirely unchangeable light shining through. And it is impossible that such a light would be a changeable creature. Therefore the mind knows in that light *which enlightens all who come into this world,* and which is *the true light* and the *Word in the beginning with God* (John 1:1, 9).

Our intellect grasps the meaning of an inference in the truest sense when it sees that the conclusion follows necessarily from the premises, and when it sees this not only in necessary terms but in contingent terms as well. For example: "If a person is running, a person is moving." It sees this necessary relation not only in existing things, but even in non-existing things. Thus, with respect to a person who exists in reality it follows that "If a person is running, a person is moving." But the conclusion is true even if such a person does not exist in reality. The necessity of this sort of inference does not come from the real, material existence of a thing, because that is contingent. Neither does it come from the existence of the thing in the mind because that would be a fiction if the thing did not exist in reality. It comes, therefore, from the exemplarity of the eternal Art, according to which things have an aptitude and a relation to each other which is grounded in their representation in the eternal Art. So, as Augustine says in his book *On the True Religion*,[16] the light of anyone who reasons truly is enlightened by that truth and seeks to return to it. From this it is clear that our intellect is united with the eternal truth itself. And if that truth were not teaching our intellect, it would be impossible to grasp anything with certitude. So you are able to see within yourself that truth which teaches you as long as unruly desires and sense images do not stand as impediments becoming like clouds between you and the ray of truth.

4. The power of choice is seen in deliberation, judgment, and desire. Deliberation consists in inquiring whether this thing is better than that thing. But a thing is said to be better only because of its closeness to the best. But closeness to the best is measured in terms of likeness. No one can know, therefore, whether one thing is better than another without knowing that this thing has a greater resemblance to the best. And no one knows whether something is more like another without knowing that other. For I do not know whether this person is like Peter unless I know and recognize Peter. Therefore, it is necessary that the notion of the highest good be impressed on anyone who is engaged in deliberation.

Moreover, a sure judgment concerning matters that are the object of deliberation takes place through some law. And no one judges with certitude by virtue of a law without being certain that the law is right and that one should not make a judgment about the law itself. But our mind does judge about itself. Since it cannot judge about the law which it uses to judge, that law is superior to our mind. And our mind is able to judge by this law in as far as the law has been impressed in the mind. But nothing is superior to the human mind except God who has created it. Therefore in making its judgments our deliberative power is in contact with the divine laws when it arrives at a full and complete analysis.

Finally, desire tends above all to that which moves it the most. And that which moves it the most is that which is loved the most. And that which is loved the most is happiness. But happiness is attained only by reaching the best and ultimate goal. Therefore, human desire is directed at nothing but the supreme Good, or that which leads to it or reflects that Good in a certain way. The power of the supreme Good is so great that nothing else can be loved by a creature except through a desire for the supreme Good. Therefore, anyone who takes the image or the copy for the truth itself is deceived and falls into error.

Behold, therefore, how close the soul is to God, and how through their functions the memory leads to eternity, the intelligence leads to truth, and the power of choice leads to the highest Good.

5. Furthermore, if one considers the order, origin, and relation of these faculties to one another, one is led to the most blessed Trinity itself. For intelligence emerges out of memory as its offspring, because we come to understand only when a likeness which lies in the memory emerges to the forefront of consciousness. And this is nothing other than a word. From memory and intelligence, love is breathed forth as the bond that unites them. These three—namely, the mind that generates, the word, and love—are in the soul as memory,

intelligence, and will. These are consubstantial, coequal, and of the same age, and mutually interpenetrating. Therefore, if God is the perfect spirit, there must be not only memory, intelligence, and will in God. There must also be the Word begotten and the Love breathed forth. And these are necessarily distinct since one is produced by the other. This production is not in the order of essence, nor in that of accident. Therefore, it is in the order of person.

Therefore, when the soul reflects on itself and through itself as through a mirror, it rises to the consideration of the blessed Trinity of Father, Word, and Love; three persons that are coeternal, coequal, and consubstantial in such a way that whatever is in one is in the others, but one is not the other, and all three are one God.

6. When the soul reflects on its triune principle by means of the trinity of its own powers which make it to be an image of God, it is aided by the light of the sciences which perfect it and inform it, and which represent the most blessed Trinity in a threefold way. For all of philosophy is either natural, rational, or moral. The first deals with the cause of being and therefore points to the power of the Father. The second deals with the basis of understanding and therefore leads to the wisdom of the Word. And the third deals with the order of living and therefore leads to the goodness of the Holy Spirit.

Furthermore, the first, or natural philosophy, is divided into metaphysics, mathematics, and physics. The first deals with the essence of things; the second with numbers and figures; and the third with natures, powers, and diffusive operations. Therefore the first points to the first Principle, namely, the

Father; the second points to the image of the Father, namely, the Son; and the third points to the gift of the Holy Spirit.

The second, or rational philosophy is divided into grammar which enables people to express themselves with power; logic, which makes people sharp in argumentation; and rhetoric, which enables people to persuade and move others. Again, this points to the mystery of the most blessed Trinity.

The third, or moral philosophy is divided into the monastic, the familial, and the political. The first suggests the unbegottenness of the first Principle; the second suggests the familial relation of the Son; and the third suggests the liberality of the Holy Spirit.

7. All these sciences are governed by certain and infallible laws that are like lights and beams coming down from that eternal law into our mind. Therefore, our mind, enlightened and filled with such splendors, can be guided to reflect on this eternal light through itself if it has not been blinded. The radiation of this light and the reflection on it lifts up the wise in admiration. On the other hand, the unwise who reject faith as a way to understanding are led to confusion. Thus the prophetic word is fulfilled: *You enlighten wonderfully from the everlasting hills. All the foolish of heart were troubled* (Psalms 75:5).

Chapter Four

THE REFLECTION ON GOD IN THE IMAGE REFORMED BY THE GIFTS OF GRACE

1. Since the first Principle can be contemplated not only *through* ourselves while we are on the way, but also *in* ourselves; and since the latter is more excellent than the former, this kind of consideration stands at the fourth stage of contemplation. After it has been shown that God is so close to our souls, it is surprising that there are so few people who are concerned with speculation on the first Principle within themselves. But an explanation for this is near at hand. The human mind is distracted by many concerns, and therefore does not enter into itself through memory. It is obscured by images of sense objects, and therefore does not enter into itself through intelligence. And it is drawn away by disordered desires, and therefore it does not return to itself with a desire for internal sweetness and spiritual joy. Totally immersed in matters of the senses, the human person is unable to reenter into itself as the image of God.

2. Just as when a person falls, it is necessary to remain lying there until someone comes near to reach out and raise the fallen person up (Isaiah 24:20), so our soul could not be raised up perfectly from sensible realities to see itself and the eternal truth within itself unless the truth, assuming a human form in Christ, should become a ladder to repair the first ladder that had been broken in Adam.

So it is that, no matter how enlightened one might be with the light of natural and acquired knowledge, one cannot enter into oneself to *delight in the Lord* (Psalms 36:4) except by means of the mediation of Christ who says: *I am the door. Those who enter through me shall be saved; they shall go in and out and find pasture* (John 10:9). But we do not draw near to this door unless we believe in Christ, hope in Christ, and love Christ. If we wish, therefore, to reenter into the enjoyment of truth as into a paradise, we must do so through faith in, hope in, and love for *the mediator between God and humanity, Jesus Christ* (1 Timothy 2:5), who is like *the tree of life in the middle of paradise* (Genesis 2:9).

3. Therefore the image that is our soul must be clothed over with the three theological virtues by which the soul is purified, illumined, and brought to perfection. In this way the image is reformed and brought into conformity with the heavenly Jerusalem, and it becomes a member of the church militant which is the offspring of the heavenly Jerusalem, according to the Apostle. For he says: *That Jerusalem which is above is free, and she is our mother* (Galatians 4:26). The soul, therefore, believes in, hopes in, and loves Jesus Christ who is the Word incarnate, uncreated, and inspired; that is, *the way, the truth, and the life* (John 14:6). When in faith the soul believes in Christ as in the uncreated Word, who is the Word and splendor of the Father, it recovers its spiritual sense of hearing and of sight; its hearing so that it might receive the words of Christ, and its sight that it might consider the splendors of that light. When in hope the soul yearns to receive the inspired Word, because of this desire and affection it recovers its spiritual sense of smell. When in love the soul embraces the incarnate Word, receiving delight from Him and passing over to Him in ecstatic love, it recovers its sense of taste and touch. With its spiritual senses restored,

the soul now sees, hears, smells, tastes, and embraces its beloved. It can now sing like the spouse in the *Canticle of Canticles* which was written for the exercise of contemplation on the fourth level. And this level *no one knows except one who receives it* (Revelation 2:17), for it consists more in the experience of affections than in rational considerations. It is at this level where the interior senses have been restored to see what is most beautiful, to hear what is most harmonious, to smell what is most fragrant, to taste what is most sweet, and to embrace what is most delightful, the soul is disposed for spiritual ecstasies through devotion, admiration, and exultation in accordance with the three exclamations found in the *Canticle of Canticles.* The first of these comes from the abundance of devotion through which the soul becomes like a *column of smoke filled with the aroma of myrrh and frankincense.* The second comes from the overflowing sense of wonder by which the soul becomes like the dawn, the moon, and the sun corresponding to the steps of illumination that lift up the soul in wonder as it contemplates the Bridegroom. And the third comes through the superabundance of joy through which the soul is brought to a *fullness of delights and rests totally upon her Beloved* (Canticle 3:6; 6:9; 8:5).

4. When these things have been accomplished, and our spirit has been brought into conformity with the heavenly Jerusalem, it is ordered hierarchically so that it can ascend upward. For no one enters into that city unless that city has first descended into the person's heart by means of grace, as John sees in *Revelation.* It descends into the heart when our spirit has been made hierarchical by the reformation of the image and by the theological virtues, the enjoyment of the spiritual senses, and the ecstasy of rapture; for then it has

been purged, illumined and brought to perfection. In this way our spirit is adorned with nine levels when within it the following are found in an appropriate order: announcing, dictating, leading, ordering, strengthening, commanding, receiving, revealing, and anointing. These correspond to the nine choirs of angels. The first three of the foregoing levels in the human mind relate to nature; the next three relate to work; and the final three relate to grace. When it has attained these, the soul, by entering into itself, enters into the heavenly Jerusalem where, as it considers the choirs of angels, it sees in them the God who dwells in them and who works in all their operations. Therefore, Bernard says to Pope Eugene[17] that "God loves in the Seraphim as charity; knows in the Cherubim as truth; sits in the Thrones as justice; reigns in the Dominations as majesty; rules in the Principalities as a guiding principle; protects in the Powers as salvation; is at work in the Virtues as strength; reveals in the Archangels as light; assists in the Angels as kindness." From all this, God is seen as *all in all* (1 Corinthians 15:28) when we contemplate God in our minds where God dwells through the gifts of the most generous love.

5. At this level of contemplation the divinely given sacred Scriptures are particularly helpful just as philosophy was at the previous level. For sacred Scripture is above all concerned with the work of reparation. Therefore, it deals mainly with faith, hope and charity; that is, with the virtues by which the soul is to be reformed. And most especially it deals with charity. Concerning this the Apostle says that charity which arises from *a heart that is pure and from a good conscience, and from genuine faith* is the whole point of the Law. As the same Apostle says, it is *the fulfillment of the Law* (1 Timothy 1:5;

Romans 13:10). And our Savior says that the whole of the Law and the Prophets depends on two commandments; namely, love of God and love of neighbor (Matthew 22:40). These two are symbolized in Jesus Christ, the one spouse of the church, who is both our God and our neighbor, both our lord and our brother, both king and friend, both the uncreated Word and the incarnate Word, both our creator and our re-creator, both the *Alpha* and the *Omega* (Revelation 1:8; 21:6; 22:13). As the supreme hierarch, it is He who purges, illumines and perfects His spouse, namely the entire church and each sanctified soul.

6. Therefore, all of sacred Scripture treats of this hierarch and of the ecclesiastical hierarchy through which we are taught how to be purged, illumined and perfected in terms of the threefold law which has been handed down in the Scriptures: namely, the law of nature, the law of Scripture, and the law of grace. Or rather, in accord with the three main parts of Scripture: the Mosaic law which purges, the prophetic revelation which illumines, and the teaching of the Gospel which perfects. Or even more, according to the threefold spiritual meaning: the tropological which purges for an upright life; the allegorical which enlightens for clarity of understanding; and the anagogical which leads to perfection through spiritual ecstasies and through the most sweet perceptions of wisdom. All this is to be seen in relation to the aforementioned three theological virtues, the reformed spiritual senses, the three spiritual ecstasies mentioned above, and the three hierarchical acts of the soul by which our soul returns to its interior where it sees God in the *splendor of the Saints* (Psalms 109:3), and in them as in her bed she *sleeps in peace* (Psalms 4:9) while the bridegroom

pleads that she should not be awakened until it is her will to come forth (Canticle 2:7).

7. From these two intermediate steps by which we enter into the contemplation of God within us as in the mirrors of created images, like the two middle wings (of the Seraph) extended for flight, we can come to understand that we are led to divine things through the powers of the rational soul itself which are implanted in the soul by nature, and through their operations, relations, and the habits of knowledge they possess. This becomes clear at the third level. We are also led by the reformed faculties of the soul itself; and this includes the gifts of the virtues, the spiritual senses, and the mental ecstasies. And this becomes clear at the fourth level. Nonetheless we are led by means of the hierarchic operations of the human soul, namely purgation, illumination, and perfection and by the hierarchic revelations of the sacred Scriptures given to us by the angels, according to that Apostle who says that the Law has been given *by the angels at the hand of a mediator* (Galatians 3:19). And finally we are led by the hierarchies and the hierarchic orders which are to be ordered in our mind as they are in the heavenly Jerusalem.

8. Flooded with all these intellectual lights, our soul—like a house of God—is inhabited by the divine Wisdom. It is made to be a daughter of God, a spouse and friend. It is made to be a member, a sister, and a coheir of Christ the Head. It is made into the temple of the Holy Spirit, grounded in faith, elevated in hope and dedicated to God through holiness of soul and body. It is the most sincere love of Christ that brings this about, a love which is *poured forth in our hearts through the Holy Spirit who is given to us* (Romans 5:5). And without this

Spirit we cannot know the secret things of God. Just as *no one can know a human person's innermost self except the spirit of that person which dwells within, so no one knows the things of God but the Spirit of God* (1 Corinthians 2:11). Therefore, let us be rooted and grounded in love, so *that we might comprehend with all the saints what is the length of eternity,* the *breadth* of generosity, the *height* of majesty, and the *depth* of that discerning wisdom (Ephesians 3:18-19).

Chapter Five

THE REFLECTION ON THE DIVINE UNITY THROUGH GOD'S
PRIMARY NAME, WHICH IS BEING

1. It is possible to contemplate God not only outside ourselves and inside ourselves but also above ourselves. Outside ourselves this is done through the vestiges; inside ourselves through the image; and above ourselves through the light that shines on our mind. This is the light of the eternal truth, since "the mind itself is formed immediately by truth itself."[18] Those who have become acquainted with the first way have entered into the court before the tabernacle. Those who are practiced in the second way have entered into the holy place. And those who are involved in the third way enter together with the High Priest into the holy of holies where the Cherubim of glory stand above the ark and overshadow the Mercy Seat (Exodus 25–28). By the Cherubim we understand two modes or levels of contemplating the invisible and eternal qualities of God. The first of these concerns the essential attributes of God; the second concerns the properties of the persons.

2. The first method fixes our attention principally and first of all on Being itself, saying that *The One who is* (Exodus 3:14) is the first name of God. The second method fixes our attention on the reality of the Good, saying that this is the first name of God. The first looks above all at the Hebrew Scriptures which are concerned to a great extent with the unity of the divine essence. For it was said to Moses: *I am who I am* (Exodus 3:14). The second looks to the Christian Scriptures, which determine the plurality of persons, by bap-

tizing *in the name of the Father, and of the Son, and of the Holy Spirit* (Matthew 28:19). Therefore Christ, our Master, wishing to raise to evangelical perfection the young man who had observed the Law, attributed to God principally and precisely the name of *Goodness* saying: *No one is good but God alone* (Luke 18:19). So Damascene, following Moses, says that *The One Who Is* is the first name of God. And Dionysius, following Christ, says that *Good* is the first name of God.[19]

3. Anyone, therefore, who wishes to contemplate the invisible qualities of God that pertain to the unity of essence looks first and principally at Being Itself, and recognizes that Being Itself is so thoroughly certain that it cannot be thought not to be, for the most pure being does not exist except in total opposition to non-being just as *nothing* is the total opposite of *being*. Therefore as total nothingness possesses nothing of being nor of being's attributes, so, on the contrary, being itself possesses nothing of non-being, neither in act nor in potency; neither in reality nor in our understanding of it. Now, since non-being is the privation of existence, it does not enter into the intellect except through being. Being, on the other hand, does not enter the intellect by anything other than itself, since everything that is known is known either as non-being, or as potential being, or as actual being. Therefore if non-being cannot be known except through being, and potential being cannot be known except through actual being, and if being names the pure actuality of being, it follows that being is what first comes to the intellect; and it is that being which is pure act. But this is not a particular being, which is limited because it is mixed with potentiality. Nor is it analogous being which has the least actuality because it has the least of existence. It

remains, therefore, that this being is the divine Being.

4. How remarkable, then, is the blindness of the intellect which does not take note of that which it sees first, and without which it can know nothing. But just as the eye, when it is concerned with the variety of colors, does not see the light through which it sees other things, or if it sees it, pays no attention to it, so the eye of our mind, intent as it is on particular and universal categories of being, pays no attention to that being which is beyond every genus even though it is that which first comes to the mind, and it is through this that all other things are known. Therefore it seems to be very true that "as the eye of a bat is related to light, so the eye of our mind is related to the most evident things of nature."[20] Accustomed as it is to the darkness of things and to the phantasms of sensible objects, when the mind looks upon the light of the highest being, it seems to see nothing. And it does not understand that this darkness itself is the highest illumination of our mind, just as when the eye sees pure light it seems to it that it sees nothing.

5. Therefore, think of the most pure being if you can, and you will see that it cannot be thought of as something received from another. For this reason it is thought of as first in every sense since it does not come into being from nothing, nor does it come from some other being. For what else could exist by itself if pure being does not exist through and of itself? Also you will understand this pure being to be totally lacking in non-being, and hence as having neither a beginning nor an ending, but as eternal. Also it appears to you to possess nothing else but being itself. Hence it is in no sense composed, but is most simple. It appears also to have nothing

of potentiality since whatever is potential in some way possesses something of non-being. Hence this being is supremely actual in the highest degree. It appears also to have no defect, and therefore as most perfect. Finally it appears to have no diversity, and therefore it is supremely one.

That being, therefore, which is pure being, simple being, and absolute being is the first, the eternal, the most simple, the most actual, the most perfect, and the supremely one being.

6. These things are so certain that their opposites cannot be conceived of by anyone who understands what is meant by *being itself.* And each one of these attributes necessarily implies the other. For since it is being with no qualification, it is first in an unqualified sense. Since it is first in an unqualified sense, it is not made by another, nor is it made by itself. Therefore it is eternal. And since it is first and eternal, therefore it is not composed from others. Therefore it is supremely simple. Then, because it is first, eternal, and most simple, therefore there is in it no potentiality mixed with act. It is most actual. Then, because it is first, eternal, most simple, and most actual, it is also most perfect. Such a being lacks absolutely nothing, and nothing can be added to it. Because it is first, eternal, most simple, most actual, and most perfect, it is supremely one. For whatever is predicated out of a sense of an all-embracing superabundance is predicated with respect to all things. But "that which is predicated by reason of an unqualified superabundance can apply to one being alone."[21] Hence, if God names that which is first, eternal, most simple, most actual, and most perfect, then it is impossible to think of God as not existing, or to think of God as existing in any other way than as exclusively one. Therefore, *Hear, O*

Israel. The Lord your God is one (Deuteronomy 6:4). If you see this with the pure simplicity of your mind, you will be filled to some extent with the illumination of the eternal light.

7. Here you have something to lift you up in wonder. For being itself is both first and last, eternal and most present, most simple and greatest, most actual and unchangeable, most perfect and immense, supremely one yet all-embracing. If you marvel at these things with a pure mind, you will be filled with an even greater light when you see further that it is last precisely because it is first. For since it is first, it does all things for its own sake. Thus the first being is of necessity the final end, the beginning and the consummation, the *Alpha* and the *Omega* (Revelation 1:8; Proverbs 16:4). Therefore because it is eternal it is also most present. Because it is eternal, it does not come from another, and of itself it does not cease to exist, nor does it move from one state to another. Therefore it has neither past nor future, but its being is only in the present. It is the greatest because it is most simple. Since it is most simple in essence, it is greatest in power; since the more unified a power is, the more it approaches the infinite. Because it is most actual it is most immutable. Because it is most actual, it is pure act. And whatever is pure act can neither acquire something new nor lose something which it already possesses. Therefore it cannot be changed. Because it is most perfect, it is immense. And because it is most perfect, nothing can be thought of beyond it that would be better, more noble, or of greater dignity. Hence nothing is greater than it. Anything of this sort is immense. Finally because it is supremely one, it is all-embracing. That which is supremely one is the universal principle of all multiplicity. By reason of this, it is the universal efficient,

exemplary, and final cause of all things as it is the "cause of existence, the principle of understanding, and the rule of life." Therefore it is all-embracing not as though it were identical with the essence of all things, but as the most excellent, most universal, and most sufficient cause of all essences. Because it is supremely unified in its essence, its power is supremely infinite and multiple in its effects.

8. Looking over the way we have come, let us say that the most pure and absolute being, because it is being in an unqualified sense, is first and last; and therefore it is the origin and consummating end of all things. Because it is eternal and most present, it embraces and enters into all things that endure in time, simultaneously existing as their center and circumference. Because it is most simple and greatest, it is within all things and outside all things, and hence "it is an intelligible sphere whose center is everywhere and whose circumference is nowhere."[22] Because it is most actual and immutable, therefore "remaining unmoved, it imparts movement to all things."[23] Because it is most perfect and immense, therefore it is within all things but is not contained by them; and it is outside all things but is not excluded; it is above all things but not distant; and it is below all things, but not prostrate. Because it is supremely one and all-embracing, it is *all in all* (1 Corinthians 15:28), even though all things are multiple and this is simply one. And because this is most simple unity, most peaceful truth, and most sincere goodness, it is all power, all exemplarity, and all communicability. Therefore, *from him and through him and in him are all things* (Romans 11:36), for he is all-powerful, all-knowing, and all-good. And to see him perfectly is to be blessed, as it was said to Moses: *I will show you all good* (Exodus 33:19).

Chapter Six

The Reflection on the Most Blessed Trinity in Its Name, Which Is the Good

1. After our consideration of the essential attributes of God, the eye of our intelligence must be raised to behold the most blessed Trinity so that the second Cherub might be placed across from the first. Just as being itself is the foundational principle and the name through which the essential attributes of God and all other things come to be known, so the good is the most basic foundation for our contemplation of the emanations.

2. See and take note that the highest good in an unqualified sense is that than which nothing better can be thought. And this is of such a sort that it cannot be thought of as not existing, since it is absolutely better to exist than not to exist. And this is a good of such a sort that it cannot be thought of unless it is thought of as three and one. For "the good is said to be self-diffusive."[24] The supreme good, therefore, is supremely self-diffusive. But the highest diffusion does not exist unless it is actual and intrinsic, substantial and personal, natural and voluntary, free and necessary, lacking nothing and perfect. In the supreme good there must be from eternity a production that is actual and consubstantial, and a hypostasis[25] as noble as the producer, and this is the case in production by way of generation and spiration. This is understood to mean that what is of the eternal principle is eternally of the co-principle. In this way there can be both a beloved and a co-beloved, one generated and one spirated; that is, Father, and Son, and Holy Spirit. If this were not the

case, it would not be the supreme good since it would not be supremely self-diffusive, for that diffusion in time which is seen in creation is a mere point or a center in comparison to the immensity of the eternal goodness. Therefore it is possible to think of another greater diffusion; namely, that sort of diffusion in which the one diffusing itself communicates the whole of its substance and nature to the other. Therefore, it would not be the highest good if it lacked the ability to do this either in reality or in thought.

Therefore, if, with the eye of your mind you are able to reflect on the purity of that goodness which is the pure act of the principle that in charity loves with a love that is free, and a love that is due, and a love that is a combination of both, which would be the fullest diffusion by way of nature and will and which is found in the diffusion of the Word in which all things are spoken and the diffusion of the Gift in which all goods are given, you will be able to see that the supreme communicability of the good demands necessarily that there be a Trinity of Father, Son and Holy Spirit. And in these persons, because of supreme goodness it is necessary that there be supreme communicability. And because of supreme communicability, there must be consubstantiality; and from supreme consubstantiality there must be supreme conformability; and from these there must be supreme coequality; and because of this there must be supreme coeternity; and from all of the above, there must be supreme mutual intimacy by which each is necessarily in the others by reason of their supreme interpenetration,[26] and one acts with the others in a total unity of substance, power, and activity within the most blessed Trinity itself.

3. But as you contemplate these matters, beware that you do not think that you can comprehend the incomprehensible. For you still have something to consider in these six characteristics that will lead the eye of our mind with great strength to a stupor of admiration. For here we find the highest communicability together with the property of the persons, highest consubstantiality together with the plurality of hypostases, highest conformability together with discrete personality, highest coequality together with order, highest coeternity together with emanation, the highest intimacy together with mission. Who would not be rapt in wonder at the thought of such marvels? But we know most certainly that all these things are involved in the most blessed Trinity if we raise our eyes to that super-excelling goodness. If, therefore, there is supreme communication and true diffusion, then there is also true origin and true distinction. And since it is the whole that is communicated and not just a part, it follows that whatever is possessed is given, and given totally. Therefore, the one emanating and the one producing that emanation are distinguished by their properties but are one in essence. Since they are distinguished by their properties, it follows that they have personal properties and a plurality of hypostases. They have emanation of origin. From this comes an order which is not an order of one after the other but of one from the other. And there is sending forth which consists not of local change but of free spiration which is related to the authority of the one producing, that is the authority which the sender has with respect to the one who is sent. Now because they are substantially one, it is necessary that there be oneness of essence and form, of dignity and eternity, of existence and limitlessness. And as you consider

these matters one at a time, you are certainly contemplating truth. But when you think of them in relation to one another, you have something that will raise you to the highest sense of wonder. Therefore you must consider all these matters together if you wish to ascend through admiration to wondering contemplation.

4. For the Cherubim that faced each other are symbols of this. There is no lack of mystery in the fact that they faced each other, *their faces being turned toward the Mercy Seat* (Exodus 25:20). In this is fulfilled what our Lord said in John's Gospel: *This is eternal life, to know the only true God, and the one whom you have sent, Jesus Christ* (John 17:3). For we must come to admire the essential and personal attributes of God not only in themselves, but also in relation to the most admirable union of God and humanity in the unity of the person of Christ.

5. If you are that Cherub who contemplates the essential attributes of God and you marvel that the divine being is simultaneously first and last, eternal and most present, most simple and greatest or uncircumscribed, totally everywhere and contained nowhere, most actual and never moved, most perfect and having nothing superfluous nor deficient, and nonetheless immense and infinite without end, supremely one and yet all-embracing, possessing in itself all things, all power, all truth, and all good, then look toward the Mercy Seat and be astonished that there the first principle is joined to the last, God with humanity created on the sixth day (Genesis 1:26), the eternal is joined with temporal humanity, born of the Virgin in the fullness of time; the most simple with the most complex, the most actual with that which suf-

fered supremely and died; the most perfect and immense with the most modest, the supremely one and all-inclusive with an individual composite distinct from others, that is, the human being, Jesus Christ.

6. Now if you are the other Cherub who contemplates the properties of the persons, and if you are amazed to find communicability together with property, consubstantiality with plurality, conformability with personality, coequality with order, coeternity with production, mutual intimacy with mission, since the Son is sent by the Father, and the Holy Spirit is sent by both the Father and the Son, yet the one that is sent does not depart from the others but remains always with them, look toward the Mercy Seat and be amazed that in Christ there is personal union together with a trinity of substances and a duality of natures. And total harmony exists together with plurality of wills. There is the mutual predication of God and humanity together with a plurality of properties. Co-adoration exists together with a plurality of rank; co-exaltation over all things exists together with the plurality of eminence; and co-dominion exists together with a plurality of powers.

7. Our perfect illumination is found in this consideration when, as on the sixth day, we see humanity made in the image of God (Genesis 1:26). For if an image is an expressed likeness, then we have already reached something perfect when we contemplate our humanity so remarkably exalted and so ineffably united in Christ, the Son of God, who is by nature the image of the invisible God; and when, at the same time, we see in a single glance the first and the last, the highest and the lowest, the circumference and the center, the *Alpha* and

the *Omega* (Revelation 1:8; 5:1; Ezekiel 2:9), the caused and the cause, the creator and the creature, that is, *the book written within and without.* Here with God we reach the high point of our illuminations on the sixth step, as on the sixth day. Nothing further remains but the day of rest when in an ecstatic insight the discerning power of the human mind *rests from all the work that it has done* (Genesis 2:2).

Chapter Seven

THE MENTAL AND MYSTICAL TRANSPORT IN WHICH REST IS GIVEN TO OUR UNDERSTANDING AND THROUGH ECSTASY OUR AFFECTION PASSES OVER TOTALLY INTO GOD

1. We have covered these six meditations, comparing them to the six steps by which one ascends to the throne of the true Solomon where we arrive at peace. It is here that the true person of peace rests in the quiet of the mind as in an interior Jerusalem. They are also compared to the six wings of the Seraphim[27] by which the mind of the truly contemplative person is filled with the light of heavenly wisdom and can come to soar on high. They are also like the first six days during which the mind needed to be trained so as to finally arrive at the Sabbath of rest. We have contemplated God outside ourselves through and in the vestiges, within ourselves through and in the image, and above ourselves through the similitude of the divine light shining on us from above in as far as that is possible in our pilgrim state and by the exercise of our mind. Now finally we have come to the sixth step where, in the first and highest principle and in the mediator between God and humanity, Jesus Christ, we find mysteries which have no likeness among creatures and which surpass the penetrating power of the human intellect. When we have contemplated all these things, it remains for us to pass over and thus to transcend not only the sensible world but even ourselves. And in this passage, Christ is the way and the door (John 14:6; 10:7). Christ is the ladder and the vehicle, like the Mercy Seat placed above the ark of God and *the mystery that has been hidden from all eternity* (Exodus 25:20; Ephesians 3:9).

2. Anyone who turns fully to face this Mercy Seat with faith, hope, and love, devotion, admiration, joy, appreciation, praise and rejoicing, will behold Christ hanging on the Cross. Such a person celebrates the Pasch, that is, the Passover, with Christ. So, using the rod of the Cross this person can pass over the Red Sea (Exodus 14:16), moving from Egypt into the desert where the *hidden manna* (Exodus 16; Revelation 2:17) will be tasted. This person may then rest with Christ in the tomb, as one dead to the outer world, yet experiencing, in as far as possible in this pilgrim state, what was said on the cross to the thief who was hanging there with Christ: *This day you will be with me in Paradise* (Luke 23:43).

3. All this was shown also to blessed Francis when, in a rapture of contemplation on the top of the mountain where I reflected on the things I have written here, a six-winged Seraph fastened to a cross appeared to him. This I myself and several others have heard about from his companion who was with him at that very place. Here he was carried out of himself in contemplation and passed over into God. And he has been set forth as the example of perfect contempla tion just as he had earlier been known as the example of action, like another Jacob transformed into Israel (Genesis 35:10). So it is that, through Francis, God invites all truly spiritual persons to this sort of passing over, more by example than by words.

4. If this passing over is to be perfect, all intellectual activities must be given up, and our deepest and total affection must be directed to God and transformed into God. But this is mystical and very secret, which *no one knows except one who receives it* (Revelation 2:17). And no one receives it except one who desires

it. And no one desires it but one who is penetrated to the very marrow with the fire of the Holy Spirit whom Christ has sent into the world (Luke 12:49). Therefore the Apostle says (1 Corinthians 2:10 ff.) that the revelation of this mystical wisdom comes through the Holy Spirit.

5. Therefore since nature is helpless in this matter, and even personal effort does not help much, little importance should be given to investigation and much to unction; little to speech but much to interior joy; little to words or writing and all to the gift of God, namely the Holy Spirit; little or no importance should be given to the creature but all to the creative essence, the Father and the Son and the Holy Spirit. So with Dionysius[28] we cry out to the Triune God: "O Trinity, essence beyond essence and God beyond all deities, and supremely good Protector of the wisdom of Christians, lead us to that which is supremely unknown, to the light beyond lights and to the most sublime height of mystical knowledge. There new mysteries—the new, absolute, and unchangeable mysteries of theology—lie hidden in a superluminous darkness of a silence that teaches secretly in the total obscurity that is manifest above all manifestations and a darkness in which all things shine forth; a darkness which fills invisible intellects with a full superabundance and splendor of invisible goods that are above all good." This was said to God. But to the friend to whom this was written we can say with Dionysius: "In this matter of mystical visions, my friend, being strengthened for your journey, leave behind the world of the senses and of intellectual operations, all visible and all invisible things, and everything that exists or does not exist, and in this state of unknowing, allow yourself to be drawn back into unity with that One who is above all essence and

knowledge in as far as that is possible. Thus, leaving all things and freed from all things, in a total and absolute ecstasy of a mind that has been liberated, transcending your self and all things, you shall rise up beyond to the super-essential radiance of the divine darkness."

6. Now if you ask how all these things are to come about, ask grace, not doctrine; desire, not intellect; the groaning of prayer and not studious reading; the Spouse not the teacher; God, not a human being; darkness not clarity; not light, but the fire that inflames totally and carries one into God through spiritual fervor and with the most burning affections. It is God alone who is this fire, and God's *furnace is in Jerusalem* (Isaiah 31:9). And it is Christ who starts the fire with the white flame of his most intense passion. Only that person who says: *My soul chooses hanging, and my bones, death* (Job 7:15) can truly embrace this fire. Only one who loves this death can see God, for it is absolutely true that *no one can see me and live* (Exodus 33:20).

Let us die, then, and enter into this darkness. Let us silence all our cares, our desires, and our imaginings. Let us pass over with the crucified Christ *from this world to the Father,* so that when the Father has been shown to us, we may say with Philip: *It is enough for us.* Let us hear with Paul: *My grace is sufficient for you* (John 13:1; 14:8; 2 Corinthians 12:9); and let us exult with David, saying: *My flesh and my heart waste away; you are the God of my heart, and the God that is my portion forever. Blessed be the Lord forever, and let all the people say: let it be, let it be. Amen* (Psalms 73:26; 106:48).

Here ends the journey of the human person into God.

NOTES

[1] For those who are interested in consulting the original Latin edition, this translation was taken from: *Doctoris Seraphici S. Bonaventurae opera omnia*, edita studio et cura Collegii a S. Bonaventura, 10 volumes, Quaracchi, 1882–1902, vol. 5, pp. 295–313.

[2] See Isaiah 6:1–2. Here we find the biblical basis for the image of the Seraph with six wings that plays such a basic role in the tradition of the stigmatization of Saint Francis and hence in this work of Saint Bonaventure.

[3] Dionysius, *Mystical Theology*, I, 1.

[4] This idea can be traced back at least to the Stoic philosophers of ancient Greece. It is taken up again in Western Christian thought by Augustine. Here we see it in Bonaventure. It refers to the active potentialities implanted by God like seeds in the world, which may be compared to a seedbed of possible forms that will be brought to actuality as time passes.

[5] Augustine, *City of God*, 8, 4.

[6] Aristotle, VII *Physics*, text. 1.

[7] Augustine, VI *On Music*, 13, 38; XXII *On the City of God*, 19, 2.

[8] Augustine, *On the True Religion*, 18, 35 ff.

[9] Augustine, *On Freedom of the Will* II, 14, 38.

[10] Boethius, I *De Arithmetica*, I ff.

[11] Bonaventure uses the Latin verb *contueor* and related forms with a special, technical meaning. J. G. Bougerol, O.F.M., in *Introduction to the Works of Bonaventure* (Paterson, N.J.: St. Anthony Guild Press, 1964), pp. 36–37, writes of "contuition": "Bonaventure avoids the word 'intuition' in designating that indirect apprehension, by thought, of an object which escapes our grasp, but whose presence is somehow implied in the effects which flow from it. He speaks of 'contuition' or 'apprehension,' through perceived effects, of the presence of a cause which cannot be discerned even by intuition. We never have any intuition of God: all we can have of God is 'contuitions' within things, within our soul, or within transcendent principles. . . ." Johnson, *Bonaventure. Mystic of God's Word, op. cit.*, p. 169, states that contuition is: "The greatest knowledge of God, albeit indirect, which the intellect can acquire." In a conversation in Spring 1999, Zachary Hayes said that "when we speak of contuition, we speak of something that is co-known. We do not see God in bare, naked divinity, but as we know things here we know something of the divine. It's tangential, not looking directly at God, but at things which direct to God."

[12] Bonaventure uses the structure of the temple in Jerusalem as a metaphor

to lay out the dimensions of the journey. He has just taken us through the outer court of the temple in the discussion of the external world and sense experience. He will now take us to the inner court of the temple, that is, the experience of that dimension of reality found within the human subject. Eventually he will lead us to the mystery of the ark of the covenant in the Holy of Holies with all that is involved symbolically in that. See Exodus 26–27; 37:17–24; 38:9–20.

[13] Aristotle, I *Posterior Analytics*, 8.

[14] Augustine, XIV *On the Trinity*, 8, 11.

[15] Averroes, III *De Anima*, text. 25.

[16] Augustine, *On the True Religion*, 39, 72.

[17] *De consideratione* V, c. 5, n. 12.

[18] Augustine, *83 Questions*, q. 51, 2,4.

[19] John Damascene, *De fide orthodoxa*, I, 9; Dionysius, *The Divine Names*, III, 1; IV, 1.

[20] Aristotle, II *Metaphysics*, Text. I.

[21] Aristotle, V *Topics* c.3.(5); also, VII. c.1.

[22] Alan of Lille, *Regulae theologicae*, reg. 7.

[23] Boethius, *De consolatione philosophiae (The Consolations of Philosophy)*, III, metr. 9.

[24] Dionysius, *The Divine Names*, IV, 1ff.; *The Celestial Hierarchy*, IV, 1.

[25] The term "hypostatic union" speaks to the question of the union of the divine and human natures in Christ, the one person. In Greek the original term *hypostasis* means "substructure" or "support." This term played a large role in the Christological controversies throughout the centuries. Of this, Zachary Hayes writes in *The Hidden Center, op. cit.*, p. 132: "The self-knowledge of God is God's inner Word. When God 'vocalizes' that inner Word, the world comes to be; and within the world, humanity comes to be; and within humanity, Christ. His human nature is the most perfect, the fullest vocalization of God's inner Word. The human nature of Christ exists in a dialectical relation to the eternal Word. Without becoming the eternal Word, it finds its truest content in that Word and embodies it most fully in the world. So intimate and perfect is this union that Bonaventure can refer to Christ as a 'single and undivided exemplar.'"

[26] The Latin term *circumincessio* is a technical term in trinitarian theology. It attempts to express the "perfect being-in-one-another of the Divine Persons in spite of their distinction of Persons." See Saint Bonaventure's *Itinerarium Mentis in Deum*, introduction, translation and commentary by Philotheus Boehner, O.F.M. (New York: The Franciscan Institute, 1956), p.

124.

[27] While the text of the Quaracchi edition speaks of a "cherub," and the symbol of the ark in the two previous chapters includes the symbolism of two cherubim, the broader structure of Bonaventure's text, which takes the reader back to the experience of Saint Francis, seems to imply a "seraph" here.

[28] Dionysius, *Mystical Theology*, I, 1.

Index

death of, 312–314
desire and union with God,
  34–35
familial love, 209
focus on God, 190
and God's loving gaze,
  43–44
handling conflict, 105
hope, 204–205
hunger for Word of God,
  226–227
hymns of praise, 231–232,
  233–234
importance of gospel for,
  223–225
mountain retreat of, 22
on obedience, 170–173
poverty rule, 178–181
and Saint Clare, 57–60
as singer, 41
on suffering and nature,
  102–104
Saint John, 210
Saint Paul, 205, 265
Schaefer, Sister Roselle,
  210–211
Second Vatican Council
  need for pilgrimage, 124
  renewal of personal rela-
    tionship with God, 35–36
  return to roots, 144, 166
  on the Word, 223
self-reflection, 25–29, 69
  See also mind, searching of
senses, spiritual
  cultivation through divine
    love, 207
  and hope, 201
  soul hierarchy, 215–216
  Word of God, 226–227
sensual experience
  appreciation of God's
    creation, 87

characteristics of, 93–94
as distraction from inner
  work, 96–97
God as beyond, 303–304
God's celebration of,
  97–100
group meetings, 331–332
limitations of, 95–96
and love, 208, 209
and memory, 141
need for inner journey,
  187–188
pleasure, 109–113
Seraph, 31, 403n2, 405n27
sexuality, 109–113
Shaw, George Bernard, 248
silence, 42–43, 287–288,
  295–301
sin, 110, 189, 267–268
  See also morality
soul mysticism, 69, 213–219
Spirituals, 4
spiritual senses
  and divine love, 207
  hope, 201
  soul hierarchy, 215–216
  Word of God, 226–227
St. Francis of Assisi
  (Chesterton), 51–52
stigmata of Saint Francis,
  51–52
structure of journey to God,
  67–73
Stuhlmueller, Carroll, 199,
  204
suffering
  and Crucifixion, 71
  meaning in, 318–319
  and nature, 102–104
  patience of hope, 204
sun as symbol of Saint
  Francis, 51–52
surrender, 72, 291–292,